The Philosophy
of the Curriculum

Other books published in cooperation with the University Centers for Rational Alternatives:

THE IDEA OF A MODERN UNIVERSITY (1974)

THE ETHICS OF TEACHING AND SCIENTIFIC RESEARCH

(forthcoming)

THE
Philosophy
OF THE
Curriculum:
THE NEED FOR GENERAL EDUCATION

edited by

Sidney Hook
Paul Kurtz
Miro Todorovich

ℙ *Prometheus Books*

Buffalo, N.Y. 14215

Published by Prometheus Books
923 Kensington Avenue, Buffalo, New York 14215

Library of Congress Catalog Card Number 75-3921
ISBN 0-87975-051-0

Printed in the United States of America

The Philosophy
of the Curriculum

Contents

THE PLACE OF SCIENCE AND THE SCIENTIFIC OUTLOOK

PROBLEMS AND DILEMMAS OF THE SOCIAL SCIENCES

REFLECTIONS ON THE CURRICULUM

Introduction

Sidney Hook
New York University

One of the most notable contributions to the literature of higher education is the five-foot shelf of books published under the sponsorship of the Carnegie Commission on Higher Education. There is hardly a facet of the mechanics and organization of higher education that it does not treat, exhaustively and objectively. What it does *not* do is address itself to the most important questions that can be asked about higher education: What should its content be? What should we educate for, and why? What constitutes a meaningful liberal education in modern times, as distinct from mere training for a vocation?

The fact that the Carnegie Commission addressed itself to these questions only peripherally by no means—some critics to the contrary notwithstanding—invalidates its contributions to the economics, politics, and demographics of academic survival. But it does make the reflective educator wonder why there has been no corresponding effort to explore what the curriculum of higher education should be in our modern age. The necessity for such a concern hardly needs elaboration in view of the curricular chaos that prevails in our colleges today. The fear of declining enrollment—and of the ensuing consequences—has intensified a process of intellectual erosion already in evidence before the current economic pinch was felt. This was reflected in the abandonment of all required courses in many institutions, grade inflation to a point where students received grades for courses they never attended, and the calm, sometimes explicit, assumption that newly enrolled college students are better judges of their educational needs than the wisest of faculties could be.

The lengths to which self-characterized liberal-arts colleges are willing to go is apparent in the advertising and promotional materials they distribute to lure students into enrolling. Their theme song is a promise to students that they will be put to no intellectual strain and that whatever they learn will be not merely painless but pleasant. Some institutions have offered academic credit to students for a wide variety of "life experiences" that have taken place prior to their enrollment and outside the context of any academic test, control, or objective assessment of achievement.

Students themselves are beginning to reject the curricular pablum and jello they are being offered—but often for the wrong reasons, chief among which is exclusive preoccupation with education for a career. But there are very few careers that can be adequately prepared for by bull sessions and innovative courses uncontrolled by competent faculty supervision. It is perfectly legitimate to expect a liberal-arts education to prepare a student through the proper combination of required and elective courses and individual faculty guidance for a meaningful vocation. In one way or another proper liberal education always has. But what we are observing today is emphasis upon a vocationalism, a kind of preprofessionalism, that regards liberal general education as a frosting on the concrete business of education. As society becomes more technological, the tendency to narrow specialization and vocational orientation becomes reinforced.

Scholars and teachers who understand the nature of liberal education cannot accept these developments with complacency. They realize that no matter how technological our society becomes there are no important human problems that are purely technical, that all of them pose choices, and that values and value judgments are at the heart of the great decisions we make, whether as citizens or as men and women. Without a liberal-arts education to undergird or accompany or interpenetrate vocational or professional education, the latter cannot be adequate. Art, literature, history, philosophy, religion, the natural and social sciences are not frosting on the cake of education. They are part of its very being, ignored at the price of our civilization, and possibly—in an age in which the sudden death of cultures is a genuine threat—of its very survival.

The real question with which all reflective educators must grapple is what a liberal general education should consist of, not whether it should be part of the prescribed curriculum of higher education. This volume addresses itself to that perennial issue—an issue that is always topical. That there should be differences among humanist scholars concerning how best to nurture the human mind should not be surprising. There is no unanimity even among natural scientists concerning what best nurtures the human body. In both cases there must be a concern for what is common and what is individual or personal. In both cases it is false to say that, because prescriptions are not universal, therefore no objective and reliable judgments can be reached in the context of this time, and this place, and for these men and women.

Every institution of higher education must periodically engage in a self-assessment of its educational goals and the extent to which they actually guide curricular practice. It can be said with confidence that the reflections contained in this book will, at the very least, serve as a powerful catalytic agent in precipitating out insights into the educational condition of our institutions of higher education and ways in which it can be improved.

This volume contains the main papers and critical commentaries developed in connection with the second national conference of the University Centers for Rational Alternatives, held at Rockefeller University, New York City, on September 21-22, 1973. Since the major drift of the papers either ignored or opposed the newer currents of "experiential education," the editors have included an essay on this theme, written subsequent to the proceedings of the conference, by Dr. John B. Stephenson, dean of undergraduate studies at the University of Kentucky, and Dr. Robert F. Sexton, executive director of its Office for Experiential Education, as a rational alternative to traditional and modern conceptions of liberal education. This essay is noteworthy for its attempt to integrate within the liberal-arts tradition certain educational practices that have hitherto been considered foreign to it. Regardless of the extent of their agreement, readers will find it intellectually challenging.

UCRA, as the sponsoring organization, takes no stand on any of the issues discussed. Each participant speaks for himself only. The third national conference of UCRA will be entitled "The Ethics of Teaching and Scientific Research."

GENERAL EDUCATION – CHALLENGE AND JUSTIFICATION

General Education and the University Crisis

Wm. Theodore deBary
Columbia University

In the calm that has mysteriously come over our campuses, it may seem melodramatic to speak still of the "university crisis." Such ominous language will sound anachronistic to some, evoking specters of a nightmarish past well put behind us. To others it will seem a cliché, signifying only that the inflation of all currencies and the escalation of rhetoric continues unabated. The crisis I refer to, however, is not the one that arose with the antiwar movement and has now subsided. It is a condition of longer standing, the creeping crisis from the neglect and erosion of general education in the last decade or so. While stirring up no immediate alarm, the situation merits more serious concern than many issues that do.

I was previously involved with the fate of general education at a large conference, in which great apprehension was expressed over the threat to academic freedom and academic standards. There was bewilderment over the seeming failure of the younger generation to respect academic freedom or appreciate what its loss could mean. There was also loud lamentation over the danger to scholarship posed by the attempted subjection of all learning to the dictates of political relevance. Young barbarians, passionate and perverse, were thought to be shattering the very foundations of rational discourse and civilized life.

ACADEMIC VALUES AND GENERAL EDUCATION

I am as concerned as anyone over the survival of academic freedom and independent scholarship, and yet it seemed obvious to me that the mere invocation of these values alone would not suffice as a remedy. Civility cannot be restored so easily to a generation already turned off on civilization (if, indeed, one can speak in such sweeping terms about today's students as a whole). The highest standards of scholarship may impress them in a lofty and remote way without actually enlisting their sympathies. "Academic excellence" appears to exist on the high plane of advanced scholarly research and training, far removed from their mundane education.

If it is too much to expect that "pure," untrammeled scholarship will be accepted unquestioningly as the highest human good and that all study be taken merely as preparation for this, may we not have to recognize a restiveness over the narrowing of educational goals and a legitimate resistance to the defining of excellence in terms meaningful only to the cognoscenti? If many in the new generation seem to care little about "pure" scholarship, perceive much of it as irrelevant, or think its freedom not their business to defend, does this not point to an educational failure for which scholars themselves, and not just others, are to blame?

At issue, it seems to me, is the question of whether in recent years the academy has not enjoyed such prestige, such fashionable attention, and indeed such privilege (I refer to the competition for "star" scholars and the improper concessions made to free them from teaching) that its members had come to take their own existence, rights, and freedoms for granted. Today nothing less than an active commitment to education—and not just the training of scholars—can reestablish these on a sound basis. Converts cannot be won over if that freedom is represented by no more than "pure" or "critical" scholarship, if it seems to set no larger purposes before the student than the scholar's right to pursue his own interests or to sequester himself in a specialty where no one else can get to him. Positive values supportive of intellectual and cultural freedom can be reestablished only if they are responsive to more widely shared concerns, so that the scholar's autonomy is exercised in behalf of something more than his own predilections, undisturbed by the needs and problems of others.

I am aware of the dangers in committing the university to such educational activism. It will seem that the university is being asked to assume a prophetic, if not pontifical, role in regard to the teaching of values or the solution of human problems, whereas, in fact, I ask only that it discuss them in as thoroughgoing a way as it knows how. I would distinguish, then, between a prophetic role or pontifical authority, which the university cannot assume without predetermining its conclusions in the search for truth, and a magisterial function that it cannot abdicate as long as it claims any competence in the intellectual preparation and training of the young.

THE NEGLECT OF GENERAL EDUCATION

Education in the basic values and the larger purposes of the human community has been one of the major tasks of what we have called "general education," and its neglect or mismanagement has been deleterious both to the university community and the larger society. By saying this, I imply neither that the raison d'être of general education is the defense of academic freedom, nor that the survival of the latter can be assured simply by a renewed attention to the former. What should be near and dear to the scholar, however, I take as illustrative of the larger problem. If he cannot cope with the challenge even in respect to his own basic needs and functions, how can the scholar discharge his responsibilities as an educator in respect to the needs of the larger community?

One explanation of our recent difficulties with youth has focused on their appetite for instant gratification and their inability to appreciate the processes, sometimes laborious and time-consuming, necessary to provide for its satisfaction. There is a similar weakness among academics, especially in the graduate and professional schools, who have expected instant recognition of their own highest values, without attending to the educational processes needed to justify and sustain them. It has always been easier to find fault with general education than to do anything about it; to dismiss it as simplistic, given to overgeneralization or lacking in rigor; and then to complain about the results of undergraduate education when it failed to produce nice people with an appreciation for the finer things in life, namely one's own brand of scholarship.

In a major study, *The Purposes and the Performance of Higher Education in the United States,*[1] the Carnegie Commission on Higher Education does not fail to acknowledge the importance of general education. Their report cites it as a prime need of students (page 13), as first among six fundamental educational responsibilities of the university (pp. 17-18), and as first among a series of sixteen university functions (pp. 65-66). Yet nowhere in the one-hundred-and-seven-page report is there a description of prime need, responsibility, and function in any but the briefest, simplest terms: "acquiring a general understanding of society and the place of the individual within it, . . . [including] contact with history and the nature of other cultures" (p. 13); and "broad learning experiences—the provision of opportunities to survey the cultural heritage of mankind, to understand man and society" (p. 65).

I do not wish to commit the common sin of book reviewers who belabor authors for what they have left unsaid rather than what they have actually written. I simply point to the discrepancy between the high priority assigned to general education and their comparative silence in regard to its nature, content, and practice. Nor is this lack made up in any of the numerous other reports issued by the Carnegie Commission. Here then is a major need, explicitly acknowledged, for which an up-to-date answer is conspicuously missing.

The term "general education" conveys the impression of something that is inherently diffuse, and when one speaks of it in the same context as "humanities," "liberal education," and even "continuing education" (with its connotations of adult education, night school and all that), one risks unlimited confusion, if not the charge of being hopelessly vague and woolly.

LIBERAL EDUCATION, GENERAL EDUCATION, AND CAREER TRAINING

General education—though to me, as to the Carnegie Commission, a vital part of liberal education—is not the whole of it. Liberal education, most people would agree, aims to liberate the powers of the individual by disciplining them; and that discipline, in turn, immediately relates the individual to the values of his or her culture and to certain social necessities. I do not, then, have any difficulty in accepting even professional training or vocational education as contributing to those aims. The educated man or woman, the member of society, even the purported citizen of the world, needs this everyday discipline if he or she is to be liberated from a sense of total dependence on others. He must have something of his own that he can contribute to the work of the world, and if he learns to do it well, that will be part of his liberal education. It is not to be scorned as "mere vocationalism."

For this reason I can appreciate the concerns that have given rise to the current drive for "career education" among public policymakers and funding agencies. The U.S. commissioner of education, Dr. Sidney Marland, is not mistaken in believing that most Americans, old or young, attach great importance to career preparation as an educational objective, and in finding much of our educational system defective in meeting this goal.[2] I recognize too that in seeking to rectify this defect Dr. Marland has not meant to advance career training at the expense of the liberal arts, nor has he set vocationalism in opposition to the humanities. For him, "career education" represents a combining of "career training" and "liberal education."

Yet it disturbs me that in combining these two terms the word "liberal" has been displaced in favor of "career." I do not suggest that combining them to produce "liberal training" is a practicable alternative, but one can nevertheless see that a shift in emphasis is taking place and that liberal education comes out second best—if it is in the running at all. Somehow the impression is conveyed that one can have the fullness of education without paying the whole price. This impression is strengthened by two related factors: the program's close identification with proposals to shorten the time spent in college, and the comparative lack of any discussion as to how the liberal arts or humanities are to be fortified to meet this all-out competition for the student's attention over such a short length of time.

One need not question the sincerity of the intention in order to demonstrate how empty is the gesture being made to liberal education. It can no longer be assumed, as both Dr. Marland and the Carnegie Commission seem to have done, that the basic elements of humanistic education are there for the taking or that general education is something for which one only needs to make a place. After years of neglect, the problem for general education is not how to make allowance for it but how to make active provision for it.

Paying tribute to humanistic education is not the same thing as working at it, and uttering the usual pieties will do little to restore humanistic values if they have been eroding away while everyone took them for granted. Without a more conscious effort being made in general education, the vocational stress in Dr. Marland's program and the pressures of the speedup will leave the humanities in an even weaker and more disadvantaged position. Thus, rather than allowing "liberal education" to be subsumed under career education in a sterile and lifeless form, I would urge restoring it to full primacy. This can only be done through the active development of general education as a vital complement to career training, and by recognizing both of these as essential to a liberal education that is worthy of the name and not just window dressing for vocationalism.

If this seems to be mere quibbling over terms, other factors in our current situation make it more than a terminological issue. Besides the crisis of values and the breakdown of language, there is today the inescapable political involvement. Quite apart from the threat of overt politicization, heavy dependence on public funding exposes us to the vicissitudes of political fortune and bureaucratic rationalization in federal and state governments. As just one example, I would cite the appealing idea that much of a college education can be achieved by examination, which has won powerful support from public agencies for external degree programs. Though unexceptionable as an adjunct to personal participation in a regular college program, this device becomes a threat to liberal education when the university is made to function largely as an external examining and degree-granting institution; it ignores the baneful effects of such a system in Europe and Asia, where the routinization of study and examination has produced a large class of students having little contact with teachers, sharing almost none of the values of university life or a common culture, and at the mercy of prevailing ideologies for some unified approach to an understanding of the world in which they live.

We are, then, in a dynamic situation, a time of pervasive flux, in which powerful forces operate on us willy-nilly and nothing of educational value can survive just by being left to itself. For this reason, too, liberal education is unlikely to be sustained if vocationalism is given a powerful forward thrust by means of public funding and if no countervailing force is exerted in behalf of general education.

Despite what I have said in behalf of both liberal and general education, there are some who will be made uneasy by my willingness to accept career training as a part of liberal education and especially by my readiness to begin it in the undergraduate years. It will seem that I have made a fatal compromise in only slightly different terms from those of Dr. Marland. To deal with this question, I must first make some important distinctions.

I conceive of liberal education as a lifelong involvement and reject the earlier idea that it is a phase of general broadening in the early years of college, followed by increasing specialization. Specialization is inescapable, but so too should general education be accepted as an indispensable continuing process. Thus we come to the notion of liberal education as lifelong learning that, both early and late, combines the concurrent and complementary activities of general education and career specialization.

It will be equally evident, however, that this process must allow for development and maturation. Each individual will experience a gradual deepening of both throughout life, but likewise, in the early stages, adaptations will need to be made in regard to what is appropriate for each person at each level. I shall discuss later what would be appropriate forms of general education at several levels. Here I need only make a distinction between disciplinary training and vocational training. The one should lead into the other, and in the undergraduate years career preparation should first take the form of training in those basic disciplines that will be essential tools in one's later work. Some students will master these sooner than others, and if they do so, in my opinion there is no reason why they should not move ahead as rapidly as possible toward the highest necessary degree of career specialization. There is no doubt in my mind that the attainment of such competence is a powerful liberating experience for almost anyone.

The danger in it comes only when this is done at the expense of one's general education, so that the achievement of specialized competence produces undue intellectual narrowing and isolation. In the best of circumstances, the more independent and original of scholars will find themselves working largely alone on their own problems, but the degree of one's isolation will depend on participation in a larger community of discourse to which they have access through their continuing general education. For most students a proper balance can be achieved by not allowing specialization to proceed more rapidly in college than is consistent with the need for general education and by stressing training in fundamental disciplines, rather than specialized research, as career preparation on the undergraduate level.

All this seems no more than obvious, but it bears repeating. Some of the most obvious truths in education are ones that tend to be disregarded when general education and career training become pitted against one another as irreconcilable interests. Those who wish to get ahead with career education regret the loss of time spent in general education, which to them is of dubious practical value. Those who struggle to preserve liberal values feel threatened by any suggestion that the student should move ahead faster toward specialization in the early years of college. Yet it is well known that many disciplines are best learned in one's early years and that it is possible to master them without sacrificing all else, if there is a maximum of flexible coordination.

We know, for instance, that much can and should be done in respect to language learning. Americans are notoriously backward in comparison to most other people in their mastery of foreign languages. At the same time, however, we have developed probably the finest instructional methods in the world for rapid language learning. It has also been established beyond question that language learning is best done in the early years. Here, then, we have an example of a specific discipline that should be learned earlier rather than later in the educational process, that should not be sacrificed either to general education or specialized training, but that should, if properly managed, contribute to both of these and thus enhance one's liberal education.

DEFINING GENERAL EDUCATION WITHOUT CIRCUMSCRIBING IT

Having oriented ourselves by defining roughly the place of general education in liberal education and suggesting its complementary relation to disciplinary training and career specialization, we can proceed to an examination of general education itself. I should like first to suggest some of the things that it is not and then attempt to describe what it could be.

First, I would renounce the idea that general education is education for the whole man, in the sense of his becoming the "complete man." In a smaller, neater world this was perhaps thinkable, but even apart from the knowledge explosion of recent years and the burden it imposes upon our learning capacity, our experience with general education itself compels us to put the emphasis on something other than comprehensiveness. General education is as much a learning of our limitations, of what we do not know, as of what we do know. It should be a humbling experience as well as a broadening one, and it should teach the impossibility of achieving all things at once.

If the concept of the whole man is still valid at all, it is for the idea of wholeness or integration, and not for well-roundedness. He who sets out consciously to become well-rounded is likely to end up intellectually flabby or overextended. Wholeness, on the other hand, implies looking for and working from a center, not trying to circumscribe all knowledge. To define general education in terms of "what every educated man ought to know" will make sense only if it is interpreted and modified to mean the knowledge that men can reasonably be expected to have in common as a basis for their individual development and participation in the human community.

Misunderstanding on this point has arisen in part from the frequent use of survey courses in general education. There is a place for surveys, including historical surveys, but to the extent that surveys imply extensive coverage and generality rather than selectivity in regard to values and priorities, they do not serve the purposes of general education as I conceive of it.

The survey approach was not inherent in general education, which got its start at Columbia after World War I with the inauguration of a course on the issues of war and peace. Later it was strongly supplemented by a reading of great books in the Humanities course, itself an evolution from John Erskine's honors program. The Humanities course was and is highly selective, not aiming even at a figure of a hundred great books. But the Contemporary Civilization course attempted increasingly to provide the essential historical background for an understanding of contemporary issues, and it developed more and more in the direction of an historical review of the "major ideas and attitudes in the development of the modern mind."[3] In the 1930s and early 1940s a second year of Contemporary Civilization still dealt with major current problems, but the difficulties of keeping the course up to date, compounded by other curriculum and staffing problems, resulted in its being reformed gradually and effectively out of existence in the 1960s.

What remained of Contemporary Civilization thereafter was only the first-year course, "seeking for some unified view of the sweep of Western Civilization."[4] It sought this "unified view" primarily through the study of concepts and attitudes in their historical evolution; the acquisition of factual knowledge and historical detail was de-emphasized. By this choice, the unmanageable burden of historical coverage in extenso was lifted from the minds of students and instructors, and attention was focused on ideas in history, with philosophical and religious thought or political and social thought predominating at different times. In any case, however, the effort to take a large view of things, historically and conceptually, has meant that contemporary problems were studied only at a considerable remove from current crises.

Thus, from the standpoint of a student eager to deal with the immediate problems of contemporary society and impatient with historical complexities or philosophical speculation, Contemporary Civilization may appear scarcely relevant to current issues. Viewed on the other hand as a survey of Western civilization, Contemporary Civilization has also had severe limitations, dealing as it does mainly with the comparatively recent past and the sources of contemporary thought. From a global perspective and against the full scale of human history and civilization, it could be belittled as parochial. If the course has, over the years, provided a liberal education for many people whose appreciation for it has deepened with time, this degree of success has been achieved without the course dealing adequately with either the "contemporary" (that is, current issues) or· "civilization" in its full sweep.

For me, this only confirms the point that no single course can satisfy all needs, and in making choices among competing claims general education usually resolves them in compromises that are inherently unstable. There is always room for dissatisfaction, criticism, and reform. The successive modifications of Contemporary Civilization should thus be taken as evidence of continuing vital concern and experimentation, not of repeated failures. In the Humanities course there is, and should be, endless dispute over the books to be read, and in Contemporary Civilization, recurrent debate over such endemic problems as the mix of idea and fact, the short and the long view, and topical treatment or problem orientation, as contrasted with historical development.

WORKING ROOM FOR AN OPEN-ENDED PROGRAM

Rather than renew such debates here, I would seek to move them into a larger arena. If there is always room for dissatisfaction and reform, there should also be room for a variety of courses that attempt to fulfill the same purposes differently. Some of the difficulties encountered by Contemporary Civilization are aggravated by having to cope with them in too cramped a space and too brief a time. Any real improvement depends, I believe, on breaking out of the confines of the lower-college program. One necessary step in that direction—reconstructing general education on the basis of a four-year college program—has been proposed by Daniel Bell in *The Reforming of General Education* (1966). I would extend the process further, beyond college and into graduate and professional school. It remains of utmost importance that the undergraduate experience be well ordered and clearly defined; it should be basic to the larger effort, and, instead of getting lost or submerged in the process of expanding general education, the college program should assume a more critical importance at the heart of a larger enterprise. But to my mind it is just as crucial that general education in the college not be thought of as terminal and that the undergraduate pressure cooker be relieved of the need to cram all of humane learning into one pot.

The unresolved issue of the Columbia College program remains: What should follow the Humanities sequence and Contemporary Civilization? The problems encountered are symptomatic of those to be met in any extension of the sequence. Some of them center around the definition of manageable course content and the recruitment of able teachers. They may well determine the success or failure of any scheme, however impressive its conception. Among these problems I would put the following difficulties encountered during many years' experience.

1. The difficulty of maintaining uniform content and a common body of up-to-date materials on contemporary problems that change rapidly.

2. The discomfort of individual instructors trying to teach a course designed by a committee, especially a committee that has met and decided things long before they arrived on the scene. Some basic required courses cannot be planned and conducted otherwise, but general education will be at a disadvantage as long as it has no other op-

tions. Successful results are precluded if the instructor does not accept responsibility himself for what he is required to teach and must compel students to learn.

3. Student resistance to the overload that results from trying to cover in one course everything considered essential by a committee representing diverse interests.

4. The faculty morale problem that arises from failure to recognize, assist, and reward teaching in general education, and the feeling that it hampers rather than furthers professional advancement.

These problems and many others that could be cited reinforce, in my judgment, the basic point that emerged from the discussion of the scope and limitation of course content: namely, that a closed program of general education is neither intellectually nor pedagogically sound and that we must project a range of courses that carry forward the work of both student and teacher into the more advanced levels of college and university work. If specialized competence in a single discipline is to be the only criterion of advancement, then there is no future in general education for either the student or teacher and, in reality, only an attenuated future for specialization itself.

PERENNIAL CONCERNS AND CONTEMPORARY APPLICATIONS

There are many ways of describing the purposes, scope, and content of the courses that we might include in an expanded and open-ended program of general education. In "A Program of General and Continuing Education in the Humanities" I stated in brief:

> The question should be viewed first in terms of the perennial concerns and problems of human life and what forms they take in the contemporary world, and second in terms of those disciplines which may contribute to an understanding, and possibly a solution, of them. This implies a recognition that the problems to be dealt with in a contemporary context are manifold, that no attempt should be made to embrace them all in an omnibus course or survey, and that a variety of instructional options in topics, format and teaching methods should be available to serve the purposes of general education beyond the introductory level. . . .
>
> From the standpoint of graduate or professional education the aim should be to demonstrate the relevance of a specialized discipline to basic human needs and to acknowledge the interdependence of the disciplines in seeking to meet them. In terms of content and approach, however, such courses would be addressed not to professionals or "majors" but to inquiring minds seeking to know the nature of the contri-

bution which a discipline can make to understanding of the human self and man in society

If we can proceed on this basis we shall be in a position to exploit a wide range of competences and be able also to honor that kind of scholarly competence which is adorned by a breadth of humane learning and inspirited by a depth of human concern. . . . As illustrations of appropriate subjects we might cite the state, bureaucracy, urbanism, political movements and organization, social protest and revolution, problems of educational, judicial and penal reform, of industrialism and agrarianism, technology, and the environment; of community planning, the family, ethnicity and ethnic relations, housing, health and welfare systems. If these are obvious examples of problems with a strong social orientation, there are other topics directed more toward the problems of the individual: individual freedoms and rights, the individual in his biological, psychological and spiritual dimensions, his need for aesthetic expression and so on. . . . These are perennial and universal concerns in the sense that they can be found in most societies, past and present. They can be dealt with both historically and contemporarily, and in many cases should be. Though we do not hesitate to stress the importance of their contemporary relevance, and the desirability of having as direct an involvement as possible with the problems that surround us, it is equally important that these problems be seen in a larger perspective and against a wide background of human experience.[5]

What I have offered as a working description of a general-education program does not depart substantially from the "working principles and commitments" of the programs at Columbia, Chicago, and Harvard, which Bell summarized in these terms:

1. Ideological. The initial impulses were the unifying needs of American society and the desirability of instilling in students a sense of common tasks, though not necessarily a single purpose. The key word here would be *consensus*.

2. Tradition. In all three schools, the main effort has been directed at making the student aware of the history of Western civilization in order to broaden his vistas, to make him aware of the recurrent moral and political problems of man in society, and to chart the travails of the idea of freedom. If there is a single conclusion to which the program points, it would be that of instilling the idea of *civility*.

3. Contraspecialism. The American university, as it emerged in the latter decades of the nineteenth century, brought with it a new religion of research. Even scholarship in the traditional disciplines was conceived, within that purview, as being concerned with detailed and specialized problems. The reaction of the liberal-arts college was to strike out against specialism. The rallying cry, in this respect, was *humanitas*.

4. Integration. The multiplication of knowledge, the rise of many new

subfields and subspecialties, the crosscutting of fields, all led to a desire for courses that emphasized the broad relationships of knowledge, rather than the single discipline. This integration was to be achieved through a survey of fields, the elucidation of fundamental principles of disciplines, the centrality of method, or a combination of all of these. Whatever the varying emphases, the underlying assumption was of the need for an *interdisciplinary* approach; and this became one of the key terms in the language of general education.[6]

Elsewhere Bell offers six purposes of liberal education (which he implies should also be served by general education) in the following terms:

1. To overcome intellectual provincialism;
2. To appreciate the centrality of method (that is, the role of conceptual innovation);
3. To gain an awareness of history;
4. To show how ideas relate to social structures;
5. To understand the way values infuse all inquiry;
6. To demonstrate the civilizing role of the humanities.[7]

Any such brief formulation as Bell's is always subject to qualification, especially as times change and emphases shift. I would myself feel that another effort is needed to deal with contemporary issues and "common tasks" as *one* important aspect of general education. This should not imply any diminution of attention to history, because history is also greatly needed. But if the past should not be sacrificed to the present, neither should the present be sacrificed to the past. It may be possible to have more of both (though never all one would want) if more time is allotted over all to general education. In the new and larger context it should become possible for values that seem inherently antithetical to be made complementary.

Similarly, we must reckon with the need to overcome provinciality in new ways, while we still have not fully succeeded with the old. The mind-expanding possibilities in surveying "the full sweep of Western civilization" are far from exhausted, but in the meantime education has fallen badly behind in the assimilation of Oriental civilizations, even while their exploration both by scholars and young people has proceeded apace. From the scholarly point of view, there has been a vast expansion in the investigation of data and translation of Asian materials, but much too little use has been made of what has become available.

Yet with all this, we cannot fail to observe how radically our situation has changed in the last decade. The seeming rootlessness and mindlessness of many persons today makes "provinciality" almost an anachronism. There are few local loyalties or parochial ties from which one might be liberated. Nostalgia for a time when people "belonged" somewhere is pervasive. With few conventional molds left to break out of, the liberal tradition of mold breaking has only itself from which to be emancipated. Thus "liberation" has come almost full circle, calling for a process of integration and consolidation as much as for expansion of the spirit. Again, general education has to deal with both of these contrasting needs—finding a human center without turning one's back on the larger world and new experience—but since these are needs not limited to the young there is every reason to expand and prolong the effort throughout the learning years.

Another point that subsequent events would lead us to underscore more heavily perhaps than Bell did concerns the social implications and consequences of specialization. I have already spoken of the effects of specialization in the undue narrowing of individuals' horizons and consequent intellectual isolation. In Bell's formulations this is dealt with as a limitation of the individual's self-development and a failure to achieve his full intellectual powers. No less significant is the positive danger to society and the whole human ecology that arises from the pursuit of special technologies in ignorance of their larger consequences. A distorted or one-sided intellectual development can unbalance not only the individual but society. This is so not only in the sense that one may have a deficient sense of social or political relevance, for even an obsession with "relevance" can be unduly narrowing; it is true also in the sense that knowledge is power and creates a potential—indeed a disposition—for its use, in ignorance of its full consequences. In this sense, one has a social as well as a personal responsibility for an awareness of one's ignorance, which can only be met, not by trying to know everything, but by cultivating an awareness of the interdependence of knowledge and a sensitivity to the contributions others can make to our own work.

It would not be difficult to cite other respects in which the Bell formulations might be somewhat amended today, but I shall limit my observations to two main aspects: *humanitas* and the humanities, and the interdisciplinary approach. My earlier statement gave rise to some misunderstanding and puzzlement as to what was intended in these areas, and I should like to offer some distinctions that may clarify them.

THE HUMANITIES, GENERAL AND PROFESSIONAL

First of all, there is an obvious need to distinguish between the humanities in the general sense and in the professional sense. General education in the humanities partakes of both, but the distinction remains valid and consequential. The general sense of the humanities expresses those areas of human experience, concerns, values, and ends that extend into virtually all forms of study and give them relevance both to the inner life of the individual and the common human enterprise. Humanities in this sense, as I have said before, include what has been known as general education but also enter into specialized branches of knowledge insofar as the latter bear upon the perennial problems of human life. In other words, I am suggesting that we need an enlarged definition of the humanities if we are not to immure them within the confines of belletristic studies, but rather keep them open to new forms of human experience and expression.

The humanities also represent, however, an area of traditional, professional study, and exhibit the characteristics of all professional disciplines, that is, a sense of commitment to precise and rigorous methods of study. For that very reason they are likely to produce the narrowness that inheres in professionalization. In other words, one does not necessarily find humanists among the professionals in the humanities, and the latter are as likely to be defensive and parochial about their own interests as any other professionals committed to a valid discipline. One hardly need add that, by the same token, humanists are found outside the humanities disciplines, and often it is they—scientists and engineers—who are more conscious of the need created by their own specialization to establish bridges to other disciplines.

The humanities professional (if I may use that awkward expression for want of a better one at the moment) brings to general education an indispensable tool, of wide use as a liberal discipline even when it is not pursued in some specialized form. This is skill and experience in reading and interpreting materials significant to the humanist. Thus the humanities professional in the various branches of language, linguistics, literature, art, music, philosophy, and religion has an indispensable role in making available for general education, texts and other forms of expression in the arts that could not be accurately and fully understood otherwise. As a humanist he may also become particularly adept at handling these materials in such a way as to make them especially meaningful to his students. In his first function as translator or scholar, he feels a professional obligation to convey accurately to the reader the original meaning of the work as it was intended by the author within the original context. Bernard Weinberg of the University of Chicago speaks of the humanities disciplines as engaged in "reading" works of art, music, literature, and philosophy "according to the principles of the art or science which generated the work."[8] As a humanist, on the other hand, a teacher would further hope to relate that

17

understanding to the contemporary context of human experience, choices, and dilemmas, and this too will lead him into the principles underlying any such work.

The humanities professional with a humanist outlook may feel particularly at home in the discussion of "great books," but he may render a service also in the areas of science and technology, where finesse is needed in the communication of knowledge or where larger human perspectives can enhance the significance of specialized findings. My colleague Amiya Sen points out that the problem in the area of technology is not only the misunderstandings that arise between the sciences and technology on the one hand, and the humanities on the other; even among scientists and engineers communication is impaired because there is a deficiency in their understanding of the humanities as a means of sharing experience and conveying meaning. On the other hand, a colleague in the English department, Joseph Mazzeo, has studied the ways in which scientific discovery and theory have affected language, literature, and the traditional humanities in general.

There is nothing inherent in general education that demands that it be done on an interdisciplinary basis or that it involve interdepartmental instructional staffs. One need not have a committee to do it, and the most elaborate teamwork will often not achieve the results of a single wise and devoted teacher. Nevertheless, a joint teaching arrangement that compels an instructor, not simply to acknowledge the value of disciplines and subjects impinging on his own, but to communicate with and confront spokesmen for other disciplines, has great advantages for general education. Indeed it imposes a special discipline of a high order upon him, for it curbs the temptation to speak as an authority on a wide range of matters and insists that he come to terms with others able to challenge his own claims. Not wide-ranging speculation, but stiff give-and-take marks general education at its best. And at its best, it provides the instructor with as much opportunity to learn from his colleagues and students as to teach.

As we move to extend general education into the professional schools and attempt to overcome the inevitable fragmentation of disciplines that professionalization naturally entails, a countervailing interdisciplinary effort is called for. The possibilities are numerous, and one can easily imagine all sorts of combinations even among the professions themselves. But my use of the term "general education in the humanities" is meant to suggest that the humanities in both the general and specific forms that I have described have a central role. We feel a particular need to draw on the traditional humanities, as disciplines in their own right, to clarify and express the human values that may serve to integrate our educational efforts. In this way the insights and methods of the humanities disciplines may be made to serve larger purposes.

INTERDISCIPLINARY EDUCATION AND RESEARCH

This effort presupposes the continuing and sustained pursuit of disciplined study in the traditional humanities. Far from displacing the latter, general education enhances their importance by bringing the fruits of such studies to bear on questions of the value orientations of the several sciences. In a larger sense, however, what is true of the humanities is also true of other disciplines contributing to general education. One cannot have interdisciplinary studies, so helpful and needful to general education, without at the same time firmly upholding disciplinary studies themselves. The interdependence of disciplined scholarship and general education must be recognized as equally essential elements of university life.

In the ordering and integrating of equally essential activities, however, general education should attempt to develop the larger implications of disciplinary studies for educational purposes. We are talking then, not about interdisciplinary research, but about interdisciplinary education. For this purpose it is vital that instructors have a command of their respective disciplines, but it is not essential that the student, as part of his general education, aspire to the same command of every discipline that may be brought to bear on a given human problem. Such a mastery would indeed become indispensable if he chose to advance, as a matter of professional specialization, to doing original research. But education cannot be solely research oriented without research itself becoming disoriented from life. No matter how rudimentary or advanced may be the state of our own professional competence, we still have a need to understand the value and relevance to ourselves of the studies pursued by others. To meet this need is the function of interdisciplinary general education, as distinct from interdisciplinary research.

John Erskine, one of the progenitors of general education, made such a distinction in advocating the reading and discussion of "great books" that had hitherto been the special preserve of classicists. To derive something of value from a reading of Plato, for example, one did not need a mastery of Greek. Erskine's explicit assumption was that Plato and other "great books" could be read, and understood to a fair degree, in translation. This clearly meant, however, that someone in particular (the translator) should have a reliable command of the original language and could accurately convey the meaning, while others without such competence (the readers) could reasonably be expected to understand it.

From this we see how general education is dependent on the contributions of scholarly disciplines and yet makes use of these contributions for purposes other than the perpetuation and multiplication of scholarly researches. What few appreciate is that scholarly discipline is in turn dependent on general education. For unless education successfully conveys the meaning and value of the humanities in contemporary terms and unless new generations succeed to their cultural inheritance, the values that sustain cultural freedom and support disciplined scholarly research are not passed on. The consequences are seen today in the disinclination of many students to undertake methodical study and preparation for research, as illustrated most dramatically by the decline in language study and the steady abandonment of language requirements at all levels of education. It is reflected in an even more fundamental way by the growing indifference, if not outright hostility, of youth to historical study and to rationality as a fundamental cultural value. The Maoist approach, which places immediate practicality ahead of cultural achievement and puts peasants and soldiers in command of the educational process, holds out a simple but profound appeal to a younger generation whose debased education no longer sustains cultural values in relation to contemporary life.

CONCLUDING QUESTIONS

I fear I have done little more than outline a framework in which to address other important questions. One practical question has to do with the organizing of the new effort. In view of past difficulties in sustaining instructional staffs for general education, the problems of a university-wide program on several levels may seem insuperable. The Carnegie Commission report reflects a common feeling that "general education may need its own enclaves" in which to sustain its existence, and the often unhappy experience of general-education teachers makes a strong argument for establishing a special status for them. Would it not then be more logical to fortify the undergraduate college against the graduate and professional schools, and in its own redoubt give a more well-defined function and a stronger identity and esprit de corps to the specialized cadre assigned this educational task?

The direction of my own thinking is clearly counter to this. General education cannot allow itself to become anyone's special preserve. Such a defensive response to divisive trends in the university only compounds them. In the end it will leave general education high and dry. Rather than a defensive posture, an offensive strategy is what is called for. Far from holing up in its own bunker, general education should try to break out into new ground where it can hope to enlist new recruits and find new intellectual sustenance. No doubt the college must have its own identity, but it should be possible for the undergraduate experience to be well defined and its teachers well supported, without shutting them up in an enclave that is almost certain to become a ghetto.

I have spoken before of the need for an open university within the multiversity. What I have in mind, organizationally, is an infrastructure for general education, with its base in the college and its branches reaching up into the graduate and professional schools. With the help of a university-wide corps of interested faculty, one would hope to work an inner revolution through existing channels. The nature and operation of this infrastructure is a problem with which I shall have to deal separately, but one cannot move on to larger issues without at least acknowledging the practical questions that must be faced and the direction in which we should look for a solution.

The larger question that must be asked, even if the answer lies beyond us now, is whether any improvement can be hoped for in general education if the changes we make are simply mechanical and remain unenlivened by some new spirit of learning. "Humanism" is the slogan commonly invoked in such discussions, and the frequency with which it is resorted to is symptomatic of our present quandary. Traditional values, which many think it the function of general education to propagate, are losing ground. Secularism and social change have undone the conventional pieties, and in default of any consensus on religious values, "humanism" serves for many as the least common denominator of secular faith. Often it appears to be no more than a cliché covering a vast unacknowledged emptiness; for a few it may express the hope, only dimly perceived, that man can still mobilize the spiritual resources to master his disordered existence.

Sidney Hook, that inveterate rationalist and foe of all dogmas including the liberals', says that resort to the word "spiritual" usually betrays an intellectual vacuum. He may often be right, but even if we grant the point, our recognition of that vacuum, or of the spiritual void that is sometimes papered over by the term "humanism," will still serve only as the beginning of wisdom and not as the end of the matter. Elusive though wisdom itself may be and uncertain though our efforts are to attain it, there still seems no alternative to it as a positive end for education. The knowledge explosion and the success of computers has rendered the acquisition of information more unsatisfying and implausible than ever as a goal for the individual.

Some years ago a disgruntled student sued Columbia University for failing to impart wisdom to him. We can all be relieved that the court upheld Columbia, exonerating it of any contractual obligation to deliver wisdom with its diplomas, but for the student to believe that wisdom should be a proper goal of education was not wrong. Nor would it be unnatural to expect that general education in particular should bear much of the burden for continually stimulating and guiding the search for such wisdom in the university.

One unfavorable circumstance of general education in the past may have detracted from that effort. Its conduct in the early years of college has associated it with a time in the life of the student when young minds were reexamining their own values and discarding much that they had taken on faith before. A skeptical and debunking attitude prevailed, sometimes consciously encouraged by instructors who found it easier to put down than to build up. In the next stage of the college curriculum such intellectual reconstruction that took place was in the hands of those who often had made their peace with the smaller, more manageable world of disciplinary specialization, whose natural tendency was to isolate problems rather than to relate them.

Even among the most articulate spokesmen for general education, whatever the other differences among them, there has been a widespread tendency to define the educational task in terms of training the critical intelligence, through increasing degrees of conceptual and methodological sophistication. I do not wish to press the point too far, but in retrospect it seems to me that even Bell's efforts to reform general education by means of so-called "integrative courses" in the fourth year tended to stress the centrality of method and the handling of concepts—"analytic modes of conceptual inquiry"[9]—with relatively little emphasis on overarching values and ends or on personal synthesis. One can share with him an instinctive distrust for anything that might claim to hold out final answers, and I would have no reason to deprecate the effort at methodological synthesis that he offers as the culmination of the college experience. It does not, however, get at the larger problem of how we keep body and soul together while the mind engages in such highly refined operations.

Though I am still only posing a question and not suggesting that there is a single answer to it, I wonder if general education has not been vitiated by too heavy a reliance on questioning for questioning's sake, or perhaps for discussion's sake, without regard to whether it produced any answers. May we not have encouraged a hypercritical attitude, disavowing any high ideals or appreciation of models in the past, and paying respect only to doubt and dissent? Or have I perhaps been overexposed at commencement, year after year, to conventional self-congratulation over the enlightening power of a college education through the hard, gemlike flame of its cool rationality, which has instilled an attitude of irreverence toward all received opinion and delivered the graduate from all illusions?

I suspect that my own dissent from the supreme value of doubt and dissent will be disquieting to many, who see it as inimical to the skepticism considered so healthy in the life of the university. To me, however, skepticism is healthy only as long as it serves constructive ends and does not itself become a religion. Our recent educational experience raises the question as to whether an overdose of critical skepticism has not bred, in reaction, a powerful trend among many students toward irrationalism and mysticism, a devaluing of reason and of the wisdom that should come from sharing the experience of the past. From skepticism of all received values we have bred a pathetic compulsion to believe in something, anything—a romantic credulousness plunging headlong into mindless exaltation of direct action or naked power, alternating with apathy and anarchy, and so on. Most conspicuous of all, and in the long run most costly, has been our failure to engender a sense of the possibilities for responsible leadership among those who enjoyed the benefits of education.

Last year, Herman Wouk returned to the Columbia campus for the dedication of a Jewish *bayit*, and he recalled with warm feelings the exhilaration he experienced as an undergraduate there, when his religious faith and training was challenged, and his thinking stimulated, by the pervasive atmosphere of critical questioning in the university. For him, he said, it resulted not only in a broadening of his horizons but a testing and deepening of his religion. Those of us prepared to respect that outcome are perhaps not safe today in assuming that quite the same process takes place, that there is the same underlying ruggedness of spirit to carry the undergraduate through that demanding test. Times have changed, and the burden of inculcating basic values or establishing some self-discipline is no longer borne to the same extent by family or church or secondary school. For the university to take up all of that burden is not possible, and no one should suffer the misapprehension that I expect general education to do it. We cannot, however, go on assuming that someone else does it and delivers to us a sturdy student, toughened for the struggle, whose only need is to be disabused of his idealism. That need may indeed remain, but something more will be needed for that idealism to be tempered and finally matured into wisdom.

Wouk acknowledged that the threat to the survival of the Jews in the late 1930s and 1940s had much to do with his own religious development. If I say that today the threat to the whole human race is almost comparable and might motivate us to a deeper concern for our common humanity, I may be straining the point. But I do not believe that we should discount either the threat or the undeveloped human resources that might be mounted against it. The living death of many Soviet intellectuals, the prolonged deep-freeze and near-extinction of any real education in China, the abuse, disillusionment, and self-anes-thetizing of young minds in the West all remind us of the fate that might easily befall our educational institutions.

Against this, though it may be more difficult to see, there are opportunities inherent in our present situation as never before for new experience and a new appreciation of others' achievements. A truly global humanism, though it may sound extravagant and overblown, is virtually there for the making. Much experience and wisdom lies em-bedded in many civilized traditions other than our own. While it may not be ready-made and directly transferable for our own use, both the sharing in other world cultures and a recognition of the neglected values present in our own pluralistic culture should infuse new blood in the old "humanities." From the standpoint of traditional Western education and scholarship, it will remain true that "nothing is sacred" and nothing should go unexamined in the light of reason. It should be equally true that in the full perspective and depth of that tradition, there is nothing human that is not sacred, nothing in the experience of other peoples or of our own minority groups that should not be approached with respect, or even reverence, with a readiness to under-stand the most and think the best of it that our intelligence will allow. There is much in human experience that we have hitherto ignored or discounted in advance, much that still can enrich the "humanities" in ways undreamed of by the codifiers of the great books and great ideas or the methodologists of general education in the past.

Drawing on this rich variety we may well come to a new under-standing of the humanities, and from this, conceivably to a new hu-manism. It is in this cause that I would argue for an open-ended, plural-istic structure of general education, while not assuming that such an arrangement alone will guarantee the result. It will have to be worked at, struggled with, brought about. But we should be grateful for the challenge and make the most of our present opportunity.

NOTES

1. Carnegie Commission on Higher Education, *The Purposes and the Performance of Higher Education in the United States* (New York: McGraw-Hill, 1973).

2. S. P. Marland, Jr., "Crisis as Catalyst in Higher Education," address before the Associ-ation of American Universities, Washington, D.C., Oct. 24, 1972.

3. *Columbia College Bulletin, 1972-73*, p. 23.

4. Daniel Bell, *The Reforming of General Education* (New York: Columbia University Press, 1966), p. 201.

5. DeBary, "A Program of General and Continuing Education in the Humanities."

6. Bell, pp. 51-52.

7. Bell, p. 151.

8. Bernard Weinberg, "The Humanities As Humanities," *University of Chicago Record*, VI, No. 6, p. 108.

9. Bell, p. 210.

General Education:
The Minimum Indispensables

Sidney Hook
New York University

Except on one point, my agreement with Professor deBary's essay is much more profound than my differences. If I stress the latter, it is with the hope of provoking discussion and avoiding a premature consensus.

First, however, I wish to say something about certain basic questions that neither he nor, so far as I can judge, the other contributors to our symposium have raised—answers to which are in effect really presupposed when we concern ourselves with the *content* of general education. When we consider the movement for the abolition of curricular requirements that has swept like a tidal wave in recent years over the academic community, we must conclude that our presupposed answers (for example, that there *should* be curricular requirements) are not merely problematic to vast numbers of our faculty colleagues; they are, seemingly, clearly unacceptable.

What makes the situation even more difficult, now that the misunderstood principles of participatory democracy have given students rights and powers in making curricular decisions, is that these answers are not acceptable to many students as well.

When we speak of general education, in the present context, regardless of how we define it we are speaking of a prescribed course of study for all students with the exception of those who can provide evidence of adequate mastery in the subject matters and skills that constitute the curricular requirement. And if our discussion is to have any point or relevance for higher or tertiary education today, we must not lose sight of the fact—deplore it as one may (and I do not deplore it)—that it must be germane to the general education not just of an elite or selected body of students at Columbia, Harvard, or Swarthmore but of *all students beginning their college careers.*

The first question we must face is this: If the course of study is to be related to the student's individual needs, capacities, and background, by what right or justification do we impose any general requirements upon him, aside from the power we have to award or withhold degrees? In the affairs of the mind, coercive power should be irrelevant. Besides, we do not need reminding that in education today power is a very uncertain and shifting commodity. It has been in the wake of student power—as a corollary of student strength and potential for disruption, not as a corollary of reasoned analysis—that requirements on many campuses have been replaced by an unrestricted elective system at the outset of the student's career. The situation has been aggravated by shrinking enrollments in many institutions; many are luring applicants to enroll with the promise that they can write their own educational ticket so long as they pay their tuition. In such institutions there is no field of inquiry, no skill, no body of knowledge that all students are expected to have some familiarity with, not to speak of competence in, before being awarded a baccalaureate degree. Each does his own thing—and not always on the campus.

The challenge to us to justify a required course of general education is often quite explicit. I recall one occasion not so many years ago when a highly vocal and not unintelligent student put it to us at a faculty meeting at Washington Square College.

"After all," she said, "the intrinsic value or interest of a subject isn't enough to justify prescribing it. Every subject has intrinsic value but not to everybody, and judging by some of our teachers, not even to those who make their living teaching it. If education is to be effective and relevant, it must be related to the personal needs of the students. Without us, you have no justification for your being as teachers." And, turning to me, the acting spokesman for the curriculum committee, she let fly: "Who are you, or anyone else, to tell *me* what my educational needs are? I, and I alone, am the best judge of what I want and what I need. What goes for me, goes for everybody. That's democracy in education."

This seems to me now, as it did then, a fair challenge. We must meet it not as specialist scholars but as educators. It is a challenge very often evaded because so many teachers in our colleges do not regard themselves as educators but as scholars, whose primary, if not exclusive, allegiance is to their subject matter. Teaching, for them, is the training of apprentices, who will someday be their successors.

We can grant two things in this challenge to us. The first is that an education that will bear permanent intellectual fruit must be related in larger measure to students' individual needs. The second is that students are aware of what they want although they may not know the consequences of what they want. But these two truths by no means entail that students know what they need, or know what is educationally good for them. Indeed, after more than forty-five years of teaching on the college level, the proposition that most students, upon immediate entry, know what their genuine educational needs are seems to me quite dubious. As a rule, they no more know what their educational needs are than they know their medical needs. Sometimes their needs, and almost always their wants, are altered as they become acquainted with different fields of study. The notion that the generality of students (I am not speaking of the precocious or exceptionally gifted) can make an informed and intelligent decision about their abiding educational needs before being exposed to the great subject matters and disciplines of the liberal tradition is highly questionable. The notion that they are capable of making sensible, lifelong vocational or professional commitments in late adolescence—which is expected of them in some institutions—seems to me gratuitously cruel, and overlooks students' natural capacities for growth and the difficulties of self-knowledge.

Granted that students will ultimately have to make their own curricular choices when the time comes for specialization or the choice of a career. Granted the important role of formal critical education in resisting the tyrannies of the peer group and other social pressures as maturing men and women make the free choice of the pattern of their lives. But so long as we believe that the wisdom of such choice depends upon its being informed, the less occasion there will be for regret. This justifies the exposure to a variety of disciplines, problems, and challenges that general education counterposes to a too early specialization.

There is another point about need. The educational needs of students cannot be considered in isolation from the needs of the society in which they live, which nurtures and subsidizes them and which justifiably expects that they will be active, mature, and responsible citizens. Indeed, the chief justification for the community's underwriting the immense costs of universal access to higher education is not that it will increase earning power or social status or even provide enjoyment but that it will enhance the prospects of developing an intelligent and responsible citizenry. But that depends on what students learn and how.

John Dewey said that there are three important reference points that must be considered in developing a curriculum on any level. The first is the nature and needs of the student; the second is the nature and needs of the society of which students are a part; the third is the subject matter by which the students develop themselves as persons and relate to other persons in their society.

Our problem, as I see it, is this: Given our society, our potential student body, the accumulated knowledge, traditions, and skills of a large number of disciplines, given the spectrum of conflicting values in the present juncture of history, can we as educators devise a program of studies (I do not mean specific courses) that we can and should require of all students on their way to adulthood and vocation? Or, to use one of the felicitous distinctions of Professor deBary: Has the university, in the exercise of its "magisterial role" rather than its "prophetic or pontifical role," not only the authority but the intellectual confidence and courage to say to all students, "Here in our considered judgment, based on experience and reflection, are the minimum indispensables of liberal or general education for the modern man and woman. We shall require a certain proficiency in these minimum indispensables before you are allowed to do your own curricular thing. We are prepared to sit down with you to discuss the educational validity of a curriculum, listen carefully to your criticisms and suggestions in the never-ending process of curricular modification, experiment, and revision, and make allowance for your special aptitudes and conditions. But in the end, the decision will be ours if you elect to stay and continue your studies."

If we were to stop at this point, we might as well have not begun. For the thrust of the argument may be accepted and yet the content of education consist of a miscellany of studies that will not reflect the common needs of students and of our society. I hope we can be sufficiently concrete to reach a consensus not only on the desirability of general education but also, allowing for some peripheral diversity and variation, on its basic content. I shall very briefly put forward some curricular proposals to that end.

Permit me first to address myself to some of the larger considerations that I fear may distract us from our task. By striving to do too much we may achieve too little. There is a danger in the overly ambitious attempt to envisage and plan for the general or liberal education of students over their entire educational career, including their technical or specialized education as well as their vocational or professional education. As I understand general education, it is an integral part of liberal education, defined as the knowledge and sensibility, the attitudes and intellectual skills that men and women, in Professor de

Bary's words, "can reasonably be expected to have in common as a basis for their individual development and participation in the human community." It introduces students in a coherent and systematic way to "those areas of human experience [and knowledge], concerns, values, and ends [and problems] that extend into virtually all forms of study and give them relevance both to the inner life of the individual and the common human enterprise."

Granted that this does not exhaust the range and depth of liberal education, that it is desirable for students to renew and strengthen their liberal orientation regardless of their subsequent experience, or subsequent specialized or professional education. But that is something we cannot plan for, for our primary concern is with the foundational years. To be sure, liberal learning is lifelong learning, but how it should be integrated into the professional education of lawyers, physicians, architects, and engineers must be worked out by educators in those disciplines, with reference to their own problems. Having served on committees that have sought to humanize the curricula of law and medical schools, I am convinced of both the relevance of liberal education and its concerns for professional education and also the wisdom of leaving the curricular broadening in these fields to the professional practitioners, in consultation with others. After all, most students do not go on to professional or graduate schools. The best we can do is to try to make liberal education so intense and meaningful an experience before the onset of specialization that the interest evoked will feed itself in all subsequent experience.

The second danger I wish to caution against is the attempt to derive the liberal-education curriculum from some metaphysical or philosophical or theological conception of the nature of man, or from some overall view of "first and last things," about which the possibility of establishing a consensus is impossible. Instead of trying to devise a curriculum that will fit some antecedent beliefs about what differentiates man from other creatures, we can probably make better progress by taking a prospective point of view, by asking what courses of study are likely to achieve more desirable outcomes than others for the men and women in our community, regardless of whether we believe that they are ultimately analyzable into complexes of electrons or sense data or spiritual emanations of the One. This makes wise decisions in curricular matters dependent upon the fruits or consequences of alternative proposals, not a matter of deduction or inference from the essential nature of man or other problematic conclusions from philosophical anthropology.

And now, I wish to sketch very briefly the areas of study that should, I think, constitute the curricular substance of general education, and dwell on some of the open problems. I classify them under six rubrics.

1. Every student has an objective need to be able to communicate clearly and effectively with his fellows, to grasp with comprehension and accuracy the meaning of different types of discourse, and to express himself in a literate way. (Judging by the student levels of reading and writing accepted at some colleges, we may expect in the future that students will sue their educational alma maters, not for failure to teach them wisdom, but for failure to make them literate or teach them the good language habits of their own tongue.)

2. Every student needs to have at least some rudimentary knowledge about his own body and mind, about the world of nature and its determining forces, about evolution and genetics, and allied matters that are central to a rational belief about the place of man in the universe. If he is to have any understanding of these things, he must possess more than the capacity to remember and parrot isolated facts. He must have some grasp of the principles that explain what he observes, some conception of the nature of scientific method. After all, the modern world is what it is in virtue of the impact of science and technology on nature and society. He cannot feel at home in the modern world ignorant of science.

3. Every student has a need to become intelligently aware of how his society functions, of the great historical, economic, and social forces shaping its future, of the alternatives of development still open to us, of the problems, predicaments, and programs he and his fellow citizens must face. Whether he wants to revolutionize the world or save it from revolution, he must acquire an historical *perspective*, without which old evils may reappear under new faces and labels. Those who act as if they were born yesterday are the great simplifiers, who mistake their own audacity for objective readiness and often wreck the lives of others in the wreckage of their hopes.

4. Every student needs to be informed, not only of significant facts and theories about nature, society, and the human psyche, but also of the conflict of values and ideals in our time, of the great maps of life, the paths to salvation or damnation, under which human beings are enrolled. He must learn how to uncover the inescapable presence of values in every policy, how to relate them to their causes and consequences and costs in other values, and the difference between arbitrary and reasonable value judgments.

5. Every student needs to acquire some methodological sophistication that should sharpen his sense for evidence, relevance, and canons of validity. He should, at least in popular discourse and debate, be able to distinguish between disguised definitions and genuine em-

pirical statements, between resolutions and generalizations, to nail the obvious statistical lie, and acquire an immunity to rhetorical claptrap. This is what I mean when I speak of the centrality of method in the curriculum. Is it expecting too much of effective general education that it develop within students a permanent defense against gullibility? It is astonishing to discover how superstitious students are, how vulnerable to demogogic appeal, to empty show and eloquence. There are, for example, more students enrolled in courses in astrology than astrophysics.

I ask this question under the influence of the report of a biazrre experiment published in the July 1973 issue of *The Journal of Medical Education*, which has a bearing on the weight now being given to student evaluations in the assessment of teachers. A medical team hired a professional actor to teach "charismatically and nonsubstantively on a topic about which he knew nothing." Under the pseudonymous name of Dr. Fox, in an inspired and seductive fashion, his lectures spiced with humor, he delivered himself of an hour-long lecture that consisted of pure gobbledegook, "nothing more than a goulash of double talk, neologisms, non sequiturs, and contradictory statements." The audience was composed of fifty-five educators, psychiatrists, psychologists, social workers, and administrators of courses in educational philosophy. All respondents were very favorably impressed. One even believed he had read Dr. Fox's papers. There seemed to be only one criticism: "The presentation was too intellectual." The topic of the lecture was "Mathematical Game Theory Applied to the Education of Physicians" and was ostensibly designed to be understood by laymen. If general education cannot immunize professionals against such farragoes of absurdity, it seems to me a failure no matter what else it does.

6. Finally, every student has a need to be inducted into the cultural legacies of his civilization, its art, literature, and music. His sensibilities should be developed and disciplined because they provide not only an unfailing occasion of delight and enjoyment in the present but also a source of enrichment of experience in the future.

These needs, I submit, define required areas of study. The creative task we face is to devise specific courses from campus to campus that will give these studies body and depth, that will truly challenge and interest students before the point of specialization, and continue to do so beyond it. I hope that others in the humanities, natural sciences, and social sciences will come forward with vital and practicable proposals for curriculum construction, and will grapple with well-known difficulties. What history, for example, should be taught, and how? Is it feasible to include the systematic study of Oriental literature and culture without cutting too much away from the study of Western literature and culture? How should the sciences be taught? Should mathematics be additionally required? Should a reading or speaking know-ledge of a foreign language be required of all students? I used to think so, on the ground that it introduces us to new ways of thought and feeling, spurs imaginative and empathetic identification with others, besides constituting the best way of getting to know a foreign culture. Today I no longer think it should be required. The time necessary to ac-quire a useful and usable linguistic mastery may be too great; it should be left to specialized education.

It is not necessary that we agree on detailed answers, but our ab-stractions about liberal education should give some guide to curricular practices. (I repeat, we are concerned here primarily with the philoso-phy of the *curriculum*, not the philosophy of the subject matters.)

Before concluding, I must say a word about objections to my em-phasis on the centrality of method in liberal education. These objec-tions assert that such emphasis results in a hypertrophic critical stance to all positive laws and institutions, to a value rootlessness that takes the forms of apathy or nihilism or exaggerated skepticism, to a demand for a shallow clarity, comparable in André Gide's words, to "the shining clarity of empty glasses." It is on this point that I find Professor de Bary's observations puzzling and rather questionable. There seems to be an intimation in his essay that a powerful cause of our academic time of troubles, its disorders and violence, is "an overdose of critical skepticism," of questioning for questioning's sake, of too much de-bunking of ideals.

Problems of causation are complex, of course, but two things seem to me to be true. First, the issues that sparked campus disruptions were most often extra-academic, related to off-campus events and not to defects of the curriculum; arguments about the latter were later brought in as sheer rationalization. Second, having confronted militant students of every sect and persuasion, I would say that, far from suffer-ing from an overdose of skepticism, they seem to be in the grip of a double dose of absolutism—cocksure, intellectually arrogant, and in-tolerant. Some are obsessed by a Marxism so crude and vulgar that it would make the doctrinaire Yipsils (Young People's Socialist League) of my own revolutionary youth blush with shame. Others are credulous prophets of immediacy or apologists of violence, while professing be-lief in the natural goodness of man. All are full of messianic zeal with-out any tincture of skepticism.

Why indeed should the awareness of method and the cultivation of methodological sophistication necessarily result in skepticism and the absence of grounded belief? After all, it is a commonplace that we can only doubt intelligently on the basis of something we believe.

Genuine skepticism is not the foundation of knowledge, but its crown. Ignorance, inexperience, naiveté are free of doubt. Methodological skepticism does not so much undermine beliefs as limit them by placing them in context. It moderates the coefficient of the intensity of belief with which they are held by relating them to the body of available evidence. What it undermines is *absolutism*, the arrogance of partial perspectives claiming a total and incandescent vision

A proper understanding of method is aware of the differences that different subject matters make—differences reflected in the varying degrees of certitude appropriate to different disciplines. It is true that students have shown an alarming distrust of democracy and the democratic process. In part, this has been an impatience with the pace of reforms, in part an understandable reaction to the abuses and failures of the democratic process. This would not be so disquieting were it accompanied by as pervasive a distrust of the alternatives advanced to cure its evils. But surely when, as many students do, they go beyond legitimate criticism of democracy and espouse unabashed forms of elitism, and even outright dictatorship of the "righteous," they are not carried there by skepticism but rather by their ignorance and innocence of the nature of ideals. Lacking an historical perspective, they are acutely aware of the ever present disparity between our ideals and existing realities. Combined with a failure to understand the heuristic function of ideals, they ignore or dismiss the substantial gains that have been made, both in the areas of welfare and freedom, and the extent to which our ideal sights have been raised with our advance. With the loss of a sense of proportion, there is loss in their sense of reality.

Nor can I accept the view that the academic and cultural barbarism that grows out of the implicit notion that *Alles ist Gefühl* came into existence to fill the vacuum created by too much intellection in higher education. I agree that man is a believing animal and that the exigencies of life and its troubles require that he act on some beliefs. I would argue, however, that the very interest of successful action reinforces the view that the ways in which he holds his beliefs, and the study of such ways, are as important as and sometimes even more important than any particular belief. I have long argued that dissent is no more virtuous than conformity, that the significant question is always whether either one is reasoned or unreasoned. On this I agree with Professor deBary, but I cannot see why the process of critical inquiry must always terminate in dissent. One widely accepted definition of science is that it is the study of propositions concerning which universal agreement is possible. Karl Popper to the contrary notwithstanding, the scientist is not always a "nay-sayer." And when he does say "nay" it is a way station in a process that terminates in warranted assertions that provide reliable knowledge.

General or liberal education studies different ideologies. It does not itself express or presuppose any ideology unless the term "ideology" is used synonymously with "ideal." In the language of ideals, general education is neither capitalist nor socialist; neither nationalist nor internationalist; neither theist nor atheist. The ideal it exemplifies is the ideal of untrammeled free inquiry, inquiry into fact and value and their interrelations. The hope is that commitment to free inquiry about nature, society, and man will lead to well-being and human happiness. But no guarantees can be given. What we can be reasonably sure about is that it will increase the range and freedom of human choice. And that is justification enough.

Where general education has been tried and failed, its failures have resulted, not from an overdose of skepticism generated by its curricular practices, but from a lack of belief in its validity on the part of those who have been responsible for its operation and especially by abysmal failures to teach it properly—a task of greater magnitude than the teaching of specialties. Here the students cannot be faulted. Like so many other things for which students are blamed, it is the faculties who are primarily responsible for the deplorable state of undergraduate education.

On Reviving Liberal Education—
in the Seventies

Joseph J. Schwab
University of Chicago

I am in general agreement with all but one of William Theodore de Bary's views. I see, however, certain omissions in his discourse and certain traps into which I think he falls. These traps and omissions call for supplements. I offer them here, most of them ad hoc, one of them systematic.

ADMINISTRATORS AND THEIR POLICIES

I agree with deBary that the Carnegie Commission Report on Higher Education is as bland as porridge and speaks nowhere of the character of general or liberal education in other than the simplest terms. If, however, deBary will look again at Clark Kerr's own contributions to this report, he will discover, I think, that this tame account arises, not from bankruptcy, but from a *policy* of demulcence, of suggesting to universities, and especially to their faculties, no more than they are presently ready to accept.

This is, I think, a mistaken policy, an obsolete policy. It was an inevitable policy in the 1950s, in the period of educational expansion, of a seller's market as far as faculty were concerned. Then, the administrator's problem was to obtain warm bodies at any cost (distinguished warm bodies, if possible); hence he wanted to run no risk of offending faculties or of asking them to do other than they wanted to do or could be persuaded was in their own interest to do.

It is no longer a seller's but a buyer's market, as far as faculty are concerned. The administrator's problem now is to preside over shrinkage, to see to it that the inevitable and accelerating shrinkage of the educational establishment be not a mere wasting away but occasion for the enhancement of quality at the expense of size. It is a time for the administrator to return to his role as first among peers and away from his role as their servant.

This point assumes relevance here because deBary, too, slips here and there into much the same hesitant posture. He is uneasily aware of the possibility of such slips, as witness one followed by a vehement denial: ". . . members [of the academy] had come to take their own existence, rights, and freedoms for granted. Today, nothing less than an active commitment to education—and not just the training of scholars—can reestablish these on a sound basis. . . . By saying this, I [do not] imply . . . that the raison d'être of general education is the defense of academic freedom . . . "

The rhetoric of direct appeal to faculty self-interest is unimportant in itself. What matters are the concrete instances in which concern for that interest is responsible for milder, less full-bodied proposals than the argument of circumstance seems to require.

DIFFUSENESS AND SURVEY

I agree that a defensible liberal education need not be diffuse and that the survey course is its perversion.

Diffuseness is worse than unnecessary. It is a failure of liberality. A course or program that is diffuse will be an object of mere acquisition. If there is to be liberal effect, the course or program must have density and coherence conferred by a unity of subject or topic (they are not the same) or a unity of discipline. Such a coherent density will appear as evidence, argument, interpretation, and qualification, whereas diffuseness arises from a rhetoric of mere conclusions. It is only by means of such densities that the challenge to students to penetrate to the problem, to attack and try to solve it arises, and it is only when challenges of that kind are recognized by students, prepared for, and met, that the disciplines that liberate arise.

As to survey courses, I was elected as a freshman to attend one of the first and better of them. It was called, modestly, "The Nature of the World and of Man." Its substance was so neat, so clear, and so slick that it required six months from its conclusion to discover its incompleteness and two years to discover that what it did teach was glibly misleading. I believed, on its conclusion, that I did, indeed, know the nature of the world and of man—and that both could be known by mere attentive listening and reading.

I know now that some of the men responsible for that course were hacks. But some of them, I know now, were luminaries of a first-rate university and "leaders in their field." The leaders and luminaries were, on the whole, as glibly clear as the hacks, as simply declarative in their rhetoric, and as responsible for the structure and content of the course as the hacks. I shall return to this point.

EXAMINATIONS, EDUCATION, AND LOCKSTEPS

I agree with deBary that routinized study followed by external examinations and the granting of degrees will not yield a liberal education. I agree that contact with disciplined and liberal teachers and a sharing of the common life and values of a college or university are necessary or almost necessary for a liberal education. But two caveats are in order, pertaining respectively to examinations and the liberalizing common life.

First caveat: deBary speaks rightly of basic disciplines that should come early in the college student's career because they are essential to his later work. And he says of these basic disciplines: "Some students will master these sooner than others, and if they do so, in my opinion there is no reason why they should not move ahead as rapidly as possible. . . " This seems to me more than a matter of mere opinion. Whatever the discipline that a student masters early, continued exposure to instruction and drill in its exercise can lead only to boredom and a low opinion of the professor and institution that subject him to such waste and boredom. But if such waste and boredom are to be eliminated, some means are required for discovering students' early mastery, and mechanisms must be prepared that permit escape from the tyrannies of required attendance, credits, and semester hours. An examination system novel in its content and novel in its frequent accessibility to students will be required. (But there is an additional question: How will professors who are willing to give courses to undergraduates react to the notion that the better student can make do with much less of the professor's personal ministrations than the professor thinks is necessary?)

Second caveat: The sharing of a common culture, the tasting and testing of the values of university life—which we think desirable for fulfillment of a liberal educational experience—will not arise from mere hours spent in a university's buildings and grounds. If a university is mainly a base for auto-entrepreneurs of expertise, there will be no point in students living there. If a university is mainly a haven for self-sequestered scholars (sequestered from one another as well as from students), there will be no point either. Yet, deBary himself speaks of the difficulty of obtaining collaborative teaching and of a morale problem that arises from "the feeling that [teaching] hampers rather than furthers professional advancement."

Unless and until we reimpart to universities a visible and palpable measure of collegiality, will there be any point to students being "in residence"? A hope for this restoration exists, I think. It can exist because of the continuation of the academic depression and its deliberate use by administrators to shrink the size of universities, especially the number of their faculties and the size of their student bodies. Continuation of the academic depression is inevitable, even if the drop in birthrate after 1960 goes no further. Appropriate use of this depression by administrators is not inevitable.

CAREER EDUCATION

DeBary rightly deplores vocational stress and pressure toward shortening nonspecialized education. He recognizes, nevertheless, that most Americans, old or young, attach high importance to career preparation as an educational objective. His solution to the problem is to abjure the notion that liberal education is entirely a function of the earlier years of university education and to emphasize the need and possibility of career education itself as the bearer of disciplinary (liberal) responsibility. This is a good solution as far as it goes. But it goes very little of the needed way, given the United States as it is here and now. It is a solution of an administrator looking, not at the national political community, but only at the university. It is a solution that can function only for those who pursue *academic* careers, or professional careers requiring graduate academic training. But "career" for most Americans and for most graduates of colleges and universities is not an academic career. "Career" is earning a wage, fulfilling the so-called American Dream—the dream that arises in the unconscious of a consumer mentality—a career, as it were, of conspicuous (and competitive) consumption and indifference to the problems and duties of polity. An effective liberal education ought at least to try to liberate us from that.

For this liberating purpose, there arises again the desirability of collegiality, of campuses that are palpably political communities in the most honorable sense of the phrase—assemblies of men and women who discern and honor their *common* goods and *common* problems and work toward their fulfillment and solution. The model afforded by such a community and the opportunity to live for a time as a member of it might go a long way toward liberating some men and women from the simplistic American Dream.

Again, we have a chance to turn necessity into a virtue. We could use the academic depression to help reestablish a balance between faculty loyalty to the learned society and loyalty to the earth-bound institution, the college or university.

THE LIBERAL FACULTY IN A CAVE OF ITS OWN

I agree with deBary that a discrete undergraduate faculty of a university, a liberal educational faculty in a fortress of its own, is a risky solution to the problem of furnishing a good liberal education. I spent ten years helping to construct and serve such a faculty. They were the most rewarding (and educational) ten years of my life. They were also the years that taught me the two major risks such a faculty runs.

The more patent risk is the risk of second-class citizenship for members of such a faculty. In an institution whose ethos is primarily an ethos of scholarship, the man who teaches more than he inquires is inevitably looked at askance by the scholars and researchers. He is alien, an oddity, at best; very often he is seen as "not really a professor." This status is likely to be conferred even if the teaching faculty is also scholarly (but never scholarly at the expense of teaching)—and even if its scholarship is good. It is highly likely too that budgets being what they are, administrators who praise liberal education will reward their teaching faculty with lower pay than other faculties, *and this fact will be known to all*. The result, of course, is poor morale in the teaching faculty and a turning in upon itself for recognition. The liberal faculty becomes a cult.

The second risk arises from formation of the cult. The teaching faculty must recruit, renew contracts, confer or withhold tenure as do other faculties. (The alternative is that these "services" be performed for it by other faculties with little interest in rewarding the teaching function.) There comes a time when the cultic teaching faculty applies to these functions as its main criterion, the criterion of orthodoxy. It sees almost every deviance from its own view of the ends and means of liberal education as heresy or treason. It eventually eliminates, instead of cherishing, diversity of view. Then it presents the unpleasant spectacle of an illiberal group of men claiming to afford a liberal education. The Platonic Divided Line becomes the Platonic Cave.

(I hasten to add that a tendency toward cultic deterioration is not limited to independent teaching faculties. It occurs in scholarly departments when their fields of inquiry enter a period of *methodenstreit*. Witness departments of political science and psychology in recent years, and sociology a few years earlier.)

AN ALTERNATIVE TO THE CAVE

DeBary and others see as the clear alternative to the independent teaching faculty that the scholars of a university—or many of them—be also teachers and that teaching be restored to honor by being rewarded. This alternative, too. has its endemic risk

I remind you that some of the most glib misrepresentations of the fruits of research and scholarship came to my freshman ears from scholars and researchers. They dealt as slickly and persuasively in a rhetoric of unqualified conclusions as any hack. And I have heard them do the same since, in classroom as well as before public audiences, and heard them with mature ears.

The universities of the United States have now lived through three or more faculty generations trained and conditioned to want to speak seriously only to their peers. They speak only *down* to others. To laymen, these faculty members retail their expertise. Conclusions are stripped of their evidence. Interpretation is purveyed as description. Qualification is omitted and doubtfulness suppressed. And all this is done in the name of "clarity," as the essence of good teaching.

That kind of discourse, that kind of "good teaching" will not be liberating. It *will* be rewarded. The Pied Pipers will pipe; the children will follow the Pied Pipers. And the rewards will go to the Piper with followers—given the usual sort of university administration.

More liberating speech will come only from scholars who have learned to respect the needs of lay audiences as they now respect peers, from scholars who understand that the limitations of lay audiences make them novices to be brought toward membership, not children to be talked down to. That kind of faculty will not be spawned by present faculties. It will arise only if tough administrators provide models of what is needed, over the heads of present faculty, and then drag the rest of the faculty, kicking and screaming, to witness what the models do and to witness their rewards. This will not be easy and it will not be peaceful.

DISCIPLINES

I come now to a systematic complement to deBary's commendations. It arises from a set of distinctions that apply to the referents of each departmental name in a university catalogue, each "-ology."

Each such "-ology" is, first of all, a *field of potential study*, a chunk of the world (or of mind, in the case of mathematics and parts of philosophy). Each such field of potential inquiry, when characterized and bounded, becomes a *subject matter*, a body of phenomena subject to inquiry. The characterization and bounding of the subject matter provide terms in which questions can be couched, indicate the data to be sought to answer the questions, and determine the principles and methods by which the data are to be interpreted. These acts—the putting of appropriate questions, the search for the appropriate data, and their canonical interpretation—constitute the *discipline* of the field. This discipline or art of inquiry, brought to bear in the subject of inquiry, yields the *knowledge* of the field sought by its *community of inquirers*.

Each of these—the field of potential study, subject matter, discipline, knowledge, and community—is interesting in its own right. Each has a contribution to make to liberal education, and each can be the planning focus of a program of liberal education.

DeBary appears to begin by emphasis on discipline: "liberate the powers of the individual by disciplining them" and "training in those basic disciplines that will be essential tools in one's later work." But nowhere are the disciplines that might constitute the liberal education of our time elucidated (apart from a reference to the mastery of a foreign language), and deBary soon shifts from the language of "discipline" to the language of "knowledge": "knowledge explosion," "the knowledge that men can reasonably be expected to have in common," "understanding of contemporary issues," "mix of idea and fact, the short and the long view," "uniform content and a common body of up-to-date materials on contemporary problems that change rapidly."

Since deBary's emphasis is upon knowledge, I shall put mine on discipline, not only the academic disciplines of inquiry but also upon certain analogous disciplines appropriate to the nonacademic, yet which require the academy and make fullest use of the academic for their acquisition. I shall call them "disciplines," "arts," "competences," interchangeably and without distinction. Five groups of arts commend themselves as speaking most directly to the temper and troubles of our time and to the most telling of our students' privations.

Arts of Access

The first consists of the arts of access. These are the arts by which we know what questions to ask of a work—a paper, a book, an oral presentation, a lithograph, a sonata, a cinema—and the arts by which we find the answers. They are the means by which we gain access to the objects of intelligence and sensibility. The questions to be asked and answered differ for works of different kinds, as Bernard Weinberg reminds us in the dictum quoted by deBary: They differ, "according to the principles of the art or science which generated the work." In reading history, for example, the ambivalent love and warfare between fact and fiction, memory and imagination, which rule the construction of history, determine that certain questions be asked an historical work that would not otherwise be asked. A scientific work poses the need to determine what problem is being attacked, what data would solve it, what data are, in fact, being sought, and what principles are used to interpret the data. Works from the social sciences again raise questions of problem, data, and interpretation. They also require hard and numerous questions about diversities of disciplines employed by the social sciences and their effects on the questions asked and answered. They require, as well, questions about the relations of knowledge and action, theory and practice.

The point in thus illustrating the arts of access lies in the fact that these are not merely linguistic arts. They have to do with much more than how to read a book or sentence; they have to do with the principles and methods of the art or science that produced the work. It follows that the arts of access are not the peculiar property of the humane professional. They know best the principles and methods out of which grow novels and lyric poetry, music and the plastic arts, history and philosophy. But not even all of history and philosophy is clear and patent to many humanists, much less the materials that arise from the social and natural sciences. In brief, transmission of the arts of access require the services of all the disciplines that constitute a university community.

The problem of locating the disciplines most useful to students here and now involves emphasis within groups of arts, as well as discrimination of the most useful groups. Among the arts of access to works of art, for example, there are many alternative avenues that could be pursued. I would commend for students of our time emphasis on the final cause and not the efficient—on the work, not the author or his times; and on the effect, not the device.

Arts of Communication

The second commended group are the arts of communication, of speaking and writing (listening and reading) with clarity and distinction. Here, too, a problem of emphasis arises. I commend two in the light of present needs, especially in the light of the long-term as well as the dramatic traumas that our political community now suffers. One of these consists of the arts of persuading and being persuaded, the arts of irenic discussion. The second is an allied art, not patently of language but of communication nevertheless: the arts of collaboration toward proximate goals on the part of men whose ultimate goals may differ.

These arts, too, are not adequately served only by professional humanists. Problems and issues should arise in all fields and be marked by expresssion of defensible varieties of view, discussion of them, and achievement of a measure of consensus—all this as a regular and legitimate part of the teaching-learning process. Irenic discussion of many such differences of view will be marked by appeal to different facts and different dicta on the part of different participants, thus posing one of the most difficult, yet most common of the problems of persuasion and collaboration, and therefore, one of the most important of problems to learn to solve. It is easy, indeed, to come to agreement with men "who agree with us in principle."

(My mention of "fact" provides occasion for mention of what I hope is obvious—that the notion of arts or disciplines is not an alternative to or opposed to the notion of knowledge. Disciplines employ knowledge and are acquired only by application to sources of knowledge. In the same way, those relevant to the arts are not opposed to or alternative to being moved or affected by works of art. They are means for locating the sources of movement and affect and of becoming sensitive to their effect.)

Arts of Inquiry

The very arts of inquiry that give rise to the need for arts of access have a limited place in the liberal curriculum. For the rightness of the questions to be asked of a fruit of an art or science is not always made clear and vivid by only experiencing a finished work. It is when we undertake to *write* a lyric poem that we become fully aware of the subtleties of device and effect and the rightness or wrongness of an imagery, the music, or the shape of a word. It is when we undertake a small piece of scientific research that we become fully aware of the problems of the propriety and reliability of data and the ambiguous difficulties of their interpretation. It is only as we undertake the study of a person or community that we recognize fully the complexity of these fields of potential study and the relative simplicity of the characterizing and bounding conceptions that make of them subjects capable of inquiry. These advantages constitute one of two reasons why a measure of the arts of inquiry might characterize a liberal education. (These arts could well be served, as deBary suggests, not in the early years of collegiate education but in a later and specialized phase.)

The second reason for their inclusion lies in the fact that few of us realize that great magnitude of most problems. We tend to assume that they are as easily solved as they are to state. It is only as we try to solve a relatively simple one that we come to know how big they are.

Overarching Disciplines

The arts of access can convey to students the illusion that subjects of inquiry are indeed the natural segments of the world—individual *and* society; living *and* nonliving; fact *and* idea (or value); free markets *and* political action. Or students may adopt from chance reading or discipleship a doctrinaire notion of the filiation of the sciences: that societies arise to fulfill individual human needs; that any human's apparent needs and values are imposed by his culture and society; that the living organism is merely the sum of its physiochemical parts; that physical-chemical events constitute a system different in no fundamental way from that of the living organism.

The dangers of such naive faiths in specialisms or in their simple connection are obvious enough to commend to us the desirability of some treatment of the many different ways in which sciences can be organized or related to one another. The paucity of expertise in such matters is so marked (among philosophers as well as others) that I shall go no further than to suggest that some treatment of the problem is desirable.

Arts of the Practical

This group of arts involves my one sharp difference of view with de Bary: on the place of practical and current problems in the liberal curriculum. I have in mind such problems as those of energy shortage, environmental deterioration, urbanism, democratization of industry, multinational corporations, individual rights and freedoms, and making democracy safe from the US presidency.

DeBary would view such problems "first in terms of the perennial concerns and problems of human life . . . and, second, in terms of those disciplines that may contribute to an understanding, and possibly a solution of them." He expands the latter point: "to demonstrate the relevance of a specialized discipline to basic human needs and to acknowledge the interdependence of the disciplines in seeking to meet them."

Thus practical problems are adapted by deBary to the present structure and interests of the academic. To view practical problems in terms of the perennial problems and concerns of human life is to ensure that practical problems are shorn of much of what makes them *practical* problems: their concrete particularity, their element of novelty, their origin in circumstances and conditions peculiar to our time, the dependence for their solution on presently available means and resources and present conflicts and differences of interest. It is to make them *instances*, members of a class, and thus to make them appear to be well within the compass of the typically academic, amenable to its great strength—which is its greatest weakness as far as practical problems are concerned—its passion for generality, neatness, and order.

What is wrong with deBary's second point—the use of practical problems to demonstrate the relevance of specialized disciplines and merely to "acknowledge" the interdependence of the disciplines—is best indicated by a statement overheard on a university campus: "I've a perfect solution to the energy crisis. All we need do is dam the Mediterranean at Gibraltar, give it ten years to evaporate, then open the sluices and generate electricity from the fall. We have all the technology necessary, including that of storage. The method is pure use of solar energy, no pollution. There are other water bodies where the same technique is possible and among them they will supply all projected energy needs. Of course, there are a few political difficulties, but that is not my problem." Thus speaks a representative of a discipline, acknowledging the interdependence of his discipline with others.

In my view, practical problems should be the focus of a part of the liberal curriculum concerned explicitly with the arts required for treatment of practical problems. Since these arts are among those least familiar to the academic (though still contingent on academic arts and expertise), I shall suggest their character.

Arts of the Eclectic

Practical problems arise from complex transactions among men and things, a web of transactions that know nothing of the boundaries that separate economics from sociology or physics from political science. Yet, our fullest knowledge of these matters lies in economics, politics, sociology, and physics. To compound this difficulty, each such science readies its subject of inquiry by separating it from the whole of the world and conferring on its part an appearance of wholeness and unity. These separations and smoothings of subjects of inquiry are reflected in the bodies of knowledge we inherit from these sciences. Each of them is couched in its own set of terms and only a few terms in each set are connected with the terms of another set.

The first of these incongruences (of practical problems and bodies of knowledge) requires that we relate science to one another. The second incongruence (of the terms employed by the various sciences) forbids a *theoretical* unification of these sciences except in rare instances, and even then too slowly to meet the needs posed by the urgency of practical problems. What is required is a practical healing of

47

the breaches among the sciences, a recourse to tentative and temporary bridges built in the course of applying these sciences to particular problems. The building of such bridges is the business of the arts of the eclectic.

Arts of the Practical Per Se

Academic knowledge is general knowledge. It is achieved by processes of abstraction or idealization, by search for uniformity and discard of the grossly variable. The very fabric of the practical, on the other hand, consists of the numerous and varied particulars from which theory abstracts and idealizes. Solution of practical problems requires recognition of and accounting for these particulars. There must be ways, then, for perceiving these particulars, arts of "irrelevant" scanning.

There are additional practical arts. There are arts of problemation, by which we assign various meanings to the perceived detail of a situation in order to shape different formulations of "the" problem. There are arts for weighing alternative formulations of a problem. There are arts for generating alternative solutions to their consequences, for weighing and choosing among them. There are arts for appropriately terminating deliberation in the interest of action.

The arts of the eclectic and the practical are necessary arts. They are necessary if institutions are to solve the problems they create when they solve the problems they were established to treat. They are necessary if institutions are to change to survive.

The arts of the eclectic and the practical are not presently arts typical of the university. Yet they depend, in part, on the fruits of academic arts. And if they are necessary arts and if they can be taught, they ought to be taught. And if they are not taught by universities, then by whom shall they be taught? Perhaps acquisition of these arts and of the arts of imparting them are two changes that universities as institutions may need to undertake in order to survive. An odd argument indeed, and ad hominem to a degree.

THE HUMANISTIC DISCIPLINES

Humanism and the Humanities

Frederick A. Olafson
University of California,
San Diego

When we speak of the humanities, we usually have in mind a loosely related group of disciplines that, by general agreement, includes at least literature, history, and philosophy. "History" is, of course, to be understood here as comprising the several branches of cultural history and notably the history of art and of music. Other disciplines like anthropology and linguistics or certain of their aspects are sometimes counted among the humanities; but for the purposes of this paper only the three disciplines which both tradition and current academic practice classify as "humanities" will be used as paradigms of humanistic study. My interest is directed to such convergent purposes and methods as this classification of literature, history, and philosophy may be supposed to imply and to the relationship between this common humanistic element, if it can be elicited, and current conceptions of inquiry and instruction within these disciplines. My guiding assumption here is that the character of the curriculum in any given field is a function of the presiding conception of the objectives and methods of scholarship within that field. If that assumption is correct, then to analyze and appraise such conceptions is also to raise questions of the most fundamental kind about the curriculum.

It is rather surprising to discover that the points of convergence of these three humanistic disciplines have not been the subject of very much sustained analysis. Although departments of literature, history, and philosophy have often collaborated in programs of general education in the humanities and a considerable body of thought has been generated that seeks to provide a rationale for such joint programs, these philosophies of the humanistic curriculum tend to be principally concerned with matters of broad civic and moral import, which, for all their great importance, may seem rather remote from the conceptually distinctive features of these disciplines as they are perceived by those who work within them. At any rate, such effective collaboration as exists among the humanities is usually at the elementary level; and I think it is fair to say that within these departments real enthusiasm is, for the most part, reserved for the kind of work that moves students ahead in their mastery of techniques of analysis that are peculiar to a given discipline. Within history and philosophy, there has even emerged a disposition to challenge their disciplinary identification with the humanities and to look to the natural and social sciences for models of self-interpretation. At times, it almost seems as though the idea of the humanities survives mainly as the object of a rather ritualistic piety and as though time were being taken off from the regular business of academic life for the purpose of some rather solemn observance that we are assured will do us a lot of good. Inevitably, one begins to wonder how it is that the humanities are accorded such universal reverence and yet seem marginal to almost everyone's deepest intellectual interests.

I believe that more is involved here than a reflex of separatistic professionalism and that there are influences at work within each of these nuclear humanistic disciplines that inspire forms of resistance ranging from indifference to outright antagonism to the common humanistic functions that have traditionally been assigned to them and to the assumptions that serve to justify that function. I will examine some of these tendencies later in this paper. Before doing so, however, I want to sketch out a set of ideas that have been very closely associated historically with the belief that literature, history, and philosophy work within a common framework of understanding. I will refer to these ideas simply as "humanism." In constructing my account of humanism, I have felt constrained to observe an absolute fidelity to any of the various senses which that term has borne in the course of the history of Western thought; and I have freely excerpted what seem to me to be centrally important themes from the several periods in the history of humanism. I will also try to show that these humanistic themes share a common conceptual framework and that it is by reference to that framework that the relationship to one another of the disciplines that compose the humanistic curriculum is best understood. But my main concern is with the challenge to the intellectual credentials of this humanistic framework and specifically the challenge that is being made within the humanities rather than by the many external competitors for intellectual and moral authority.

I

There has been a good deal of controversy in recent years as to whether humanism and, specifically, the humanism of the Renaissance, is in any proper sense a philosophy; and it has been very cogently argued by a great authority on these matters that humanism should be regarded as a movement of educational and curricular reform rather than as a set of philosophical theses that claim acceptance on the basis of reasoned argument.[1] One can accept this view and yet wonder what implicit grounds motivated the humanist's preference for subjects like grammar, rhetoric, moral philosophy, poetry, and history, even though these grounds may not have been formulated in explicit philosophical terms until the time of Giovanni Battista Vico or even later. I suggest that these implicit grounds should be sought in the conceptual scheme to which the humanist is at least tacitly committed and which is most coherently and effectively deployed in the various departments of thought of which he is the custodian and the interpreter.

Paradoxical though it may seem, the most general characteristics of that scheme can best be suggested by drawing attention to the deep affinities that bind the language of history, literature, and philosophy to the world of myth, on the one hand, and to that of common sense, on the other. With respect to the first of these, I think it is generally agreed that literature in its broadest sense, which embraces both history and philosophy, originates as the product of a mythopoeic imagination for which the cosmos as a whole is instinct with life and intelligible in terms of categories of personality and agency. The world of myth is comprehensively a world of persons, who often combine natural and human attributes that we now think of as quite distinct. It is also a dramatic world in which only teleological forms of explanation can finally be adequate.[2] It is a remarkable fact that even in this embattled time literature is still on occasion the vehicle of such a unitary mythopoeic imagination of the world; but for the most part the humanities have accepted the fundamental conceptual revision through which there emerges from the world of myth a world of common sense, by which I emphatically do not mean the common sense contaminated by half-understood science that passes by that name today. I mean rather a world that is still a world of persons, but in which nature is denied personality and intention and agency. This is the world to which Edmund Husserl gave the name *Lebenswelt* and which Professor

Wilfred Sellars has aptly called the world of the "manifest image," which is contrasted with that of the "scientific image."[3] It is a world that is coordinate with and dependent upon the existence of man; the most fundamental fact about it is that, while it restricts their sphere of application, it retains the teleological categories of explanation it inherits from the world of myth, and it treats these as ultimate in the sense of not being derivative from anything that is fully independent of the world of persons. It is, rather, the world of human purpose and agency and thought that provides the framework within which nature itself becomes intelligible, both at the humbler level of everyday human contrivance and at the more exalted one of scientific theory construction. It is a world in which one's most significant vis-à-vis is another person and in which the mode of understanding appropriate to a human life as well as to human relationships retains the dramatic and narrative form that characterized myth. It would, of course, be a mistake to impute the sophistications of the philosophical terminology I am using to the mass of mankind, who are, of course, the users and not the analysts of the person-based conceptual scheme I am characterizing. But I am claiming that, without being in any way reflective or self-conscious, the most comprehensive framework of understanding that prescientific common sense deploys is one that radiates out from the concept of the person as knower and as agent. At one and the same time, this ordering yields a picture of the world that is the field of action of the human person and of the principal traits of the person that are coordinate with the structures of its world.

Among the latter, no feature of personality is more important than the capacity for self-determined action; it has always enjoyed a correspondingly important place within the conceptual scheme of common sense. A satisfactory statement of what this capacity involves is not readily available; but it is clear that in virtually all its major interpretations it involves taking very seriously the experience of choice between alternative courses of action, and presupposes a corresponding element of indeterminacy within the object domain or world, in which human action is seen as a kind of intervention from without. This is an experience that can be undercut in a variety of ways, ranging from the theological to the scientific. On occasion, philosophers—humanists among them—have adopted extreme formulations of the kind of indeterminism that seemed to them to be required in order to safeguard human freedom and responsibility against the devaluations they have suffered at the hands of one or another of these parties. But what seems more characteristic of the mainstream of humanism than any particular interpretation of human autonomy is simply its tenacious— some would say simpleminded—commitment to the commonsense picture of man as having certain options, as capable of exercising a certain control over his fate and of drawing on his knowledge of the natural and social world for the purpose of devising strategies of action.

This is not to imply that humanism is straightforwardly rationalistic in its treatment of human conduct and thus insensitive to tragedy and the human tendency to self-destructive action. The point is that these failures and the "tragic" significance that attaches to them are possible only within a context of life that is envisaged as being susceptible of some degree of control and volitional direction. It is also true that, although all human beings are presumed to be endowed with this capacity, occasions for exercising it in really significant ways may be more frequent among persons whose position in society is privileged. There has been a tendency for humanism to concentrate its attention upon such persons in whom a general human capacity finds an exceptional opportunity for realization. This tendency has, in turn, caused humanism itself to appear to be exclusively concerned with an elite minority of the human race. So it may, in fact, often have been; but in its broader and truer inspiration it has addressed itself to what may be called the internal teleology of human life in all its forms. By this I mean that humanism has been interested in human life, not primarily for the practical and technological achievements it has to show, but rather as standing in a certain relationship to itself, as conceiving itself and its accomplishments in terms of their relation to standards and images of good and evil that inform the feelings and intentions of a human life in a way that is supremely interesting to the humanist.

In this connection it is sometimes supposed that this interest can be effective only if there is available to the humanist some authoritative ordering of human goods against which the movements of thought and intention of the human protagonist can be plotted; and from this assumption, it is just a step to the conclusion that the humanities must in some sense teach values. The trouble with this view of the humanities is that it compulsorily situates them at a point of achieved moral knowledge from which they look back, as it were, to the more limited human protagonists who are still groping their way toward such apprehensions. What is true in all this is the implied claim that the consciousness of the humanist, like that of the real or imaginary persons in whose lives he interests himself, is organized by a concern about intentions and outcomes and the evaluative ordering of human life; and it may also be true that he is in a position to perceive and assess these matters a little better than one can in the midst of life. There is no reason, however, to conclude that the perception of the humanist must therefore claim the finality of definition that is implied in that rather unsatisfactory word "values."

What has been said about autonomy clearly implies an ordering of human time in which the future becomes the locus of an indeterminacy that is to be resolved through responsible human choice. That ordering of time also construes our relationship to the past in a certain way that has been so important a feature of humanism as to deserve separate treatment. The primitive fact here is, of course, that human beings, unlike animals, are capable of explicit recollection of past events and, beyond that, of forming general images of the past that stand in a validating relationship to their own current practice. The development of an historical consciousness of the kind that has been so characteristic of Western humanism—but not apparently of the Chinese humanism it otherwise resembles in so many respects—is, of course, something else; and it is often traced to the peculiarly discontinuous character of Western history and above all to the destruction of ancient civilization. A quite immediate and practical task—that of recovering the lost monuments of ancient thought and eloquence—was the origin of an historical interest that was eventually to go far beyond it. The excellence that was attributed to these ancient models was initially conceived to be timeless in nature and the motive for rediscovering them was that of emulation: the belief that knowledge of these great originals was a necessary condition for any comparable performance on one's own part. An unavoidable preliminary to such independent performance was thus the hard work of mastering an alien tongue, and that, in turn, required a grasp of the wider context of life in a society in many respects quite different from one's own.

Gradually, the earlier, rather simplistic, notion of a literal rebirth of ancient culture was forced to give ground to a more realistic interpretation of the relationship of the modern world to its past. In some cases this relationship was seen exclusively in the terms set by a conception of exact historical scholarship that no longer bothered to ask itself any broader questions about the humane significance of historical knowledge. Justification for such abstention was provided by a skeptical historicism that seemed more and more inevitable as the horizon of historical inquiry widened to include non-Western cultures. Intermediate between an ahistorical conception of the authority of a particular past and skeptical doctrines of the normative equivalence of all times and places, however, there is an attitude that finds the past, and especially certain major human achievements in the past, to be deeply interesting and relevant to our present situation without thereby according to the past or to any part of it the status of a unique authority or model.

In this view, which I believe to be the characteristically humanistic one, our relationship to the past is a complex one marked by many ten-

sions; and the liabilities that have been incurred by preceding generations and passed on to us are as important a part of our story as are their
glorious achievements. In any case, a fully human life is one in which
we try to transform our relationship to that past from something that is
suffered or undergone into one that is characterized by consciousness
and critical judgment. The continuity with the past that is thus realized
is not the static continuity of fidelity to an unquestioned model of perfection, but rather one in which the elements of tradition carry both
positive and negative valences, but in both cases serve as sources of
self-knowledge and as instruments of self-definition. What is truly and
radically incompatible with this humanistic conception of our historicity is an attitude of blank indifference to the past or a temporal perspective so short and so subordinate to the immediate interests of the
ego that no speaking parts can be assigned to anything or anyone in
the past that is at all remote or unfamiliar; the only voice that is heard
finally is our own.

Considered simply as very general modes of conceptual ordering,
both the temporal and practical structures of the human world that I
have been discussing presuppose the linguistic capability that is
uniquely human. This is the third derivative from the concept of
the person that has received extensive elaboration at the hands of humanism. There can, in fact, be little doubt that the power that looms
largest in the humanistic concept of man is the power of speech. Recent scholarship has shown the central place that was accorded to the
orator—man as speaker—within the pedagogical program of humanism and the practical basis for this emphasis on the *artes sermonicales*
in the life of ancient society. It was assumed that the orator would be a
statesman or leader of his community and that the public life of that
community would provide the themes he would have to treat and the
audience to which he would address himself. Indeed, it was not uncommon to go so far as to claim that the beginnings of organized
social life were attributable to the persuasive power of the orator-state-
man, who thus also emerges as a culture hero. In actual practice, of
course, this public role was more often than not closed to the graduates of the schools of eloquence, who had to accommodate the
civilizing function of eloquence to the more modest and private circumstances in which they found themselves. Even so, they held onto the
belief that the act of expression through language is the supreme human act, in which our highest potentialities are most fully realized, and
that all other human achievements are in one way or another dependent upon it.

It is this conception of man as the "language animal" that explains the overwhelmingly verbal character of the culture of human-

ism—its dominating concern with the text, as well as its sensitivity to grammatical and rhetorical intricacies, and its delight in the complex play of allusion and limitation that an easy mastery of language permits. It is true that logic or dialectic did not enjoy the degree of favor accorded to grammar and rhetoric, but it is hard to believe that the acute sense of grammatical and rhetorical organization fostered by this training was not in itself a kind of training in logic. Then, too, humanism was, almost from the beginning, based on assumptions about the importance of mastering the language of an earlier and more mature culture; and so, what has been called the "second-language experience," with all it implies in the way of an ability to note features that are peculiar to a particular instrument of expression *as such*, was implicit in the humanist curriculum of studies. It is, of course, possible that the *artes sermonicales* were so highly developed and so highly valued because the *artes reales*—the sciences and technologies whose language makes possible the prediction and control of natural processes —were in such an early stage of their development and because speech was still the primary available field in which human ingenuity and invention could be exercised. But, however that may be, when the sciences did establish their own secure identity, the language-based culture of humanism maintained itself for a very long time, and it is only quite recently that a society has emerged in which the old pleasure taken in the written and spoken word has become a rarity.

With this conception of verbal expression as the essentially human act was associated a new conception of society as an association of persons who communicate with one another through the literary medium. This is what was often referred to as a "republic of letters." It was never even remotely coextensive with any actual society, if only because most persons remained illiterate. The medium of communication was a public discourse of a nonspecialist kind that was addressed to an educated audience assumed to be interested in a wide range of subjects. A certain common stock of readings in the Bible and classical literature was typically assumed as a common reservoir of allusion and illustration; but it was also believed that the persons entering into this literary commerce with one another did so simply in their capacity as human beings. This notion of addressing oneself to a "common reader" and a general audience has been of the greatest importance in the history of humanism. When it came to be thought of as a disadvantage, through the constraints it imposed upon the development of a thoroughly technical vocabulary, this was a clear sign that humanism itself was in trouble. In any case, one major purpose served by such nonspecialist communication was to give one a larger imaginative grasp of the inner life and feelings of persons who might be as different from oneself and from one another as Petrarch from Richardson's Pamela. Through literary portrayal, the dramas of the self acquired a kind of public existence and availability for common reference that were to be of central importance in the mapping of the social world for the purposes of broad human appraisal. And, however muted it may have been, an appraisive and critical intention was never wholly absent from such re-creations of a personal and social world—and it could on occasion become quite explicit.

The elements in the humanist scheme to which I have been drawing attention relate to a number of human powers that organize our experience of the world in certain fundamental ways. In one sense what humanism has to tell us about ourselves—that we are capable of discourse, that we stand in a certain relation to our past and to our future, that we are social and moral beings and, as such, capable of choice and action—is nothing new, for these are all features of our common-sense conception of ourselves. But humanism is more than a repetition of such—as they may seem—trivially true propositions. It takes these familiar and almost routine aspects of our nature and gives them a new emphasis and centrality within the conception we form of ourselves. It does so, to an extent, at the expense of other powers and attributes we have or may believe we have. By intensifying our consciousness of capabilities we had previously just taken for granted as part of our standard operating equipment, it brings home to us their susceptibility to being exercised in a progressively more highly developed way.

Originally, the persuasive force of this way of conceptualizing our distinctively human powers lay in the implied contrast with animal existence and with the more brutish and savage forms of human life that were supposedly akin to the latter. Now, the contrast is more likely to be with forms of human life that are highly developed in a technological sense, but which at the same time seem to deny adequate expression to, or even suppress, the very facets of human nature to which humanism assigns primary value. Along this line, it is possible to go much further and to assert on philosophical grounds the integrity, and indeed the ontological primacy, of this stratum of concepts and of the ordering of the Lebenswelt they jointly define against any possible encroachments of the kind of scientific theory that eschews moral and teleological concepts altogether. But these inquiries cannot be assayed here. The general point about humanism that I want to make is, rather, that it not only defines as essentially human a stratum of functioning in which language, purpose, and a certain ordering of time are paramount but it also initiates a continuing inquiry into man so conceived—an inquiry that is to be conducted under the auspices of this same set of focal human capabilities. In other words, as humanists we are to be interested in ourselves and in others as persons, and it is as persons and with the motivating interests of persons that we are to conduct this inquiry.

This conception of an interest that is brought by the humanist to the works he studies and that is informed by a concern that responds to that reflected in the works themselves, is so central to my thesis that it must be further clarified, especially since it is subject to at least two possible misinterpretations. One of these would unceremoniously assimilate these works to the situation of the contemporary humanist by authorizing the latter to read his own personal concerns freely into the work under consideration. The other asks the reader to set aside his own personal concerns so that he can assume those that are reflected or expressed in the work itself. The latter proposal, if taken literally, strikes me as unworkable since, for the life of me, I don't think I can have the feelings or the world view of either the author of the *Iliad* or of his characters, although I may be able to understand them reasonably well. The former proposal may be all too feasible; but it would mark the end of any effort to understand, rather than absorb, the matters under consideration. The view I am urging recognizes that, as a person, the humanist remains distinct from the author (or the characters) he is considering; and it does not require any special sympathy between the two beyond what is implied in an honest effort to understand a writer's meaning and intentions. What *is* required is that the humanist's response to the work be at the level of the primary human substance of the work itself. This response may take the form of an acknowledgement or a correction of the moral or imaginative insights that work affords, but in either case it signifies that contact has been made with something that was felt to be humanly significant in the world of the work under study and that it has been made by a person who still has some kind of stake in the matter at issue, if only because it represents a possible permutation of his own experience. Such interventions need not be obtrusive nor do they require an explicit declaratory form. Their informing influence on the consideration of a given subject matter may be most effective when the humanist is least aggressive about them. What they signify is simply that the humanist is in the same existential boat as those whose treatment of human themes he has made his special subject of study. Although much of his work bears on aspects of these matters that do not require a response of this kind, these narrower scholarly aspects of his work cannot be isolated from the concern they serve. In other words, humanistic inquiry, though at two removes from "life" itself, is expressive of and finally motivated by interests that we have as human beings. The concerns we have as humanists can never be finally isolated from the concerns we have as human beings.

At this point something should be said, however briefly, about the role played by this set of concepts within each of the three humanistic disciplines I have singled out. Of these, it is clearly literature that displays the strongest and most consistent commitment to the conception of human personality outlined above. The world of imaginative literature has been, since its inception, a world of persons and it continues to be so. Indeed, it is a real question whether literature, by contrast with history and philosophy, has unambiguously made the transition from the mythical to the commonsense treatment of the concept of the person. This is not to say that there have not been efforts to challenge or to modify in one way or another the operative conceptions of character and agency by means of which the presentation of an imaginary world is organized. Although some of these have had the effect of making the telling of a story much more difficult (and sometimes more interesting or interesting in new ways), I think one can say that an outright abandonment of the story form and of the whole organization of human time and of interpersonal space by means of the teleological categories that constitute the story form would be the demise of literature. It may be that because the notion of fidelity to particular fact has no clear application to imaginative literature, the informing influence upon the presentation of events of what, following Kenneth Burke, one might call the dramatistic schema is purer and more unobstructed than it is in the case of history. Another difference is that in history agency is divided and extended over time and generations in a way that makes it impossible to treat the unities of history as unities realized within a single life or generation. Nevertheless, when the great Greek historians made Athens the protagonist of their histories, this was not so much a misguided tendency to personification of social events (parallel to the earlier personification of natural events) as it was a perception of the transferability of the categories derived from mythical and dramatic presentation of events to actions that have no single agent. Broadly speaking, one can say that the tradition of narrative history that they founded was one that remained, in this respect, very close to literature, and even the extraordinary expansion of the evidential base of history that took place in the eighteenth and nineteenth centuries did not expel from history the concept of the story or the associated apparatus of teleological concepts.

The case of philosophy considered as one of the humanities is quite different. Philosophy does not tell a story and in fact came into being under the sign of a certain hostility to the mythopoeic imagination and comprehensively to the world of appearance, in which common sense feels most at home. Then again, the ordering of human experience that philosophy effects is not dramatic but logical, and while the categories of myth are still at work in philosophies as different as those of Aristotle and Hegel, the level of abstraction at which the philosopher works is one from which the dialectic of human agency, which is so central to literature and history, is often difficult to descry. It has, however, often been remarked that if the theses put forward by a philosopher may display little in the way of affinity with the concerns of the poet and the historian, philosophical confrontation and exchange can have a conspicuously dramatic character. And beyond that, philosophical reflection itself has a quality of motivation that has to be understood within a context I would describe as moral. This is because philosophy expresses a disposition on the part of the individual human being to assume full and final responsibility for what he believes to be true and for what he believes to be good and right. Within the context of a human life, what this means is that a new reflective and critical consciousness supervenes upon all the conceptual dimensions of personal life that have been noted above. As a professional activity, philosophy has often become entirely absorbed in issues that can scarcely be said to have any bearing one way or another on the concerns of an individual life. Nevertheless, considered as a principle of responsibility and coherence governing the conduct of life and belief, philosophy amounts to a radical internalization of those activities by which we constitute our relationship to the past or to our fellowmen or to a future that is to be determined at least partly by our own actions. As a broadened and more explicit framework of belief, philosophy thus becomes an element in the moral world with which literature and history deal. While philosophers have not often exhibited any great interest in literature and history—since the form of knowledge they represent is not ranked very high by comparison with that of the sciences—scholars in those two fields have shown a considerable interest in philosophy, as the background of belief out of which the character and action of individuals and societies can be understood.

II

I turn now to contemporary scholarship and teaching in the humanities and to the relationship in which these stand to the leading ideas of humanism that I have been outlining. More specifically, I want to consider three quite general styles of intellectual work in the humanities that have also had a strong influence upon the design of the curriculum. One of these, which I will refer to simply as the historical paradigm, has been the dominant mode of humanistic inquiry in Europe and America for more than a century. My discussion of it will also serve as background for a characterization of two other quite distinct styles that are currently challenging it. One of these, which seems to be motivated to a considerable extent by the study of formal systems and by developments within linguistics and logic, might be described as "formalistic," but I will more often refer to it as an "objectifying" interpretation. The second is of a type that seems proper to describe as "visionary" or "prophetic." It has been enjoying a considerable vogue of late, largely as a result of widespread disillusionment with its better-known rivals.

In approaching the analysis of these styles of humanistic inquiry, it will be useful to bear in mind a distinction that bears on the concept of humanism itself. In a sense for which there is good historical authority, the humanist's work begins only after the primary act of creation, typically in the form of verbal or artistic expression, has taken place. The humanist is thus the one who recovers, restores, and interprets works of which he himself is not the author; or if he is, say, a poet as well as a critic or scholar, what he does in the one capacity is distinguishable without much difficulty from what he does in the other. For the most part, this conception of the humanist's work fits the case of history and literature well but not so well that of philosophy, where it virtually identifies the study of philosophy with the study of the history of philosophy. This is, however, the aspect of philosophy that is most frequently thought of as being specifically humanistic, and the point I want to make applies to it, if not to philosophy as a whole.

That point concerns the nature of the operation that the humanist performs upon the works that other men have created. As the fundamental task of discovering and reconstructing such works advanced toward completion in the course of the modern period, questions about the nature of the cognitive enterprise in which the humanist himself is engaged became more pressing. Implied in these questions was an expectation that the humanist's work must satisfy rigorous cognitive standards. I want to argue that the effort to meet this expectation has gradually altered the humanist's perspective upon the works he studies and that it has done so in a way that progressively deepens the contrast between his perspective and the perspective that is reflected in those works themselves. There has been introduced into the humanist's scholarly activities a strong tendency to self-objectification in the sense of abstraction from the context of personal concern that informs the works he studies. In saying this, I am not implying that cognitive motives are wholly absent from, say, works of imaginative literature but, rather, that in such works intellectual interests are not independent or autonomous but are closely integrated with a vision of life that the work expresses and in which relative values are assigned and imperatives for action are generated.

What I am saying is that, typically, a great poem or a history like Thucydides' or even a philosophical work like Spinoza's *Ethics* locates the matters it deals with on an axis of concern and that the descriptions under which events and persons figure in such an account are expressive of a personal and existential stand that the author has taken, at least symbolically—an evaluative ordering he has introduced into his relationship to the matters with which he deals and one which is not susceptible of the kind of objective validation that requires it to be rigorously disassociated from the moral being of its author. The question all this raises for the humanist is simply whether, consistently with the cognitive claims it has to satisfy, his treatment of such works can be informed by any vision or evaluative ordering comparable to those that inform a great work of the imagination. The difficulty is that, if the answer must be negative, the response of the humanist to a work informed by such a vision will be in the nature of a *fin de non recevoir*, and the fundamental humanistic nexus to which I have alluded earlier, in which concern responds to concern, will have been broken.

The historical paradigm of scholarship in the humanities, to which I now turn, can be viewed as a compromise between two ways of resolving the question I have raised. One of these would assign to the humanist a point of view on the creative work of others that is informed by an evaluative ordering of human experience that is every bit as comprehensive as the visions that inspire the works under study, although not necessarily in harmony with the latter. An example might be the interpretation of ancient culture by a Christian humanist who quite explicitly interprets and judges facets of his subject matter in accordance with the canons of significance and value that he derives from Christian doctrine. The other answer is to insist on a bracketing of the humanist scholar's own personal criteria of significance and value. It would concentrate his scholarly work on matters that can be abstracted from the total context of belief in which they may be existentially imbedded, so as to provide a solid terrain on which scholars of all persuasions can meet and cooperate.

The compromise of which I speak can be effected by historical humanism in two different ways and at two different levels. To begin with, the great bulk of historical work is of an essential but preliminary kind that involves rather little in the way of the kind of interpretative ordering of which I have been speaking, that is, the establishment of reliable texts, translations, inquiries into dating and influences, the construction of sequential histories, and so forth. This is the indispensable work that makes an author available to us in the first place and supplies the essential data without which any response to his work or any effort to come to terms with his imaginative vision would be doomed to run aground on the shoals of ignorance. Very often, humanistic scholarship of this kind strikes even the literate and well-disposed outsider as terribly dull, as indeed it often is. Too prolonged and too exclusive an immersion in it can decisively inhibit any capacity for imaginative response to the works under study with which we may begin, but this is hardly a danger at the present time, when even the barest minimum of such training is too often scanted in our schools and colleges.

It may, therefore, be useful to point out not only that scholarly work of this type is essential but also that the kind of instruction that derives from it has the advantage of not forcing the imaginative response, if it is forthcoming, into any particular channel and of permitting the highly trained reader a substantial measure of freedom in his personal appropriation and enjoyment of an author. At its best, historical scholarship represents a compromise, in that it really just leaves open the possibility of a more intimate form of engagement with the mind of the author at the same time that it supplies the elements of understanding that it takes to be essential for any interpretation that is more than an exercise in self-expression. This is a compromise between what might be described as the interests of the self and the interests of humanistic scholarship as a responsible and collective undertaking. The doubt that arises about it is clearly whether the massive apparatus of historical scholarship that dominates the public manifestations of humanistic activity in the area of publication and instruction and deals for the most part with matters of subsidiary interest to the nonspecialist reader, will not finally swamp even that area of private enjoyment and response to which it assigns every other form of interest in the cultural properties it claims as its own.

There is another form of historical scholarship in the humanities that is not content to confine itself to the substructures of humanistic understanding in the manner just described. Yet it remains sensitive to the hazards of arbitrary personal judgment, which increase dramatically as one moves to levels of interpretation that bear directly on the "form of life" implicit in the perspective of the author. Indeed, historicism—the name I will use for this kind of historical scholarship in the humanities—itself developed *pari passu* with a recognition that the past is not simply a storehouse of moral examples and that much of it is too remote and different from our own world to be judged or even interpreted in terms of current assumptions about human motivation and goals. The inhibition this perception imposed upon our natural tendency to treat men in the past as though they were contemporary with us and could therefore be judged by the same standards was unquestionably a salutary one at a time when whole new historical worlds were being opened up that could hardly have been understood if they had simply been forced into the parochial framework suggested by Western history. But the point I want to make about historicism is that it did not completely abandon the idea of ordering, in terms of criteria of significance and value, the extraordinary wealth of materials with which the historian and the humanist have to deal. While it was accepted that the subjective preferences of the individual human person—whether humanist or not—lacked the cognitive authority to establish such an ordering and that God no longer seemed available to perform that function, a displacement of such authority to the historical process itself seemed both feasible and attractive.

The nuclear thesis of historicism is that, in spite of all its appearance of chaos and conflict, the order to historical time is also the order of realization of a goal toward which history moves. A convincing entelechy for world history as a whole might be difficult to agree on for those who lacked the inspired audacity of a Hegel; but within more manageable and familiar unities like the history of Western civilization, there was a real plausibility to the notion that history is a cumulative process in which, at the deepest level of interpretation, things happen because they are required by the inner logic of the process itself. Within that process conflicts among limited perspectives and standards of judgment would be progressively overcome and resolution effected at a higher level. And, what was most reassuring, it seemed that the whole business of "values" was being transacted in the third person and thus constituted a perfectly satisfactory object of inquiry for the humanities or *Geisteswissenschaften*, as they came to be called. The "compromise" thus effected between the evaluative and the cognitive claims made on the humanities permitted the humanist to take a strongly relativistic view of the forms of life he studied, including his own, while still maintaining a teleological conception of the historical process in which the fulfillment of some momentous, if vague, goal was promised.

The version of historicism I have presented is an explicitly philosophical, indeed Hegelian, one. I am not suggesting that it was principally or exclusively in this form that historicism became a reigning methodology in the humanities. But as Professor E. H. Gombrich has recently pointed out, the broader kind of *Geistesgeschichte* that derives from Hegel has dominated humanistic scholarship for more than a century, most conspicuously in Germany, but also elsewhere.[4] It attaches primary interest to the placement of a writer or thinker or artist within a stage or period of an evolving process in which each stage is a necessary condition for the one that follows upon it as well as the implicate of the one that precedes it.

For many critics—among them Professor Gombrich—the forms of continuity introduced into historical sequences by these Hegelian assumptions are spurious and finally detrimental to historical understanding itself. Other writers have drawn attention to the peculiarly anonymous character of the self that takes its directives and its critical perspective from some hypothesized schedule of historical development and is always second-guessing the historical process in order to determine what part has been assigned to it in the latter. In the background of all these contemporary critiques of historicism is Nietzsche's great attack on what he called historical *Bildung* and on the imbalance between past and present that characterizes it—an imbalance that results from a belief that all meaning and direction come to us from the past we study rather than being brought to the past, as Nietzsche thought it should be, by a sense of identity and purpose in the present, which seeks out the past it needs.

These are powerful criticisms, and to the extent that historicism has made possible this peculiar kind of ventriloquistic role-playing on the part of scholars whose work thus lacks any definable relationship to what they are or stand for as persons, it has clearly run counter to the central inspiration of humanism. If the motivational interests of the inquirer remain wholly unrelated to his concerns as a person and as a member of a community, and if both he and the figures in the past to whom he turns his attention are defined entirely in terms of the position they occupy within some historical entelechy to which they contribute but which they cannot control or perhaps even understand, it is really not clear what the point or possible human benefit of an encounter between them might be.

For all these justified strictures on two major aspects of the historical paradigm for humanistic inquiry, it seems to me that it has effected a permanent enrichment of such studies and that it has conferred benefits on those who pursue them that dwarf the liabilities I have been recognizing. While it is true that many of the continuities historicism introduces into the historical process have been specious and derive more from a priori postulations than from empirical evidence, many of them were very well founded indeed. The notion of a tradition, which has become so central to humanistic studies, is one that is capable of empirical validation; and while there are many logical and empirical problems connected with the use of generalizing concepts like those of period, style, culture, and so forth, it would be absurd to suppose that these stand or fall with the metaphysical principles of synthesis with which they may have been associated.

Beyond these questions of method, the point is that historical inquiry in the humanities has made available to us a wealth and diversity of human experience and of symbolic orderings of experience by comparison with which the extension of the concept "man" in the earlier days of humanism seems narrow indeed. Nor is this a merely quantitative gain that might be overbalanced by the diminished sense of attachment to one's own local tradition, as on occasion it may indeed have been. Our widened range of comparative reference has changed in important ways our understanding of features of our own intellectual and artistic and moral tradition, as witness, for example, the work of E. R. Dodds on the status of the irrational within the Greek mind.[5] And as for fears that the burden of historical erudition inevitably has a negative effect on the fineness of apprehension and sensitivity to delicate nuances of feeling, it is reassuring to recall the example of Erich Auerbach, in which all these attributes of the humanistic mind seem in such perfect balance.[6] The best examples of scholarly work along historical lines in the humanities are very good indeed, and this suggests that the historical paradigm does not stand so much in need of radical correction from some external source as it does of closer contact with its own best inspiration, as exemplified in the work of scholars such as those I have mentioned.

At this point, it will be useful to draw into the discussion the two counter-conceptions of the humanities to which I alluded at the outset. Both build on the critique of historical humanism and both move toward a conception of the humanistic enterprise in which its special orientation toward the past is subjected to quite drastic revision. But then they part company and resolve the ambiguities inherent in the historicistic compromise in utterly different ways. One of these seeks to complete the objectification of humanistic inquiry. In order to do so, it is prepared to abandon virtually the whole person-based conceptual scheme of traditional humanism as well as any notion that cognitively responsible inquiry might be the vehicle of existential or personal concern. The other view, which I have described as visionary and prophetic, holds that the objectification of the humanities—their transformation into a research field and their resulting skewed relationship to the primary vision of the creative artist and the seer—has already gone much too far. For the ambiguous compromise of historicism they would substitute, not a yet more rigorously defined ideal of scholarship, but rather a direct vatic utterance by the humanist.

I do not think it is fanciful to suggest that both of these counterinterpretations are straining, though in opposite directions, against the boundaries of the conceptual domain which, I have suggested, has traditionally been the domicile of humanism, that is, the teleologically organized *Lebenswelt* that was separated out of the organic cosmos of myth at an early date. The visionary interpretation would, if I understand its spokesmen correctly, undo that conceptual revolution, and by restoring the integrity of the world of myth, incorporate human life once again into a wider cosmic life. The objectifying interpretation would subvert the *Lebenswelt* in a quite different way by applying to it categories and methods of inquiry that definitively prescind from the basically teleological forms of order that have been the substance of humanism. What is especially striking is the common hostility to "man"—*homo humanus*, who is at once the denizen and the demiurge of the human world—that runs through the rhetoric of these otherwise so profoundly different schools of thought. It is as conspicuous in the writings of Michel Foucault as it is in those of Martin Heidegger.[7]

Such characterization and assessment of these views as I can offer must be extremely condensed.[8] The secession from humanism in the direction of a scientific objectivism is clearly motivated by a feeling that there is something shallow about the humanist conceptual scheme, that it is lacking in theoretical power, that it is, in Spinoza's phrase, an asylum of ignorance. Such charges are not new. Attacks on final causes and the whole apparatus of teleological explanation formed an important part of the elaboration of the modern scientific concept of method. Nor are precedents lacking for the effort to expel these offending concepts from the sciences of man as well. Although the efforts that have been made to apply the insights of a Marx or a Freud to the analysis and interpretation of literature and art may not, as many commentators have noted, have been wholly successful in abstracting from the finalism and even the moralism of the older humanist, there can be no doubt that they have displaced the focus of interest from conscious intention and the language in which it expresses itself to structures and relationships which, if they do not absolutely transcend the *Lebenswelt*, have at best a problematic status with respect to it. Nevertheless, efforts to transfer biological and economic categories to the internal analysis of the discursive and imaginative structures with which the humanities deal have always been marked by a certain crudity. In practice this fact has assured a large measure of continuing autonomy for the humanistic kind of internal analysis that is still conducted in a language that is conceptually much closer to that of the works under study.

What is new, however—and I refer here to current structuralist tendencies in the humanities that are already immensely influential in Europe and are gaining ground here—is the attempt to undertake the task of the internal analysis of discourse with a set of concepts that are not drawn from independent sciences like psychology or biology nor from the conceptual repertory of humanism as I have presented it. While these concepts have no single source and may at times betray points of affiliation with external disciplines like anthropology and psychoanalysis, the purest manifestations and core inspiration of this approach are clearly logical and linguistic in character. Its focus of attention is on the semantic and syntactical properties of the discursive structures being studied. Here there are obvious similarities between what is happening in analysis of literature and current trends in philosophy, which has become increasingly a kind of extended logic, setting forth the most general structural features of conceptual systems as such. In other areas, such as the nondiscursive arts, metaphors based on the vocabulary of linguistics and the study of formal systems are everywhere to be found. At times one even gets the rather disquieting impression that under this new dispensation literature has become a form of cryptography, in which the business of encoding and decoding monopolizes the interest once given to what would have been described as more substantive concerns, and the ultimate addressee of the literary message appears always to be the structuralist decoder himself.

It is certainly not my intention to try to evaluate the work that has been done under the auspices of the type of interest I have been describing. My concern is solely with its bearing on traditional humanistic concerns and especially with the question of whether these forms of analysis should be understood as supplanting those that were carried out in the idiom of the older humanism or whether they should be regarded as presupposing the person-based conceptual scheme of the latter at the same time as they effect a kind of abstraction from it for special purposes. In other words, does the analysis of the corpus of rules, concepts, syntactical and logical structures, and so forth, under which human beings operate in various contexts, presuppose the *Lebenswelt* as the milieu in which these logical structures become applicable and intelligible? Or, do they represent a form of reconceptualization that is so radical as to escape from the world of the manifest image altogether and constitute a new and independent characterization of human and social reality?

It seems to me that it is on the answer given to this question that the issue as to the humanistic character of the study of conceptual systems depends. There can be little doubt that the traditional notions of the "author" and the "book" have suffered a devaluation as a result of attention being concentrated on the invariant properties of the discursive system that they are now thought of as instantiating. More generally, the role of the individual human being as something more than the vehicle for a symbolic system, of whose internal complexities he need have no idea, and as standing in a relationship to his own conceptual instruments that is expressive of his active nature, does not appear to constitute a significant set of issues for those of the structuralist persuasion. Some expressly condemn it as a set of illusions. It is, of course, in the historical dimension of human experience that the capacity for detaching oneself from a set of conceptual constraints and for revising them or replacing one set with another becomes most evident. Conceptual history, if such a discipline ever takes form, may indeed represent the deepest stratum of human development. But history is never much in favor with those for whom formal systems are a paradigm of intellectual achievement; and there are many indications that the cerebral cortex is regarded as a more plausible existential base for such systems than the human person. In any case, the idea that the sequence of conceptual orderings—the "epistemes" and "paradigms" of current discussion—might form a central element in a wider human history, with its own internal teleologies, is one that most structuralists apparently regard as a transcendental fantasy.

From all these considerations I would draw the conclusion that, in intention at least, the structuralists repudiate the very notion of the sort of existential context and temporal continuity with which the concept of the person has been associated. Their explorations of the formal systems undergirding discourse and society are presented in much the same way as discoveries in physics or astronomy would be, that is, as standing outside and having no particular relevance to what was once called the moral history of mankind. From such forms of inquiry the humanist may be able to learn a great deal by bringing their results into some fruitful relationship to his own concerns, just as he can on occasion find much of interest in the finding of the natural sciences. But it would surely be seriously misleading to describe intellectual work done in this degree of abstraction from and indifference to those interests, as being itself humanistic in character, much less as an adequate replacement for the humanities as they have been traditionally understood.

With regard to the second alternative interpretation of conduct of the humanities referred to, I can be a good deal briefer. I have already characterized it as being in the nature of an effort to reverse a vitally significant conceptual shift in the course of which a human world organized in terms set by the concept of the person emerged in contradistinction to the natural world. The divorce thus established between man and nature is felt to be a painful state of alienation and the abstract manipulative stance vis-a-vis nature in which we find ourselves is contrasted unfavorably with a lost sense of consubstantiality conceived in strongly animistic terms. There have, in fact, been a number of attempts in our own time to propose new mythic readings of this desiderated cosmic unity. There is every reason to think that they respond to an authentic sense many of us have of the impoverishment of our imaginative relationship to the natural and cosmic environment. In an era in which virtually all facets of intellectual and social life have been bureaucratized to an extraordinary degree, it is hardly surprising that there should be great appeal in a conception of the humanities that reasserts, in a paradoxical and even violent way, the claims of the self and of personal vision. But is it really possible to model that vision on an archaic and mythic state of mind that we could realize in ourselves only by carrying out the most drastic kind of surgery on our current body of beliefs? And supposing that we were able to use our detested autonomy one last time for the purpose of disqualifying it and inducing in ourselves the desired state of receptivity to the intimations of meaning in the world process, are we ready to accept the primitive terror and ignorance that would be its certain accompaniment? The world of animistic myth is certainly a vivid world in which experience takes on a salience and a depth of suggestion that make it unlikely that one would be bored in the modern manner. But what sense could we retain of our own human nature or that of others?

In this connection, I would also like to take note of a suggestion that comes from Nietzsche and writers influenced by him, to the effect that humanism and historical consciousness prosper in ages in which the will to live has slackened somewhat and that, when the energies of the self achieve a greater intensity, they tend to make a clean sweep of the cultural bric-a-brac with which weakness and sterility surround themselves. Such a profound renewal of vitality generates its own myths and imposes its own emphatic style upon whatever images of the past it is interested in entertaining. There is some truth in this view, and I think it would be best to acknowledge that by comparison with the dramatic intensity of the world of myth or of the titanic self-assertion that produces its own myths, humanism is a non-starter. But precisely because its sense of meaningfulness is not obsessive and total and also because its apprehensions of meaning and intention are in the intermediate range and on the human scale, it is in a position to take a kind of interest in human beings and in the way they conceive and define their own situation that would hardly be possible if they were subsumed under the drastic abstractions of myth.

For those who think in harsh dichotomies, it may seem that we can listen to a tale told by others only at the price of passing over into a rather passive and unassertive mode and thus breaking our own personal momentum. Once again there is an element of truth in this view. While the world of humanism is unquestionably organized by vectors of moral concern, it is also the locus of a great deal of ambiguity. There is no single plot line and the moral identities borne by its protagonists are rarely stable or univocal in character. A measure of detachment and of skepticism is therefore likely to serve the cause of understanding better than is a commitment of belief that is irreversible because it lacks the critical instruments that would correct and modulate its own affirmations. Whether an individual, or for that matter a society, can in fact maintain a sense of direction and purpose that both informs and is informed by an understanding of its past and of the record of human experience available to it, is of course a matter that cannot be decided a priori. What can be said is that the effort to maintain such a balanced and fruitful relationship between the two is the humanistic ideal.

There is a great deal more that could be said about the three models of humanistic inquiry outlined above and about the distortions they may introduce into the kind of interest in persons and the past that develops within the conceptual scheme I have characterized. Nevertheless, as a tentative conclusion I would suggest that the historical paradigm, in spite of the tendencies to self-objectification it reveals, can claim a substantially higher degree of congruence with the central inspiration of humanism than can the other two. It would seem, too, that the positive insights developed by those alternative models are susceptible of at least some degree of incorporation into the practice of historical humanism.

While I have argued that it is not the business of the humanist to assume the mantle of the prophet, it would certainly be entirely proper and desirable for him to assume in a more explicit way the obligation of setting his work in what I have called a context of concern, that is, the set of intellectual, moral, and other assumptions on the strength of which that work is entitled to claim general human interest. Again, while I have argued that the language of everyday life has an absolutely fundamental importance for the humanities, it would surely be a mistake to assume that no light at all can be cast on human thought and motivation by forms of analysis carried out in the various technical idioms that have been developed recently within the sciences of man. Indeed, it should be of the greatest interest to the humanist to explore the points of juncture of the manifest and the scientific images of the world, provided that it is understood that the former is a genuine term in this relationship, with its own integrity, and not simply a halfway house on the route to authentic scientific knowledge. If he can learn from these competing conceptions of the humanities without surrendering his own mode of self-understanding, the humanist may be in a better position than he is now to understand the pressures under which the conceptual scheme of humanism has already suffered such severe erosion, as well as its prospects for survival in a time in which humanity seems more and more a survival from another age.

NOTES

1. P. O. Kristeller, "The Humanist Movement," in *Renaissance Thought: The Classic, Scholastic and Humanist Strains* (New York: Harper Torchbooks, 1961).

2. Since I use the words "teleology" and "teleological" a good deal in the course of this paper and since they have an important role in the argument I develop, some clarification of the sense they bear is needed. That sense is for the most part the one set forth in Charles Taylor's *The Explanation of Behaviour* (London: Routledge, Kegan Paul, 1964). It is not a metaphysical notion and it does not postulate the existence of any unobservable entities. It concerns rather the logical form of explanations that are given of human conduct. The latter are such that "to offer a teleological explanation. . . of the behavior of some being is . . . to account for it by laws in terms of which an event's occurring is held to be dependent on that event's being required for some end." (p. 9) Taylor's whole discussion of this matter and his argument showing that teleological laws are not derivable from nonteleological laws is of great interest. My discussion assumes that at least at the levels with which the humanities are most likely to be concerned, human beings are teleologically organized systems of the type he describes.

3. Husserl developed the concept of the *Lebenswelt* most fully in *Die Krisis der europaischen Wissenschaften und die transcendentale Phänomenologie*, Husserliana, vol. 6 (The Hague: Martinus Nijhoff, 1962). The discussion of the "manifest image" is to be found in Wilfred Sellars, "Philosophy and the Scientific Image of Man," in *Science, Perception, and Reality* (London: Routledge, Kegan Paul, 1963).

4. E. H. Gombrich, *In Search of Cultural History* (Oxford: Clarendon Press, 1969).

5. E. R. Dodds, *The Greeks and the Irrational* (Boston: Beacon Press, 1957).

6. I refer especially to Auerbach's *Mimesis* (Princeton, N.J.: Princeton University Press, 1953).

7. Heidegger's *Brief über den Humanismus*, reprinted in *Wegmarken* (Frankfurt am Main: Klosterman, 1967) is one of the classic statements of opposition to humanism; much of his later philosophy reads as though he were calling for a return to a mode of "indwelling" that has obvious affinities with much of what I refer to in the paper as being characteristic of the world of myth. The writings of Michel Foucault that I have in mind are *Les mots et les choses* (Paris: Gallimard, 1966) and *L'archeologie du savoir* (Paris: Gallimard, 1969). What appears to be an attempt to synthesize these points of view can be found in Jacques Derrida, "The Ends of Man," in *Language and Human Nature*, Paul Kurtz, ed. (St. Louis: Warren H. Green, 1971).

8. The account of the two movements of thought to which I turn here is based on a great many sources, but what I say about the antihumanistic implications of the theses in question derives to a very considerable extent from Foucault and Heidegger, or perhaps I should say from my understanding of the positions of those writers. My treatment of the second movement has been influenced also by the recent writings of Theodore Roszak, notably *The Making of a Counter-Culture* (Garden City, N.Y.: Doubleday, 1969), as well as by a good many other statements by dissident humanists, some of which can be found in *Liberations: New Essays on the Humanities in Revolution*, I. Hassan, ed. (Middletown, Conn.: Wesleyan University Press, 1971).

Justifying the Humanities

Ronald Berman
*National Endowment
for the Humanities*

Professor Olafson began by noting, not altogether endearingly, that the federal government is in the business of arts and humanities. I hate to say this because it may make us feel superfluous, but the federal government has indeed gone to the trouble of defining the humanities. Public Law 89-209 has stated for the people of the United States what humanities are—so all the problems of definition that we have faced have naturally evanesced. This law defines the humanities as a set of fifteen disciplines ranging from archaeology to the study of comparative religion, including on the way literature, linguistics, history, social studies, jurisprudence, and so forth. Knowing this, it would appear that there is really not much difficulty either in the enterprise now engaging us or in drawing out the implications of the congressional mandate. However, a difficulty does remain, because the most persistent question asked at congressional hearings (by the people who have themselves defined the humanities) is: "What are the humanities and what are you doing about them?" They are all quite dissatisfied when I simply repeat the definition that they have given me. I have therefore been driven to find some supporting arguments.

We begin with the propriety of describing humanities as a set of disciplines ranging from archaeology to comparative religion. That is the way humanities are commonly understood at universities. And that is the way we understand our profession. But there are some things not satisfied by that definition—or even identified. One of them is the particular work; another is the life that formed it. What, in short, embodies the humanities? There is then, in addition to the disciplines we stipulate, the work and the men who made it. Finally, we have to take account (and with this Congress has been at least mildly satisfied) of certain ideas. I have concluded that the humanities are *practiced* by professionals very much like those at this symposium. Shakespeare, Milton, and many others, ancient and modern, form our natural *subject* because of certain ideas that are inherently necessary. At this point I shift ground evasively to say that we cannot get mathematical or even moral certainty out of Shakespeare. Nor should we. But there are at least two kinds of certainty. One kind admits that we are never going to get absolute political or philosophical knowledge. But there is another kind of certainty—an educational necessity—that obliges us to confront students (and ourselves) with great minds. The student does not have to drink at any particular well, but he should understand that, say, in the period from 1580 to 1610 Shakespeare had little competition and that *King Lear* is intellectually serious. This certainty should exert an imperative, for it implies that education means *access* to the best of what has been thought and said; *belief* may or may not follow.

The National Endowment for the Humanities (NEH) has gone into ventures that tend, we hope, to bring out some of the concerns that teachers of the humanities have expressed. One of the things that struck me most in this symposium is the idea that the humanities have been isolated in the liberal-arts curriculum. I would like to expand on that and point out not only that they are isolated but also that they are virtually absent in elementary or secondary education. Except in the disciplines of the humanities themselves, the same may be said of professional, graduate education. Thus, study of the humanities is confined to young middle-class Americans, ages seventeen to twenty-one, and the humanities are neither transmitted nor really used at any other time in life.

The first thing to do, in the most pragmatic way, is to try to break out of this. But there are real complications. It has been pointed out that it is obviously not the duty of the university to inculcate values that a student should already possess upon arriving at the university. That is perfectly true. But students now come to the university without essential knowledge of values and ethics—even of themselves. There is probably no other institution in American capable of teaching them either to believe or to criticize usefully. Whether we like it or not, we are in the value-commentary enterprise. Furthermore, it is anomalous that faculty should be expected to give students opinions on virtually everything and beliefs about practically nothing.

In an attempt to partially remedy some of this, NEH has tried to disseminate learning. The Princeton School of Engineering, the Harvard Law School, the Michigan School of Journalism all have humanities programs now which are, although conventional enough, new in the general education of a profession. They are, I think, more or less the kind of humanities program that you are familiar with at Columbia University in the traditional and excellent freshman humanities course. In addition, at a great many institutes and centers of research previously known for their restriction to behavioral science, natural science, or political science, there is going to be some kind of entry for the humanities. This will take the form of special support to attract humanists in order to broaden the intellectual scope of the professions. We are reminded in this connection of Professor Olafson's remark that the association of people from different disciplines is in itself an intellectual boon.

I should also comment on some of the issues already raised. The thing we should remember about the humanities right now is that, although they are under the aspect of eternity, they are also situational: they exist in the light of both past and present. One recent fact has been turmoil at the university. Then there is the normal difficulty in retaining belief in a technological world. Affluence itself seems to have damaged our disciplines. Cadres of people, some of them uncommitted to teaching and learning, have come into the profession. Expansion has vitiated quality. Curricula have been offered as entertainment. The poetry of T. S. Eliot—with its fragmented, whirling, centrifugal images—is perhaps the correlative for the recent past. The knowledge explosion has brought to the humanities so much information and so many structural changes that they could not be contained. Part of the trouble then is not simply the failure of people inside the profession to cope with things in the old way but the failure to adapt to a culture of epistemological revolution. The other, as I have indicated briefly, is the social historical event: the doubling, tripling, and quadrupling of the graduate-student population, the entering into our disciplines of those whose major interest has not even been vocational. These people came simply to find in the university some kind of refuge from the problems of the outside world, a congenial environment, a private world without war or injustice or, finally, simple answers to their questions.

There have been necessary evils—and unlikely virtues born of them—the institution of enormous lectures, the star system, the imitation of scientific and corporate models. There has been transmission of knowledge via graduate assistants rather than directly by faculty. There has been intense and narrow specialization. I have seen it written recently—amusingly enough but I think with serious implications—that there is no reason to suspect a man of being a humanist because he is intimately knowledgeable about Near Eastern philology. That, like accounting, is a vocation.

One problem is so familiar that it really does not need to be dwelt on at length. The boom gave us one set of problems, the bust another. From the latter came political problems, emotional problems, problems having to do with social equity, with classes and races, with wars, and with foreign and domestic policy. The humanities especially become a cockpit of oppositions.

When I turn to some of the problems that have been identified, I can only say that I agree with the speakers. I think they have been well identified, and I intend to add only a few others. I think, for example, that the deviation into scientifically inspired structuralism, which Professor Olafson has remarked upon, is entirely true. I think it also true that we have entertained the vices of historicism. But I would add as factors of almost equal weight those of politics and mass culture. The issue of relevance is mentioned continuously to the point of stultification. Universities are vulnerable to insistent demands of what I take to be false utilitarianism.

I agree wholeheartedly that vocationalism is one of the things that we have to worry about most, not only philosophically but also politically. There are several reasons for this. I think it is inherent in the American character to want to do things in a narrowly productive way. There is a native strain of materialism, "applied humanism," so to speak. A second reason for vocationalism is that virtually all educational lobbies like the idea. The third is that after the bust of the last decade it is a safe and attractive idea.

The university is now a place between secondary school and graduate school. Part of its work must be rehabilitation and another part preparation for the immediate future. That is to say, it will continue to repair the damage of secondary education while training those to whom the idea of disinterested knowledge is not compelling. The professional school is going to get more professional; that is, I think, because the principal way to success is increased specialization. We will probably see greater refinement of those procedures that have made our professional schools narrowly disciplinary. And of course there is our competition.

The humanities face some tough going. We sometimes like to think that "interdisciplinary" means cooperation between academic interests, but that does not seem to be the case in the modern university. Competition for the budget is going to be ferocious, and the scientific and statistical disciplines are going to be better off than the humanities. This conclusion in part is the product of observation and in part is drawn from those familiar with the difficulty of raising money for the disciplines of value. It is relatively easy to raise money for their more directly productive rivals. Finally, there is the question of pop culture, which has reached the universities and become "relevant." Seymour Martin Lipset has pointed out to me that the life cycle of a craze is four or five years. Some intellectual fashions are going to fade of their own weight or perhaps lightness. Others, happily, may transform themselves. Still others will be excised with no great reluctance.

I shall close with this observation: There is less difficulty than has been asserted in isolating the humanistic. Sidney Hook's six ways of justifying a course of study seem quite right to me. For my part, I think that there is even less difficulty than appears. I am surprised not by how much there remains of the past but by how little. The museums of America and Europe contain only the skeleton of our culture, and they can be exhausted within a few years. Without being an Erasmus, Milton, or Dr. Johnson, it is still possible to read the essential books of our history. And it is clearly possible to teach them. The problem, then, consists not so much in identifying what is worth teaching as in transmitting our knowledge to our students. That, I should guess, is a much more finite task than we are ready to believe.

Observations on Humanism and History

Gertrude Himmelfarb
City University of New York

Professor Olafson has stated very clearly and sensitively the twin evils to which the humanities are prone: an excessive, or misplaced, objectivity on the one hand; on the other, an excessive subjectivity, an over-indulgence in the self. In the first case, the subject being studied—an historical event, philosophical idea, or literary work—is regarded as fixed, given, predetermined in its form and substance, having no necessary relation to the present, no necessary relevance to the concerns and interests of present-day human beings, even those presently engaged in studying it. In the second case, the subject is deprived of its independence and integrity, becoming little more than a vehicle for the present, a means of expressing the personal interests of the inquirer; it becomes, in fact, almost anything one cares to make of it.

These twin evils, Mr. Olafson implies, are not fortuitous but rather inherent in the humanistic enterprise itself. It is precisely because the humanist is concerned with the past (the historical, literary, or philosophical past) that he would like to endow it with an objective status, respecting it in and for itself, quite apart from his own personal, utilitarian, transient concerns. But it is also and as much a part of the humanist enterprise—and here Mr. Olafson puts the case very eloquently —to be concerned with humanity, our own humanity as well as the humanity of the past, so that we cannot divorce our personal, human concerns from our aesthetic or scholarly ones. Moreover, it is also part of the humanist endeavor to claim a freedom for the past as well as the present, to see the past not as fixed, given, inviolate, but rather as indeterminate, open to choice and change. Just as contemporaries in the past had alternative options of which they could avail themselves (they were not the prisoners of history, of blind, irresistible forces), so the scholar has alternative ways of looking at the past. He is not bound by any authoritative interpretation; he is free to understand the past as best he can, however he can.

So far, in the diagnosis of these aspects of humanism, I have no quarrel with Mr. Olafson. And perhaps I have none with his way of reconciling them. But I would like some clarification of exactly what it is he is proposing. As I understand him, he is proposing something by way of "compromise," as he puts it, a compromise that will respect the objectivity of the past—of the event, work, or idea under consideration —and at the same time respect the legitimate, necessary, sometimes urgent concerns of the present. He finds the essential ingredients of that compromise exemplified in "historicism." For what the historical does is to combine objectivity and subjectivity in a single, viable schema. He sees the past in all its uniqueness and remoteness; he refrains from judging the past in terms of the present; he refuses to be—and this was Lord Acton's great complaint against Leopold von Ranke—a "hanging judge"; he tries to understand and explain the past in its own terms. But he does not make the past a series of discrete events; he does not see it as so unique and remote as to have no bearing on the present. On the contrary, he posits a movement and meaning in history that necessarily relate the past to the present and encompasses both within a larger pattern. History for him is a continuous and cumulative process; and if values cannot be imposed on history (as Acton would have liked to impose them), they can be seen as working themselves out in history.

This is not to say that Mr. Olafson endorses all forms of historicism. He is sufficiently aware of what he himself calls the mythopoeic imagination that is so rife in historicism, the impulse to drown the self in the irresistible tide of history, to deny commonsense reason and freedom in the name of a higher, Hegelian, hypostatized Reason and Freedom. Mr. Olafson is assuredly not holding up this kind of historicism as a model for us. But as I understand him, he is recommending a more modest version that is both humanistic and humane, which does not impose absolute standards on history but which does find "values" in history, which appreciates, as he says, the "wealth and diversity of human experiences" but which can also discern a "tradition" behind those rich and diversified experiences.

If this is what Mr. Olafson is suggesting, he is more sanguine than I about the ability of historicism to sustain that compromise. The practical effect of historicism today, it seems to me, is to reinforce the relativistic temper of our time, a relativism, or subjectivism, that I sometimes think borders on nihilism. In the nineteenth century, Nietzsche may have had cause to complain of the "imbalance" in historicism that tilted it heavily, as he saw it, on the side of the past, that drew all meaning from the past and saw the present only as an extension or extrapolation from the past, and that therefore denied to the present the freedom that Nietzsche sought for it, the freedom to know and create itself. But that was in the nineteenth century. Today, the tilt in historicism is overwhelmingly in the opposite direction. Today, when so many people, and young people particularly, regard the past as so discredited that they can hardly take it seriously in itself, let alone as a guide to the present, when the Hegelian idea is incomprehensible to them even as a philosophical concept, let alone as one that could conceivably inform their own sense of reality, the thrust of historicism is completely relativist and subjectivist.

In the nineteenth century the historicist dictum—that all values are relative, that the past can only be understood in its own terms—was taken as a warrant of historical objectivity; indeed, it was held out as the promise of a new "scientific" history. All that was required, it was thought, for an objective, scientific re-creation of the past was an immersion in contemporary—that is, historically contemporary—sources, and an identification on the part of the historian with the values, attitudes, beliefs, and concerns of the historical period he was studying. Today we have taken historicism a giant step forward—or backward, as the case may be. We have discovered that if all values are relative, they are as relative for the historian as for the historical epoch he is studying. If there is no common morality binding the past and present, if each age is unique unto itself, then the historian, being a product of his own age and of his own person, is incapable of objectively re-creating the past. He can only re-create it in his own image. In relativizing history, we have also relativized the historian—and the historical enterprise itself. It is not Hegel, or even Ranke, who has triumphed, but rather Nietzsche.

Mr. Olafson's discussion embraced all the humanities—philosophy, literature, and history. I will confine myself to some observations about history, although I think they are pertinent to the other disciplines as well. I do not want to engage in that time-honored strategy of academic one-upmanship—"my discipline is worse than yours"—but I do have the impression that history *is* in a worse state than the others. We historians cannot, to be sure, compete with the Modern Language Association, whose president not so long ago declared the study of literature (or was it only Milton?) to be obsolete. The only comparable statement we can boast of comes from outside our profession—Henry Ford's famous pronouncement that "History is bunk." But if we have not quite conferred an honorary presidency upon Ford, we have dignified and popularized his sentiment in ways he could not have anticipated. It was an eminent historian, one I much admire, who coined the equally famous maxim "Everyman his own historian." There is a long slippery slope leading from "Everyman his own historian" to "History is bunk." A skillful and tenacious spirit like Carl Becker can keep his footing on that perilous incline, but most of us find ourselves sliding inexorably downward.

This nihilistic tendency is fed by the pervasive relativism of our culture, the prevailing conviction that anything is possible and everything is permitted, that truth and falsehood, good and bad, are all in the eyes of the beholder, that in the free and democratic marketplace of ideas, all ideas are equal—equally plausible, equally valid, equally true. The corollary of "Everything is permitted," Nietzsche said, is "Nothing is true." Real freedom is the freedom from truth—and not only from truth, he reminded us, but from the "*will* to truth." It may be that we are finally witnessing our liberation from that ultimate bondage.

This may seem a rather exalted and fanciful way of describing the present state of historical studies. Yet it does correspond to what we are now experiencing. Let me start with what seems to be a trivial point —and this takes us to the subject of curriculum. I know of no major graduate school in history—I hope I am wrong about this but I am afraid I am not—that still has a required course on what used to be called "Historical Method." Such a course would now be regarded as presumptuous, as suggesting that there is a prescribed method for historical inquiry, for the validation of historical facts, the proper use of sources, the proper presentation of the evidence, and so forth. What graduate schools do offer, however, are courses on "New Methods in History"—quantification, psychoanalysis, sociological history, history as drama or psychodrama, and the like. If there is no one method we feel competent to transmit to our students as a model or standard, there are a multiplicity of methods—the newer the better—that we offer for their delectation and, we hope, edification.

Apart from the zest for the new, what is interesting about these "New Methods" or "New Approaches to History" is the tolerance extended to all of them. An outsider might think that some of these methods or approaches are mutually exclusive, contradictory. But that is not as they appear in the multitude of symposia and conferences devoted to this theme. At one such conference I attended, the quantifiers were entirely prepared to concede the validity of the psychoanalytic approach so long as the psychoanalysts extended the same courtesy to them, which the latter promptly did. I might add that it was not simply claimed that quantification might be appropriate to one historical problem and psychoanalysis to another; with this, one would not quarrel. What was claimed was that the same problem might, with equal legitimacy, be subject to either approach, however discordant the results might be. The refrain of the conference was quite simply, and vulgarly, "doing one's thing."

The same tolerance is extended to "new interpretations" or "revisionist theses." If the aspiring historian cannot come up with a new method or approach to establish his reputation, the next best thing is a new interpretation—or "interp" as my students familiarly refer to it. A good deal of controversy may be generated by these interpretations, but behind the controversy is a quite extraordinary amount of latitude. All that is required to get a hearing, to become the subject of discussion, is that the interpretation be "interesting." The question of its truth is entirely secondary, and indeed, may never be decided.

Now the point is not that the truth about any particular subject is difficult to come by or agree upon. Historians have always known that; that is what historical scholarship is all about. What is new about the present situation is the prevailing conviction, as I see it (especially among young historians), that there is no truth, that there is, in fact, no history but only historians. This is what "Everyman his own historian" has come to mean—that every man creates his own truth and that that truth is true only for him. This is not, I believe, what Carl Becker meant by that dictum, but it is the meaning that is currently attached to it. The personalization of history—the reduction of history to the person of the historian—has never gone as far as it has today.

We have long been familiar with the Marxist insistence that the class interests of the historian are necessarily reflected in the history he writes. More recently we have been advised that psychoanalysis is not only a necessary tool for the historian to understand his historical subject—Martin Luther, Gandhi, Woodrow Wilson, or whoever—but also that the psychic character of the historian himself necessarily enters into the history he writes. So too we are told that only Black historians are competent to deal with the history of Blacks, and women historians with the history of women.

Instead, then, of truth or truths what we are left with is a variety of opinions—and opinions that are assumed to derive not from reason but from interest and passion—the interest and passion of the historian. The only truth available to the historian is thought to be the truth of self-confession, the confession of his own interests and passions, or as it is fashionably put, his "commitments." It is not about history that the historian is presumed to speak with any authority but only about himself. The most he can be expected to do is to declare his interests, to be candid about his commitments.

I am not suggesting that all or even most historians are taking this position, or even that all those who do profess it carry it out consistently and systematically. Old habits die hard, and even the young, fortunately, exhibit signs of cultural lag. But the cultural tendency is unmistakable and difficult to resist, so that even the most benighted of us are hard put to justify a view of history, and a practice of history, that is not thoroughly relativist and subjective. Confronted with this situation, historicism, in my opinion, is not very helpful. If historicism does offer a "balance," a "compromise," as Mr. Olafson suggests, it is so precarious a balance that it cannot withstand the pressure of the *Zeitgeist*. It is a compromise, I suspect, that has conceded too much to the enemy.

And finally I suspect—and here I am on more dangerous, certainly on more unpopular, ground—I suspect that humanism itself, as Mr. Olafson describes it, is not very helpful. For humanism can only speak, as Mr. Olafson does, of "values" in quotation marks—that is, diffidently, apologetically, as if they were not quite real, as if, in fact, they are what our culture has made of them, "norms," as we say, that are relative, subjective, personal, conventional, arbitrary. There is very little in such a conception of values that can sustain the historian—or the philosopher or literary critic—in what used to be called the "pursuit of truth." In addition, humanism, as Mr. Olafson also reminds us, must have constant reference to "human beings," to their "commonsense" image of themselves, their common interests, concerns, needs, and passions. But this regard for common humanity, commendable as it is, does not encourage an equally high regard for the "humanities," which consist in large part, after all, of the study of the *uncommon* products of uncommon human beings: great ideas, great books, great works of art, great events, great men. To the familiar accusation against the humanities—that they are "elitist"—it used to be enough to say that there is a necessary relation, a continuum between the uncommon and the common, that the humanities are in the service of humanity, that they instruct, edify, elevate even the lowliest of us. But this reply no longer serves when the very idea of the uncommon, of the great, is denied. Who is to say—this is the question that is always put to us—by what right can anyone presume to say, that art is greater than artifact, that Shakespeare or Milton are greater, more worthy of study and respect, than Bob Dylan or Kurt Vonnegut?

This, as I see it, is the situation in which the humanities now find themselves. And in this situation humanism seems to me to be at best irrelevant, at worst mischievous. For it is fighting the wrong war. It is battling against a dessicated, inhuman, impersonal, authoritarian enemy, at a time when that enemy has long since been routed; it is urging the claims of the present, of relevant human needs and concerns, at a time when we have a surfeit of present-mindedness and relevance. At this time, humanism, however subtly conceived—and Mr. Olafson's is a subtle view of it—may be a symptom of our malaise more than a cure for it. Perhaps what is required now is not so much a reaffirmation of humanism, as a critical philosophical and historical study of humanism itself, so that we may better understand how we have arrived at our present predicament.

The Language and Methods of Humanism

M. H. Abrams
Cornell University

I find enlightening and useful Professor Olafson's sketch of the conceptual scheme—the frame of often implicit assumptions—that has been a distinctive feature within the various disciplines traditionally grouped as "the humanities." This scheme establishes coordinates that enable us, in a preliminary way, to map out what is humanistic, what is nonhumanistic, and what is antihumanistic; it also enables us to detect recent tendencies within the humanities themselves that threaten to subvert, or else to abandon silently, the very premises on which the Western humanist, through the centuries, has undertaken to understand and assess man, his actions, his history, and his intellectual and imaginative productions.

Mr. Olafson finds that the traditional humanistic concern is with the world of the distinctive person, for whom nonhuman nature is the theater for his activities, and who confronts in the world other persons similarly endowed and engaged. These persons are thinking and feeling agents who manifest intentions and purposes and have some measure of control over, and thus responsibility for, their own destinies. The term "purpose" means something that is real and essential in the person. If there is purpose, there is also a choice between alternative actions, and the choice and its consequences can be judged by criteria of better or worse, right or wrong, good or evil. Human life and history are viewed as a narrative sequence, or drama, in which there are conflicts within a person, and between persons, and between a person and the conditions of his milieu. This drama, as it evolves, displays love and hate, mutual achievements and mutual destruction, individual successes and failures, comedy and tragedy, the sublime and the ridiculous. In his intellectual and imaginative products, man expresses his human concern—his "form of life," his informing vision, his assumptions and structure of values—and the humanist scholar who undertakes to understand and place and assess these products views them, ultimately, through his own perspective of concern.

What I want to do is bring these traditional humanistic concepts to bear on two topics that have emerged. The first topic is the risk of skepticism and relativism to the modern humanistic enterprises; the second is the question of whether effective teaching in a liberal education is primarily a teaching of "arts" or methods in the humanistic disciplines, or whether it is primarily a teaching by example, by instancing in the person of the individual humanist a stance and procedure that is representatively humanistic.

I

The humanist typically addresses himself to texts that are not written in the highly refined and specialized languages of the logician or the scientist, but in the ordinary language that has been developed over many centuries to express and to deal with the complexities, the ambiguities, the nuances, and the contradictions of the human predicament—the predicament of purposive, fallible, perplexed, and feeling persons, who, for better or worse, act and interact and manifest what Keats called "the fierce dispute/Between damnation and impassioned clay." As Mr. Olafson has suggested, the traditional language of humanistic critics and scholars, despite some technical elements specific to a particular discipline, remains the ordinary language of the persons and documents with which they deal—and it has to do so if humanists are to carry our their traditional functions.

From this fact follows a conclusion that a number of us find hard to accept; namely, that in many of the central and most distinctive judgments of the humanistic scholar and critic we can never achieve certainty. In fact, one way to identify the humanities is to say that they are those disciplines whose concern is with the areas of human action and production where valid knowledge is the aim, where a rational procedure is essential, but where certainty is impossible.

I agree with Professor Himmelfarb's concern about the dangers to the humanities of threats from within—the threats of radical skepticism and relativism, and of giving up the old search for truth. I recognize—with equal dismay—the same tendencies in literary studies that she finds in historical studies: a surrender to irrationality, a stress on multiple "interps" instead of meaning, the drift to a profound skepticism, even to nihilism, with respect to values. It would be a bad mistake, however, to combat such tendencies by the counterclaim that humanistic studies, in all their central enterprises, can yield certainty and a single and ultimate truth. Some parts—some basic parts—of these studies are indeed factual, and therefore subject to the criteria that govern the sciences: the criteria of valid empirical reasoning and the established ways to support or falsify hypotheses. But when you get down to matters of explanation, interpretation, and evaluation—whether of *Hamlet* or of Aristotle's *Poetics* or of the French Revolution or of the nature of justice—then you are out of the realm where certainty is possible and where universal, or even very widespread, agreement is to be found.

Even when I, as a literary critic, feel quite certain that I am asserting the truth about a complex work, I have long since given up being surprised to find that other men, who are indubitably expert, sensitive, and rational critics, sharply disagree. If we should be so misguided as to claim to our students that in this realm our conclusions are certain and at least approximate the single and universal truth of the matter, then we shall be quickly found out and discredited, with the risk of discrediting as well the whole humanistic enterprise in which we are engaged. And if the denial of the possibility of certainty in many humanistic undertakings entails skepticism and relativism, then "that's the way the cookie crumbles"—as my students put it.

But I do not believe that the denial of certainty entails radical skepticism and relativism. To say that the humanist operates in a realm where, in large part, certainty and the single truth is impossible is not to say that it is a realm where uncertainty reigns, where no truths are achievable and therefore anything goes. What produces confusion in the use of the terms "certainty" and "truth" is that, in professional discourse about rational procedures, they are closely tied to highly specialized verbal and symbolic models. In the distant past, when divine authority yielded the ultimate certainty, there was also a symbolic enterprise—formal logic—that was the model of the certainty that could be achieved by human endeavor. When what we think of as modern science developed, apologists had a difficult time justifying the validity of their new systematic procedures, and they tried to mitigate the differences from the deductive logical model by bridge-concepts such as the law of sufficient reason. But after the exact sciences had triumphantly established their own validity and authority, the codified rules of scientific language and scientific reasoning achieved a status equivalent to that of logic in guaranteeing certainty, in the sense that all qualified practitioners would consent to its conclusions.

The criterion of certainty, as applied to the humanities, is usually tied to one or both of these alien and highly specialized models for achieving formal certainty or practical certainty, deductive truths or empirical truths. The language of the traditional humanist, however, is very different from the specially developed, sharply defined, and strictly rule-bound ideal languages of logic or the natural sciences. For the humanist's language, although responsible to the formal rules of logic and in its own fashion empirical, must perform its central functions beyond the point where these drastically simplified calculi of logic and the exact sciences come to a stop. To achieve its traditional aims, the language of the humanist is necessarily flexible, loose, uncodified, nuanced, and lacking sharp definitional boundaries. Ultimately, it is also what Mr. Olafson calls the language of concern—that is, it engages with its subject matter in an area in which it is subject only to such soft-focus criteria as good sense, tact, insight, aesthetic sensibility, and a sound sense of moral values. Such discourse is rarely capable of rigid codification, and therefore rarely capable of achieving strictly conclusive arguments; but it can and should be responsible and rational—with the kind of rationality that alone is adapted to fulfill its own humane purposes and to achieve sound knowledge in its elected area of understanding. And if (when judged by the alien criteria of simplified calculi) it is not certain, neither is it, strictly speaking, uncertain. The reasoning and conclusions of humanistic discourse are subject to criteria, but these are criteria appropriate to its own intellectual enterprise, such as coherent or incoherent, inclusive or omissive, sensible or outré, disinterested or partisan, central or overly ingenious, clear or obfuscative, sound or unsound.

"The kind of certainty," Wittgenstein has said, "is the kind of language-game." Now we can, if we choose, apply the word "certain" to a humanistic conclusion that satisfies the positive criteria I have listed. But if we are to avoid confusion and error, we must keep in mind that this is often a very different kind of certainty from the formal certainty of logic or the practical certainty of an exact science. An even more serious error is to try to make the humanities capable of the scientific kind of certainty by "objectifying" (to use Olafson's term) humanistic inquiry; that is, by substituting for its ordinary, loose, and flexible language of interpretation, evaluation, and concern the specialized and codified language of science and, above all, by translating the langauge of purpose and responsibility into a calculus of causality. Either this translation is no more than a merely lexical substitution, which results in scientism—a mere simulacrum of scientific procedure and conclusions—or else it is inherently incapable of accomplishing the central humanistic functions. For the language of science has achieved its precision, the codified rigor of its reasoning, and its kind of certainty by systematically eliminating from consideration all those aspects of human experience and judgment that, to the humanist and to all of us with our human interests and concerns, matter most. And when the humanist genuinely commits himself to a language modeled on that of the sciences, he finds that the specifically human aspects of his subject matter, such as individual personality, purpose, passion, drama, and value, ineluctably elude his linguistic grasp.

What I have said about humanistic language and rationality does not entail a radical skepticism or relativism, but it does, I think, entail a very different thing: an essential pluralism in the humanistic pursuits. All nondogmatic humanists recognize in experience (and in practice, if not in theory, they make constant allowance for these things) profound differences in the elected cognitive perspectives, favored frames of reference, distinctive kinds of reasoning, and individual forms of sensibility in their fellow humanists. These differences permit individual inquirers, by diversely coherent and rational procedures, to produce sound but divergent conclusions about the matter in hand, whether it is *Hamlet* or the *Poetics* or the French Revolution or the nature of justice. And what each perspective does—if its application through the medium of an individual sensibility is rational—is to bring out different aspects of a subject, to locate it in a different context of relevant considerations, and to force us to see it in a way we have not seen it before.

I am as little disposed as Professor Himmelfarb to surrender the term "truth" and to yield it up for the exclusive use of the logician and the scientist. But it is important to keep in mind that, as the kind of certainty is the kind of language game, so the kind of truth is the kind of language game too. And the truth that each of us, as individuals engaged in a common humanistic enterprise, ought to claim is not the final truth, the whole truth, and nothing but the truth; for that is to convert our disciplines into dogmas. The superposition of multiple, coherent, and rationally exploited perspectives yields a vision in depth; and this multidimensional knowledge constitutes what is the distinctive humanistic truth about a subject. If this claim implies that the humanistic search for truth is always in process and is never finished, I find nothing to be dismayed about such a conclusion. It is, in fact, precisely this feature that gives to our group of disciplines their importance and indispensability in the energetic intellectual life of a vital culture.

II

And now I shall say a few words about my second topic: the role of method as against personal example in teaching the humanities. I spend much of my own time in teaching method—that is, the forms of sound reasoning in a humanistic discipline, the kinds of questions that are relevant, and the nature and weight of the evidence for and against answers to these questions. This kind of teaching is essential in the academy and, I agree with Mr. Olafson, has been injuriously neglected in recent years. But here too it is important to remember that rational procedure in many humanistic areas can be identified and loosely described, but not codified; that it is thus (in the traditional distinction) an art rather than a science; and that to attempt to rigidly define and regulate what is by its nature and aim necessarily a flexible and elusive way of proceeding is to transform a humanistic process of reasoning into a calculus that systematically leaves out of account everything that really matters.

Because normative procedures in the humanities are variable and much easier to recognize than to categorize precisely, teaching by force of example is so much more important than it is in logic or the sciences. Judging by my own experience as a student rather than as a teacher, I find that what has counted most has been a model of the humanist as a normative personage, who instantiates a humanity that becomes representative of what the humanities are. This model, ideally, is a composite of the stance and procedure of one's own teachers and of the great humanists of the past, who have projected their individual ethos in almost every page of the documents they have bequeathed to us. These humanists have managed to deal extraordinarily well with areas of experience in which rationality is essential but certainty is impossible, meeting concern with concern, yet maintaining an equilibrium between dogmatism and skepticism.

The tide most threatening to the traditional stance of the humanist in our own time, as Olafson has pointed out, is a reaction against skepticism by a kind of dogmatism that speaks in the vatic voice of the prophet and the visionary. The truth is that when you go to the liberal humanists, hot for certainties, you get what seems to be very dusty answers. As a result, some of our students turn increasingly to such prophets of the past as Nietzsche, or much worse, to some of the small and seedy prophets of our own day. The world of the prophet is a hot, intense world of total assurance that you have the humanistic truth, that you know what we must do to be saved—and as such, it has great contemporary appeal. In comparison with the hot world of prophecy, the world of the humanist is a cool world. What we need to get our students to recognize is that the stance of the liberal humanist is a very difficult one, which takes poise and courage to maintain. It takes a secure balance and a firm will to conduct, rationally, a discipline in which many of the premises, procedures, and conclusions are essentially contestable, without surrendering either to an all-dissolving skepticism or to the inviting dogmatism of the visionary and the fanatic. Our aim, by example as well as precept, must be to show the dignity, as well as the comfort, of maintaining the humanistic poise, of searching for answers to our inescapable human problems, answers that are neither ultimate nor certain, but are the best and most rational ones we are capable of making.

The normative personages of the humanistic tradition, from Socrates to Solzhenitsyn, offer instances of ways to cope with the human predicament, while steering between the rocks of nihilism and the whirlpool of fanaticism. I have the hunch—I certainly have the hope—that the instinct for survival in civilized humanity is great enough to ensure the persistence of the humanistic stance which these models, each in a diverse and distinctive way, represent to us.

III

I was certain that, in the brevity and omissiveness with which I had to present my views, I would evoke counterclaims, and that I would agree with a number of these counterclaims. Thus, I consent to the assertion that, in the humanistic disciplines, we are justified in rejecting some interpretations and arguments and conclusions out of hand. A large fraction of humanistic problems are factual, or close to factual (though these are often preparatory to the enterprise of interpretation and explanation), and here we often find ourselves capable of denying the factual claims or producing counterfacts or falsifying the hypotheses. And though the modes of humanistic rationality are diverse, we are able to recognize and reject patent irrationality, as well as overt dogma. Certainly, also, within the domain of interpretation itself we are often readily able to identify an impossible, inept, radically inadequate, or outrageously implausible interpretation. In fact, our jobs as teachers confront us again and again with such patent errors by students (not to speak of fellow-critics and scholars) that it is incumbent upon us to reject them and to identify the criteria by which we judge them unacceptable.

My emphasis in these remarks, however, has been on that area of interpretation that involves central principles of organization, of theme, structure, characterization, and authorial intentions (to use literature as an example). And here we find contestable conclusions, in the sense that expert, knowledgeable, sensitive, and reasonable critics come out with very different results. Take Shakespeare, for example. In our own century the interpretations of Shakespeare's plays—and the kinds of evaluation dependent on particular interpretations—have multiplied remarkably. We have eliminated very few of the alternative interpretations of earlier centuries, while adding many others. And some of the newer interpretations yield valuable insights, bringing into our ken aspects of the plays that enrich our ability to experience Shakespeare's plays in ways outside the range of even such great critics of the past as Johnson or Coleridge. Each validly innovative critic who exploits, rationally and responsibly, his distinctive perspective and frame of reference (whether Marxist, Freudian, new critical, structuralist, or whatnot) adds depth to our perception of one or another of Shakespeare's plays; and I would not hesitate to say that each adds to our knowledge of the truth about that play.

This also bears on another question that has been raised. Given what I have said about the absence of criteria of certainty in some central humanistic enterprises—hence our frequent inability to resolve with finality radical differences in critical judgments and conclusions —how are we to distinguish between greater and lesser works of art? And on the pedagogical level, how are we to decide what works to teach our students?

I think it is only when we are theorizing about the humanities rather than practising a humane discipline—only when we are writing metacriticism rather than criticism—that we are dismayed about the lack of anything approximating logical or scientific certainty in our elected province. What it comes to is this: to demand certainty in the humanities is in fact to ask for a set of codified rules and criteria such that when, say, a work of literature is presented to any expert critical intelligence, it will process the work and come out with a precise meaning and a fixed grade of value that will coincide with the meaning and evaluation arrived at by any other critical intelligence. When a humanist really faces up to these consequences of his demand for certainty, he finds such a mechanical process to be disquieting and repulsive—and with good reason—because in fact it is approximated only under an authoritarian cultural regime in which the codified rules and universal criteria are not discovered in the language and practise of individual critics but are established by edict. In our free humanistic activities, we all take for granted the human predicament that the humanities both deal with and express, and we manage as a matter of course, and quite well, to cope with a situation in which tenable perspectives are diverse, individual sensibilities and proclivities are distinctive, many judgments are contestable, and few basic disagreements are in any final way resolvable. The nature of that human predicament, in fact, is what makes the free humanistic enterprise an indispensable, difficult, and deeply and endlessly interesting pursuit.

As a matter of everyday practise, however, we in fact possess various ways for checking our individual judgments and for establishing the difference between the better and the worse, the greater and the lesser, by criteria that transcend our personal predilections and judgments. Chief among these is a revised form of what used to be called the *consensus gentium*, which used to be considered the ultimate criterion of humanistic truth, goodness, and beauty. In the revised form, we can state the principle in this way: agreement among diverse humanists as to the importance and value of a work at any one time, and still more, the survival value of a work—general agreement as to its importance and value over an extended period of time—serves as a sound way to distinguish the better from the worse and to identify which work is a classic. The consensus that emerges when an imaginative work is viewed from a diversity of critical perspectives and through a diversity of sensibilities—and especially a consensus that emerges despite radical cultural changes over many centuries—is a reliable index to the fact that the work is central in its human concerns, broad in its imaginative appeal, and rich in its inherent aesthetic and other values.

As humane critics and teachers, we in fact employ such criteria as a matter of course. Thereby, we are certain that *Hamlet* and *Twelfth Night* are greater and more worthy of attention than *The Spanish Tragedy* or *Gammer Gurton's Needle*; as teachers, we may for good reasons decide to teach the second two plays, but we do not make the mistake of letting them displace the plays of Shakespeare. But of course, expert critical consensus and survival value are no more than a prima facie index to a classic work; what matters to us as individuals is what has been called our "participation" in the work—our full intellectual, imaginative, and emotional engagement—as well as our response with concern to the author's concern, our consent to the consent of the ages because we feel the greatness of the work on our own pulses. The aim of good teaching is to get the student to respond humanly, with power, passion, and concern to the literary classics from Homer and Sophocles on—and *mutatis mutandis,* to the classic works in other humanistic areas.

THE PLACE OF SCIENCE AND
THE SCIENTIFIC OUTLOOK

Science, Science Teaching, and Rationality

Gerald Holton
Harvard University

INTRODUCTION

I feel honored to be asked to address this conference dedicated to a rational examination, at a fundamental level, of educational programs at the college and university level.

Recently, I made my way through a happy sea of students just arriving at college, unloading armfuls of books and records that have helped shape the cultural background they bring along. A look at what is unpacked in freshman dormitories at various colleges today would be fascinating and instructive. I suspect that the balance is heavily in favor of Carlos Castaneda, J. B. R. Tolkien, Ray Bradbury, and R. D. Laing, rather than, let us say, Spinoza, Bertrand Russell, Thomas Mann, and Norbert Wiener. And if such students wander into the huge Harvard Cooperative Bookstore in search of general reading in science, they will find that the whole category "Science" is banished to one distant set of five-foot shelves, largely devoted to ecology, Isaac Asimov, gardening, Immanuel Velikovsky, and manuals on the care of cats and dogs. To reach that section, in this and most similar stores, one must take care lest one gets lost in labyrinthine spaces given over to what really seems to sell today—the occult, sci-fi, transcendental musings, handbooks on shamanism or mushrooms, and the achievement of joy through various types of athletics.

I note all this with some trepidation, for every few years I give a course on the concepts and theories in physical science for some hundred of these freshmen—largely nonscience students. It is from this practical point of view and with this particular audience in mind that I want to approach my topic. For I am aware that I shall not only try to teach science; I shall often be struggling with very intelligent persons, whose *Weltanschauung* I want to change and expand.[1]

It therefore behooves me to ask myself: What are the epistemological bases from which we start, both my students and I, in our different ways? What are the unwritten assumptions in my and their approaches to nature? (I recall that some two decades ago the most striking characteristic on the whole was my students' unreasonable *belief* in the efficacy of science and the "scientific method.") Having been influenced early by the philosophical thoughts of working scientists such as P. W. Bridgman and Philipp Frank, Einstein and Wiener and by philosophers such as Wittgenstein, Ernest Nagel, and Carl Gustav Hempel, what do I regard now as most essential to communicate to my students (and graduate assistants on the staff), and how can it be done? What future research programs on the philosophy of the curriculum seem to be needed today as the result of these recognitions? In sharing some thoughts on these topics, I shall not make a thorough philosophical analysis, but I hope at least to start a discussion.

This is also not the place to discuss my own credo in any detail as it concerns science teaching, and in particular, teaching that large group, the nonscientists. It is embodied in two texts I have written, a national curriculum-development project I initiated—the Project Physics Course—and some essays.[2] The chief elements of this credo are:

1. The major concepts, theories, and methods should be known by any person who claims to be educated, for four reasons: to serve as basic cultural background; to permit career-based opportunities for conceptual or methodological overlap; to make one less gullible and hence able to make more intelligent decisions as a citizen and parent where science is involved; and last but not least, to make one truly *sane* (for while scientific knowledge is no guarantor of sanity, the *absence* of knowledge of how the world works and of one's own place in an orderly, noncapricious cosmos is precisely a threat to the sanity of the most sensitive persons).

2. To bring a respectable level of knowledge and understanding of the "hard" sciences to the kind of person who has traditionally shied away from contact with science, it is not enough merely to make a course compulsory or to hope that the usual, departmental introductory course that science concentrators do not openly rebel against will be adequate for the nonscientist too. No, I believe a special effort

must and can be made for this larger, second group. In various colleges, there exist examples that cover a wide variety of styles, from purely research-oriented case studies to largely historical, semiqualitative courses. I am not doctrinaire on what will work best. But I suspect that the approach at either extreme is unlikely to succeed, since it avoids coming to grips with three needs: to tell what we now know about the physical world (a relatively easy thing to do); to tell how one came to accept it, hence how one can check on the veracity of the claims without having to rely on the flat, authoritarian statements characterizing most textbooks; and to tell of the effects on and by science.

In my own courses, therefore, I try to infuse the presentation of the chief results of scientific research—which necessarily is the major focus of attention throughout—with materials introduced at chosen points to explain the epistemological, the historic, the societal, and humanistic contexts of scientific work. By this, I mean allowing some room in the course—perhaps 10 percent of the total lecture time—for discussing how theories are tested and modified; for showing science as a human achievement of historic persons, who usually acted within their cultural context; for showing that the scientific community is a social institution with traditions, canons of workmanship, a large range of agreement, and ways of distinguishing rather well between sound opinions and dubious ones; for showing examples of short-range and long-range effects of scientific work, both in technology and in so-called intellectual revolutions outside science; and for demonstrating that one of the motivations for and results of scientific understanding can be the exhilarating and psychotherapeutic discovery that one lives in a universe that can be grasped by the effort of one's own individual mind.

In short, science courses need not be exempt from the larger task of education, but should and can try to contribute to the aims of education in its widest meaning: "the physical, intellectual, emotional and ethical integration of the individual into a complete person." [3]

Anyone who has such ambitions is not going to be satisfied with drilling F = ma. Not only must he be prepared to convey to students the traditional lessons of mechanics, heat, light, quantum physics, and so on, as they are related to new frontiers (for example, cosmology) but also he must help his students learn equally hard lessons of another kind, concerning the complex and sophisticated rationality at the center of science: that science is built up to a large extent of impotency laws; that there are rules and procedures for testing the adequacies of scientific ideas and that they usually work well but sometimes fail spectacularly and hence may need occasional revision; that understandability does not necessarily mean certainty in science any more than in humanistic studies; that neither classical rationalism nor classical empiricism leads to unshakable knowledge; that scientific knowledge, while not always gained by oversimplification, does not lead by itself to the ability to deal with the complexities of the science-society link; that there are two kinds of science—one public, the other private; that objectivity is achieved, not by a lonely act of individual decision, but by an ongoing process of criticism and social consensus; and that, nevertheless, there is a unique, understandable, and fundamentally simple universe characterized by harmony, parsimony, and necessity.

Anyone who has such ambitions for science teaching and science learning has a difficult task, made more difficult than ever by the fact that today he also finds himself between a large anvil and a fearful hammer. Both exert mighty and opposing pressures on the concept of rationality held by teacher and student alike.

The anvil is provided by the group that I might call the New Dionysians—Charles Reich, Theodore Roszak, Lewis Mumford, Kurt Vonnegut, and others. With all the differences between them, they are alike in their suspicion or even contempt of conventional rationality. They would "widen the spectrum" of what they regard as useful knowledge. They not only urge the introduction of aesthetic and psychological elements at the highest level of priority but in general tend to celebrate the private, personal, and the mystical. Their appeal is large, and they sell well at the college bookstore.[4] In fact, they are writing the liveliest and most readable material available.

The hammer on the other hand, is wielded by the group I shall call the New Apollonians, who urge the educator to confine himself to precisely the opposite: the logical and mathematical side of science, the final fruits of memorable successes, the conception of rationality that depends on criteria of objectivity derived from public science. They would "shrink the window" emphatically, discarding precisely the elements that the other group takes most seriously.

Both groups present themselves with the apocalyptic urgency of rival world views. Their chief attack, as is usual in a polarized situation, is not so much on each other as on anyone caught in the middle. Indeed, they seem to reinforce each other's political position, as any two Cold War antagonists do, for example, by exacting close discipline and loyalty in their own camps and administering punishment for suspected heresy. Each limits the circle of allowable thought and action in the face of its enemy—one ritualistically heaping scorn on a caricature they call rationality, the other on a caricature they call irrationality.

This middle ground is the situation in which I find myself as an educator and which I wish to analyze. For this confrontation is notable, not for any useful results nor even for any entertainment derivable from it, but chiefly for its costs. One of these is, in my view, that it has been a chief obstacle to a more rigorous or rational study of the imaginative process, of the sources of scientific creativity—a study that would seem a contradiction in terms to each side, whereas in reality it may be the ground of their most obvious common interest. To an educator trying both to teach rational procedure and to shape the quality of the imagination, and trying to elicit respect for both the deliberate and the spontaneous sides of creative thinkers, the current polarization is a grave handicap.

THE NEW DIONYSIANS

Evidence for the existence and influence of the New Dionysians is not hard to find. *Time* magazine, in a series called "Second Thoughts About Man," had an installment entitled "Reaching Beyond the Rational." There it was announced that *Time* had "been examining America's rising discontent with entrenched intellectual ideas: liberalism, rationalism and scientism. . . . this week, the Science section considers the repercussions for science and technology. It finds a deepening disillusionment with both, as well as a new view among some scientists that there should be room in their discipline for the nonobjective, mystical, and even irrational." [5]

Time, of course, is not the only discoverer of such trends. We all have seen evidences of it. Don K. Price has pointed out that even the Congressional Research Service, which is not addicted to radical and esoteric ideas, noted solemnly not long ago that the new trend in American culture "implies throwing out the scientific method, the definition of effects, and the search for cause. . . . through the process of rational analysis." [6]

As we turn now to an examination of the views typical of the Dionysians, I must stress that while they may be fashionable they are not transient fads. Indeed, they are pale versions of a long-lived tradition. When Roszak, in *Where the Wasteland Ends* or in a new essay on science called "The Monster and the Titan," proposes to redefine true knowledge as a "gnosis," within which traditional science is only the small part of a larger spectrum (that part that seeks merely to gather "candles of information"), one recalls that it is almost exactly one hundred years ago that DuBois-Reymond's essay "Die Grenzen des Naturerkennens" led to the controversy that culminated in the slogan "the bankruptcy of science." Or one recalls the view of George Santayana in *Reason in Science*: "Science is a halfway house between private sensation and universal vision . . . a sort of telegraphic wire through which a meager report reaches us of things we would fain observe and live through in their full reality. This report may suffice for approximately fit action; it does not suffice for ideal knowledge of the truth, nor for adequate sympathy with the reality."[7]

The current version of this sentiment, more extreme and less eloquent, comes to us, for example, in a book that graced the best-seller lists for a long time after it first appeared in 1970. I refer to Charles A. Reich's *The Greening of America*. While some details have become out of date in the heavy industry of counterculture publications, the basic attitude toward science, nature, and rationality has not changed much in that movement. As a matter of fact, I still find Charles Reich's book more interesting than more recent ones as a source for the study of that world view. If one measured the book only by its wide readership, it is easy to take him perhaps too seriously. If one measures it in terms of a coherent program, on the other hand, it is too easy to dismiss him. There exists a whole book of largely hostile reviews called *The Con Three Controversy*, edited by Philip Nobile; a few are much to the point, but on the whole there is some justice to Reich's rejoinder that most of the critiques have not been thoroughgoing and serious enough.

Reich's is, on the whole, an optimistic book, with a kind of paradisiacal utopia for the United States—but not beyond these shores. There is surprisingly little said about the problems the majority of the world's people face. His relatively parochial platform is not the only evidence for a fundamental solipsism that pervades the book. Indeed, Reich's "first law" of what he calls Consciousness III is that it "starts with self. . . . The individual self is the only true reality. Thus, it returns to the earlier America: 'Myself I sing.' "[8]

Right here we see that this ptolemaic, self-centered conception of the world order directly conflicts with the basic attitude necessary for doing or understanding science. This was expressed quite beautifully by Einstein in his essay "Motiv des Forschens," written in 1918.

> To begin with, I believe with Schopenhauer that one of the strongest motives that lead men to art and science is flight from the everyday life with its painful harshness and wretched dreariness, and from the fettles of one's own shifting desires. One who is more finely tempered is driven to escape from personal existence into the world of objective observing and understanding. . . . Man seeks to form for himself, in whatever manner is suitable for him, a simplified and lucid image of the world, and so to overcome the world of experience by striving to replace it to some extent by this image. . . . Into this image and its formation he places the center of gravity of his emotional life, in order to attain the

peace and serenity that he cannot find within the narrow confines of swirling, personal experience. [9]

Later, in the essay "Religion and Science" (1930), Einstein reiterated the point in these words: "The individual feels the futility of human desires and aims, and the sublimity and marvelous order which reveal themselves both in nature and in the worlds of thought." Einstein thinks of this sympathetically as "the beginnings of cosmic religious feelings," a feeling that he recognizes as "the strongest and noblest motive for scientific research," together with the "deep conviction of the rationality of the universe."

In the constant struggle to go beyond what he called the "merely personal," Einstein came in the end to agree fully with Max Planck's remark that a basic aim of science is "the complete liberation of the physical world picture from the individuality of separate intellects." One must add of course that this search for a world picture that is covariant with respect to differences in individual observers did not and does not contradict the centrality of human concerns in those activities that have direct societal impact. Thus, Einstein said, "concern for the person must always constitute the chief objective of all technological effort." Moreover, the escape path from the "merely personal" through the projection of a rational world order does, after all, lead back to the solution of complex and pressing problems (physical, biomedical, psychological, social, and so forth), and indeed is the only known method for finding such solutions.

Another commandment of Consciousness III, Reich tells us, is that it is open, "to any and all experience. [Elsewhere: Experience is "the most precious of commodities."] It is always in a state of becoming. It is just the opposite of Consciousness II which tries to force all new experience into a pre-existing system, and to assimilate all new knowledge to principles already established." [10]

This commandment announces a very important theme: the primacy of direct experience—unreconstructed, nonreductionistic, unanalyzed, unordered. This extends on the one side to music ("the older music was essentially intellectual; it was located in the mind . . . ; the new music rocks the whole body and penetrates the soul"[11]), and on the other side it is the guiding attitude taken toward nature itself. The Dionysians are, of course, all for experiencing nature, but in a specific manner. In one of the most revealing passages, Reich says that the Consciousness III person "takes 'trips' out into nature; he might lie for two hours and simply stare up at the arching branches of a tree. . . . He might cultivate visual sensitivity, and the ability to meditate, by staring for hours at a globe lamp."[12] He might also find at that point that "one of the most important means for restoring dulled consciousness is psychedelic drugs." (Although Reich does not advocate the use of drugs stridently, he holds that "they make possible a higher range of experience, extending outward toward self-knowledge, to the religious [the only time, I believe, that Reich speaks about religion in the book], and to vision.")

Nature, thus, is what one takes "trips" out into. Nature means "the beach, the woods, and the mountains." And it is "perhaps the deepest source of consciousness. . . . Nature is not some foreign element that requires equipment. Nature is them."[13]

This homocentric view of nature, in which man and nature overlap in the total uncritical experience of natural phenomena, is quite obviously diametrically opposite to the attitude needed for the rational understanding of nature. And of course it is meant to do so: "Consciousness III . . . does not try to reduce or simplify man's complexity, or the complexity of nature. . . . It says that what is meaningful, what endures, is no more nor less than the total experience of life."[14] Even to a mystic such as Johannes Kepler, experience was the trigger of a puzzle that raised itself in the mind. It was through the working out of such puzzles that men, in Kepler's view and in that of the neo-Platonists in general, could consider themselves as directly communicating with the Deity. As Kepler said: "Those laws [that govern the material world] lie within the power of understanding of the human mind; God wanted us to perceive them when He created us in His image in order that we take part in His own thoughts."

Total, unanalyzed experience itself would never lead one to the experience of rationality in nature. For, as Einstein put it in the 1918 essay I referred to, we have to be satisfied with "portraying the simplest occurrences which can be made accessible to our experience." More complex occurrences cannot be constructed with the necessary degree of accuracy and logic of perfection. One has to make a choice: "supreme purity, clarity, and certainty, *at the cost of completeness*." Only after we have constructed a valid world image may we find that it applies, after all, to every natural phenomenon in all its complexity and completeness. The effort to encompass the totality of experience is possible in principle, but only *post hoc*.

It is at this point that Einstein introduced a warning, an essential demurrer, which he made frequently and which we shall soon have to treat seriously: the reality of human limitations puts limits on the efficacy of logic, and it would be foolish to hide it, or deny it, or restrict the permissible use of reason to such narrow ground. From the general laws on which the structure of theoretical physics rests, "it should be possible to obtain by pure deduction the description, that is to say the theory, of natural processes, including those of life, if such a process of deduction were not far beyond the capacity of human thinking. To these elementary laws there leads no logical path, but only intuition supported by being sympathetically in touch with experience [*Einfüh-lung in die Erfahrung*]. . . . There is no logical bridge from experience to the basic principles of theory. . . . Physicists accuse many an epis-temologist of not giving sufficient weight to this circumstance." [15]

Reich's message, however, is that nature is to be studied or under-stood, not by analysis, not even ameliorated by an intuitive, specula-tive leap where human limitation makes it necessary and human ingen-uity makes it possible, but by total experience, first and last. One rea-son for reaching this conclusion is his basic attitude toward rationality itself. Throughout the book it is not science, not even the corporate state but rationality, defined quite narrowly, that is the true enemy. Thus, we read that the corporate state "has only one value, the value of technology-organization-efficiency-growth-progress. The state is per-fectly rational and logical. It is based upon principle." [16] One might think that the vision of Saint-Simon had really triumphed in our day!

Just what is wrong with rationality? Reich gives the answer on the second page of his book, where we read that the rationality of the modern state must be "measured against the insanity of existing 'rea-son' "—and this reason is one that makes for "impoverishment," "de-humanization," and so forth. "So-called rational thought" is discussed at greater length later in these terms: "Consciousness III is deeply sus-picious of logic, rationality, analysis, and of principle. Nothing is so outrageous to the Consciousness II intellectual as the seeming rejec-tion of reason itself. But Consciousness III has been exposed to some rather bad examples of reason, including the intellectual justification of the Cold War and the Vietnam War. At any rate, Consciousness III believes it is essential to get free of what is now accepted as rational thought. It believes that 'reason' tends to leave out too many factors and values." [17] And later: "Accepted patterns of thought must be broken; what is considered 'rational thought' must be opposed by 'non-rational thought'—drug-thought, mysticism, impulses. Of course the latter kinds of thought are not really 'non-rational' at all; they merely introduce new elements into the sterile, rigid, outworn 'rationality' that prevails today." [18]

Or again, "One of the most important means employed by the new generation in seeking to transcend technology is . . . to pay heed to the instincts, to obey the rhythms and music of nature, to be guided by the irrational, by folklore, and the spiritual, and by the imagination." [19]

As Charles Frankel has accurately noted in an article in *Science*,

"The Irrationalist's theory of human nature is steeped in the tradition of the dualistic psychology it condemns. It talks about 'reason' as though it were a department of human nature in conflict with 'emotions.' But 'reason,' considered as a psychological process, is not a special faculty, and it is not separate from the emotions; it is simply the process of re-organizing the emotions. . . . As Hume said, 'reason is, and of necessity must be, the slave of the passions.' " [20]

The place of reason in the counterculture world is so low therefore because, first, it is defined as the seat merely of the instrumental analytical faculty, and then is discredited by association with the failures of technological and political planners. And having undercut the usefulness of reason, Reich has no tool left for organizing and validating a realistic attack even on the ills he deplores. Whether this position has had an influence on or merely reflects a *Zeitgeist*, any student or curriculum effort depending on it is in direct conflict with the basic conditions for working in science, teaching science, or understanding it.

THE NEW APOLLONIANS

Now to the hammer. The New Apollonians, too, are members of a long tradition. In their most recent form, they could be found among the logical positivists of the pre-World-War-II period, the inheritors of the long battle against blatant obscurantism and metaphysical fantasies that had haunted science in the nineteenth and early twentieth century. Rereading today, for example, Otto Neurath's influential essay "Sociology and Physicalism" (1931-1932), one can glimpse the magnificent arrogance that helped them to their victories: "The Vienna Circle . . . seeks to create a climate which will be free from metaphysics in order to promote scientific studies in all fields by means of logical analysis. . . . All the representatives of the Circle are in agreement that 'philosophy' does not exist as a discipline, alongside of science, with propositions of its own. The body of scientific propositions exhausts the sum of all meaningful statements. . . . They wish to construct a 'science which is free from any world view.' "

How long the road since those days and how much more sophisticated the fruits of this journey are now clear; we find this, for example, in works such as Hempel's grand survey, *Aspects of Scientific Explanation* (1965). On the subject before us, we find in Hempel's survey room for the "non-consciously rational" or "non-deliberately rational" and similar conceptions and for the speculation that a rationality of nondeliberate actions may be granted.

The most influential offspring of the prewar movement, however, is associated today with Sir Karl Popper and his disciples. As is well known, he holds that the rationality of science presupposes a common language and a common set of assumptions that themselves are subject to conventional rational criticism. The contrary opinion—namely, that there may exist cases of scientific work within an accepted framework that have not been or perhaps never can be subjected fully to such a critique—is labelled "the myth of the framework." Popper writes that this myth "is in our time, the essential bulwark of irrationalism." [21] Similarly, the progress from one stage of scientific theory to another, in his view, does not and cannot take the form of a leap, unlike, say, conversion in the religious sense.

But as if to shield the analysis of this point of view from any discipline other than an approved portion within the philosophy of science, Popper announces that it is dangerous and useless to turn to sociology, psychology, or the history of science for "enlightenment concerning the aims of science and its possible progress." He sees sociology and psychology as "riddled with fashions and with uncontrolled dogma," and refers to them often as "spurious sciences. . . . No, this is not the way, as mere logic can show." [22]

The difficulty is that most historians of science who have actually immersed themselves in the way a particular person, in his painful "personal struggle," achieved an advance will be forced to disagree with this severe analysis. Yet, their testimony and their examples, in Popper's catechism, would be inadmissible, since the analysis of actual case histories would use techniques from one of the "spurious sciences." The presentation of the work of real individuals groping their way to discovery—the very same material that can be shown to be one of the most successful tools for science instruction along the lines discussed earlier—is frowned upon, if not forbidden. In this framework, individual case studies are simply dismissed, as in a typical passage:

> [Consider first] the way in which objective scientific knowledge is arrived at. We may leave aside here the question of *ways of discovery*, i.e., the problem of how a new scientific idea arises, how a novel hypothesis or theory is first conceived. For our purposes it will suffice to consider the scientific *ways of validation*, i.e., the manner in which empirical science goes about [as against the scientist himself going about] examining a proposed new hypothesis, and determines whether it is to be accepted or rejected. . . . As is well known, empirical science [rather than, it appears, the scientist] decides upon the acceptability of a proposed hypothesis by means of suitable tests.[23]

An educator sensitive to and wishing to heed philosophical criticism is therefore almost necessarily left with a view of science as precisely the routine of rational reconstruction that has for so long been the chief content of science textbooks of the traditional kind. Otto Neurath's dictum that " 'philosophy' does not exist as a discipline alongside of science, with propositions of its own" has been turned on its head: the study of the actual work of scientists does not exist as a discipline, alongside of philosophy, with propositions of its own.

In the writings of the more extreme members of the group of Apollonians, one senses that one is not merely watching the development of a philosophical position for its own sake and for the sake of its possible evaluation in the crucible of rational critique. Their ambitions are much larger. One of these is the hope to save scientists from the threat of the irrational and from their suspected inability to do a good job without help from those who can decide which theories are truly scientific and which are merely pseudoscientific.

But the ambitions seem to go beyond even that: to save mankind as a whole from obscurantism, error, madness, astrology, and revolution. Thus, Popper's disciple and successor at the London School of Economics, Imre Lakatos, writes about a theory of scientific change that bases itself on historical case studies, and—a fact that he does not respect—the studies seem to him to deal with "a mystical conversion which is not and cannot be governed by rules of reason and which falls totally within the realm of the (*social*) *psychology of discovery.*"[24] [Italics in original—GH] It makes "scientific change a kind of religious change." This dangerous view, Lakatos says, poses a threat not only to technical epistemology, but "concerns our central intellectual values," hence has effects on "social sciences . . . moral and political philosophy." The position of his hapless victim, Lakatos says, "would vindicate, no doubt, unintentionally, the basic political credo of contemporary religious maniacs ('student revolutionaries')." Elsewhere, Lakatos is led so far as to speculate ad hominem on the same author's possibly sinister influence: "I am afraid this might be one clue to the unintended popularity of his theory among the New Left busily preparing the 1984 'revolution.' "[25]

What is at stake seems to be the defense of civilization itself. The apostle of rationalism is now revealed as the soldier at the gates, fending off the horde of barbarians. The mirror-image symmetry is familiar —for the alarms, rhetoric, and invectives are very similar to those of the New Dionysians, protecting their own vision of civilization from their enemies.

There is, however, a problem with Lakatos' hopes for the history of science. He admits that "if we look at the history of science, if we try to see how some of the most celebrated falsifications [of hypotheses] happened, we have to come to the conclusion that either some of them are plainly irrational, or that they rest on rationality principles radically different from the ones we just discussed."[26] He sees a way out: to replace the "naive" version of methodological falsification with a "sophisticated version . . . and thereby rescue methodology and the idea of scientific *progress*. This is Popper's way, and the one I intend to follow."

It is a small price to pay, Lakatos says, considering that the alternative is a view of scientific revolution that he variously calls "irrational," "a matter for mob psychology," "psychologism," "vulgar Marxism"—a view that would trigger a "new wave of sceptical irrationalism and anarchism." On the other hand, he says that his own "sophisticated methodological falsificationism offers new standards for intellectual honesty."

What emerges is a directive of what constitutes a valid historical study. Lakatos announces it in these words: "In writing a historical case study, one should, I think, adopt the following procedure: (1) one gives a rational reconstruction; (2) one tries to compare this rational reconstruction with actual history and to criticize both one's rational reconstruction for lack of historicity and the actual history for lack of rationality." [27]

Examples of what happens to an historical case study when done in this style are given too. One is "Bohr's plan . . . to work out first the theory of the hydrogen atom. His first model was to be based on a fixed proton-nucleus with an electron in a circular orbit . . . ; after this he thought of taking the possible spin of the electron into account. . . . All this was planned right at the start."[28] Of course, as it happens, Bohr's early work has been very carefully studied by historians of science, and this version produced by "rational reconstruction" is an ahistorical parody that makes one's hair stand on end. At the very least, it is of no help at all to one like myself, who will soon be presenting to a class "Bohr's plan"—the very case study that can be both excellent history and philosophy of science on the one hand, and memorable physics on the other. [29]

PROGRESSIVE RATIONALIZATION

The neglect, the "reconstruction," the distortion of historic cases would be merely an amusing sideshow if it did not fit in so well with and reinforce the tacit aims of many writers of scientific textbooks and unphilosophical scientists, at whose mercy the science educator finds himself. The hammer of the New Apollonians finds there its most malleable material, for they would like nothing better than to believe that science is an always rational pursuit of an elite, progressing inevitably (with the use of "progressive problem shifts") to objective truths.

The reasons for the persistence of the "irrationalized" view of science in the curriculum are several, and mutually supporting. Indeed, the view of science that reaches the student is only the end product of the process of rationalization that has several discernible stages. At the very beginning of scientific thought, Niels Bohr pointed out, there is a complementarity between clarity and truth (*Klarheit* and *Wahrheit*). "The attempt to express the thought in words involves some change, some irrevocable interference with the essential idea." [30] At the next stage—what Einstein called the "personal struggle"—the scientist is required to focus his ideas from private reverie to public testability.

The discontinuous elements of an individual's scientific reasoning in actual cases has been studied by many authors, from Jacques Hadamard to our day.[31] What is clear is that the process of a tentative working out of relations between experience, axioms, and deduced assertions on the way to a verifiable or falsifiable statement does not fit the models of the Apollonians; nor does it usually become part of scientific literature. Over the desk of every scientist the admonition of Louis Pasteur hangs implicitly: "Make it seem inevitable." Journal publication is (necessarily) designed to maximize clear and unambiguous communications between individuals of vastly different backgrounds in all parts of the world, and across time. Therefore it accentuates the "information" yield of the knowledge process and persuasively sets it forth in a rational, causal sequence. There is a high premium on neutral presentation, on operational definitions of concepts, on the sharing of data, and the description of techniques in a way that permits them to be repeated everywhere. Conversely, one must, in such publications, submerge as far as possible other essential components of the process of discovery—one's individual motives, provisional hypotheses, guesses, epistemological assumptions, and above all the actual unique historical sequence.

The process of rationalization is, necessarily, carried even further at the next stage, in the *didactic presentations* that follow from the publication of actual research results. The last and highest stage of rationalization takes place when these didactic presentations become grist for the mills of axiomatizers.

The result of this multistep process is, of course, gloriously successful. It condenses the labors of generations and yields the celebration of the crystallized achievements of positive, public science. For the training of most science-bound students perhaps we need nothing more. However, for better or worse, those not already caught up by science are usually repelled by this product. If they cannot see at some point the human actors that stand behind the linearly programmed reconstruction, the progress of science may well appear to be a collectivist story, an anti-individualistic or even totalitarian construct, free of doubt, error, and criticism—as a glance at most textbooks in science will quickly confirm—devoid of personal participation within a social milieu, bereft of thematic choices, in short, lacking all those elements that, together with the rational input and methods, do in fact shape the progress of precisely the most important scientific work. It may well be that the absurd, anarchic reconstructions of science on the part of the New Dionysians are overreactions to the view of science that emanates from the rationalistic reconstructions of the Apollonians; for that is perhaps all that they, like many students, ever get to see of science.

To conclude, I do not of course propose that we abandon all rational reconstruction for pedagogic purposes or that scientists try to do without progressive rationalization. As educators, we have to show our students the key areas in which rationality is of the essence for actual scientific work, and we must insist at least on these four: rationality in the deductive portions of private theorizing; rationality in the structure of the theory once it has been worked out moderately well; rationality in the process of communication and validation among scientists, operating in the area of public science; and the perception, at least among our more exalted spirits, of the underlying rationality and uniqueness of the world order as seen through science—perhaps the only order open to human perception that is not a Rashomon story.

If we can secure this much, we have gained a great deal indeed. But to obtain this end with the audience I am speaking about—or even in order to gain an interested hearing—we must not pretend that "all this was planned right at the start." At least for the sake of pedagogic effectiveness (though also for the sake of truth), one workable policy I have advocated is to embed these aims in a course that from time to time allows an honest account of actual scientific work, not hiding its human complexity.[32] It is precisely the course directed to the largest number of students—the introductory course—that can take advantage of occasional specific case studies in the context of discovery to demonstrate the complex powers of the reasoning faculty, that can learn to honor the critical part that can become objective without having to demean the energizing part that is largely subjective. They should be able to appreciate what scientists such as Peter Medawar meant when he wrote: "Scientific reasoning is an exploratory dialogue that can always be resolved into two voices or episodes of thought, imaginative and critical, which alternate and interact. . . . The process by which we come to form a hypothesis is not illogical but non-logical, i.e., outside logic. But once we have formed an opinion we can expose it to criticism, usually by experimentation."[33]

This is not accepting a compromise between rationality and irrationality. On the contrary, it is widening the claim of rationality, as well as the scope of still much-needed research on the nature of scientific rationality in practice. Precisely in opposition to the narrowly rationalistic school of philosophy, Medawar holds that "the analysis of creativity in all its forms is beyond the competence of any one accepted discipline. It requires a consortium of the talents: psychologists, biologists, philosophers, computer scientists, artists and poets would all expect to have their say. That 'creativity' is beyond analysis is a romantic illusion we must now outgrow."[34] A student who is given the more ecumenical view of science of this sort is more likely to see that the raging of the high priests of the counterculture against what they attack as overly rationalistic science is largely a war against an army of bogeymen of their own making—although some of our scientific pedagogues have, alas, unwittingly given them an excuse.

Precisely because the student comes to us at an age when there is still hope for triggering the internal imaginative growth of the mind, neither the Dionysians nor the Apollonians can be our guides. I fear that each, in their very different ways, would doom our charges to mediocre, ineffective lives, not only as individuals but also as members of a species that now, more than ever, depends for its long-range survival on contributions that are both imaginative and workable.

It is evident now that even this middle road brings us, in the end, to the edge of the apocalyptic abyss. I do not apologize for that. It was inevitable, given the fact that mankind seems to have chosen that particular place as its own ecological niche. Like all educational reformers since Plato, we too can hope that science, properly taught, may help secure our foothold a little better on that storm-tossed precipice.

NOTES

1. Some of my comments will have relevancy also to science teaching for prospective scientists. One remembers Einstein's remarks that he found the cleverest of his students were precisely those who were most interested in the foundations of knowledge and not only in the scientific content. But since only a thousand out of nearly four million young people of a given age go on to take a PhD in physics, my main concern is with the large and difficult group, the nonscience-oriented student, between about seventeen and nineteen years old, who encounters his or her first and "terminal" course in physical science on a serious level. Moreover, my concern is heightened by the statistical fact that the percentage of students taking any physical science course, from the last year of high school on, has now dropped to about 20 percent in the United States.

2. See "Physics and Culture: Criteria for Curriculum Design," and "Modern Science and the Intellectual Tradition," in Holton, *Thematic Origins of Scientific Thought* (Cambridge, Mass.: Harvard University Press, 1973). For a good programmatic statement on

what is and should be taught in science today in the United States, see Paul Doty and Dorothy Zinberg, "Science and the Undergraduate," in *Content and Context: Essays on College Education*, Carl Kaysen, ed. (New York: McGraw-Hill, 1973), pp. 155 ff.

3. Edgar Fauré et al., *Learning To Be—the World of Education, Today and Tomorrow* (Paris: UNESCO; London: Harrap, 1972), p. 156.

4. The atmosphere they produce may help to account for a whole rash of new "science" courses with such titles as Physics for Poets, Physics and Antiphysics, Relevant Science, and Science and Science Fiction.

5. *Time*, April 23, 1973.

6. "The Evolution and Dynamics of National Goals in the United States," prepared by F. P. Huddle, pursuant to Senate Resolution 45, serial number 92-9 (Washington, D.C.: U.S. Government Printing Office, 1971), quoted in Don K. Price, "Money and Influence: The Links to Public Policy," *Daedalus*, Summer 1974.

7. George Santayana, *Reason in Science*, Vol. 5 of *The Life of Reason* (New York: Scribners, 1905-1906).

8. Charles A. Reich, *The Greening of America* (New York: Bantam Books, 1970), pp. 241-242.

9. The essay "Motiv des Forschens" has been republished in an English translation in *Ideas and Opinions by Albert Einstein* (New York: Crown, 1954).

10. Reich, p. 251.

11. Reich, p. 266.

12. Reich, pp. 279-280.

13. Reich, p. 285.

14. Reich, p. 426.

15. For a further analysis of the Einsteinian methodology, see my article "The Mainsprings of Discovery," *Encounter*, April 1974, pp. 85 ff.

16. Reich, p. 95.

17. Reich, p. 278.

18. Reich, p. 394. Startling though these recommendations for three types of nonrational thought are, it must be said that they seem almost pale compared with those made in the 1920s and 1930s by groups wishing to legitimate their political action by pointing to the failure of conventional rational processes.

19. Reich, p. 414.

20. Charles Frankel, "The Nature and Sources of Irrationalism," *Science*, 180 (1973), p. 930.

21. K. R. Popper, "Normal Science and Its Dangers," in *Criticism and the Growth of Knowledge*, I. Lakatos and A. Musgrave, eds. (Cambridge: Cambridge University Press, 1970), p. 56.

22. Popper, pp. 57-58. For another discussion of what he dismissed as the "subjectivist" approach, see Popper, *Objective Knowledge* (Oxford: Clarendon Press, 1972), p. 114.

23. Carl Gustav Hempel, *Aspects of Scientific Explanation* (New York: Free Press, 1965), pp. 82-83.

24. Imre Lakatos, "Methodology of Scientific Research Programmes," in *Criticism and the Growth of Knowledge*, p. 93.

25. Imre Lakatos, "History of Science and Its Rational Reconstructions," in *In Memory of Rudolf Carnap: Boston Studies in the Philosophy of Science*, Vol. 8, R. C. Buck and R. S. Cohen, eds., (Dordrecht, The Netherlands, and Boston, Mass.: D. Reidel, 1971), p. 133.

26. Lakatos, "Methodology . . . ," p. 114.

27. Lakatos, *Criticism and the Growth of Knowledge*, p. 138.

28. Lakatos, *Criticism and the Growth of Knowledge*, p. 146. A footnote after the words "into account" laconically adds: "This is a rational reconstruction. As a matter of fact, Bohr accepted this idea only in [his paper of] 1926."

29. There is no time to go further into the distorting effects of this view of the progress of science. One or two short examples must suffice. Lakatos assures us that a theory has to undergo "progressive problem shifts" to remain scientific. If the advance is made with the use of ad hoc proposals, the "progressiveness" is spoiled, and such programs become "degenerating," so that one has to "reject" them as "pseudoscientific." Since, however, ad hoc proposals frequently do figure in what is widely acknowledged to be successful scientific work, Elie Zahar is forced into making a strenuous attempt to rescue Lorentz' ad-hoc-prone work from any possible charge that it might not be a single theory constantly undergoing "progressive problem shifts." To do this requires, however, new definitions of "ad hoc," "novel fact," and so forth, that are patently ad hoc themselves; moreover, they in turn entail a number of distortions of well-known historical fact, as demonstrated by A. I. Miller in "On Lorentz's Methodology," *British Journal of the Philosophy of Science,* April 1974.

A similar strenuous attempt to "rescue" Einstein has recently prompted Gerig Gutting in *Philosophy of Science,* 39 (1972), pp. 51-68, to an analysis that solemnly concludes that "any intuitions Einstein had . . . took their place in a logically coherent argument." The clear evidence from Einstein's own testimony that there were occasionally elements that did in fact not yield to conventional, rational analysis is dismissed by amplification: to allow that would amount to making a case that the discovery of the relativity theory as a whole "was derived essentially from a private intuition."

30. V. Weisskopf, introduction to H. Yukawa, *Creativity and Intuition* (Tokyo: Kodansha, 1973).

31. Perhaps the clearest presentation of Einstein's thoughts on this subject is in a letter written on May 7, 1952, to his friend Maurice Solovine.

32. A number of careful, statistically validated studies exist that test the effectiveness of this approach, most recently a report by A. Ahlgren and H. J. Walberg, "Changing Attitudes Towards Science Among Adolescents," *Nature,* 245 (Sept. 28, 1973), pp. 187-190.

33. P. B. Medawar, *Induction and Intuition in Scientific Thought* (Philadelphia: American Philosophical Society, 1969), p. 46.

34. Ibid.

In Defense of Scientific Knowledge

Ernest Nagel
Columbia University

Dr. Holton's views on the nature of the scientific enterprise and on some of the problems facing the teaching of physical science in liberal-arts colleges seem to me cogently and persuasively argued. In any case, I am in substantial agreement with most of his views, and therefore find it difficult to perform the function commonly expected of a commentator, namely, raising fundamental objections to what the principal speaker has said. Accordingly, my comments are not primarily about difficulties I find in his essay but are, for the most part, expansions of some of his points or explorations of some issues his essay suggests.

I

The scope of Dr. Holton's discussion is limited by two factors. The first is his exclusive attention to problems related to the teaching of general courses in physics intended for students who do not expect to have careers in some branch of natural science. The second is his aim to design such a course that would avoid the inadequacies of, and would mediate between, two opposing and extreme conceptions of reason and science—the philosophies he attributes to those he calls the New Dionysians and the New Apollonians. He believes that, to be successful, such a course not only must provide students with sound ideas and information about the nature of the physical world but also must have a genuine "humanistic" dimension. And he thinks this latter requirement can be satisfied by presenting the facts and theories of physics, not as finished products without a history, but as the outcome of emotionally colored activities of passionate individuals inquiring into the nature of things, that is, in terms of actual case histories in the development of physics, in which the uncertainties, the personal travails, and the human drama of scientific discovery become evident. Students are thereby enabled to realize that science has a "private" and not only a "public" aspect; that knowledge of nature's ways is gained neither through a passive immersion in the flux of experience, as the New Dionysians recommend, nor by mechanically following definite rules of discovery, as the New Apollonians maintain; and that creative imagination, intuitive insight, feelings of ectasy and despair are to be found as much in the work of individual scientists as in the efforts of artists.

It is not a criticism of Dr. Holton to note that he devoted his essay to the desirable content of general courses in physics suitable for non-science students and that he says nothing explicitly about courses for such students in other sciences nor about science courses in liberal-arts colleges designed for students headed for a scientific career. (In this respect, he continues the emphasis introduced into the teaching of science by the former president of Harvard, Dr. James Conant, who used case histories in general-education science courses for nonscientists.) But surely these are matters that deserve serious attention in considering the aims and content of higher education. For it is not evident that Dr. Holton's way of exhibiting a "humanistic" dimension in the teaching of general physics is feasible for other subjects. For example, as Jacques Hadamard's *The Psychology of Invention in the Mathematical Field* makes plain, very little is known about the circumstances of mathematical discovery. Nor is it clear that the use of case histories is either practicable or desirable in more-advanced science courses, especially if the students are already familiar with the relevant case histories. However, if this is so and if it is assumed that science courses in liberal-arts colleges should not be narrowly professional in content and should include a "humanistic" component, ways need to be employed for achieving this objective other than the introduction of biographical and other historical information.

Materials dealing with what Dr. Holton calls "private science" are doubtless frequently fascinating, and the examples he cites from the history of physics can be easily matched in other disciplines. I cannot resist the temptation to repeat the not-so-well-known story that the late Otto Loewi tells of how he came to make the discovery that eventually won him the Nobel Prize in physiology. He was working on the chemistry of neural impulses in the muscles of the heart, and one night he had a vivid dream of just what chemical substances will produce a rhythmic contraction of the heart muscle. The dream woke him, without getting out of bed he jotted down its contents on a scrap of paper within reach, and fell asleep again. When he rose in the morning he found to his dismay that his jotting was undecipherable. He spent the day without food or drink, walking around in agonizing but futile efforts to recall the content of the dream, and when he returned home he went to bed completely exhausted. The dream that eluded him all day recurred that night and again awakened him. But this time he dressed immediately, ran to his laboratory, performed the experiment described in the dream, and so discovered the chemistry of the heart's rhythmic action.

Such incidents from the lives of major scientists show unmistakably that much research is not a routine affair and that neither the facts nor the theories of science can be obtained by following a cut-and-dried procedure. Nevertheless, the rationale for including materials about "private science" in science courses needs to be made explicit. The major objective of science courses, even those designed for non-science students, is surely not to inform students either about the history of the subject or about "private science," and it would be preposterous to suppose that such information could be a substitute for instruction concerning the substantive experimental and theoretical ideas of a discipline and the ways in which those ideas may be validated. The use of case histories may indeed be an effective pedagogic device, whether for making the comprehension of difficult concepts easier or for serving as honey around the edge of a cup whose contents are not otherwise palatable to certain students. However, it is not the sole effective device either for achieving these ends or for exhibiting the humanistic content of natural science.

Moreover, despite recently revived claims for a "logic of discovery" (in the sense of definite rules for attaining the goals of scientific inquiry), its existence has not been established and its possibility remains questionable, so that as Dr. Holton's discussion indicates, the presentation of case histories cannot be justified on the ground that they illustrate the operation of such a logic. To be sure, as he suggests, the study of case histories may yield *causal* explanations for scientific inventions and discoveries—for it is not absurd to suppose that causal mechanisms are involved in successful scientific inquiry and it is not inherently impossible that historical analyses will disclose such mechanisms. However, our present knowledge of those causal conditions is at best meager. And it seems unlikely that the study of case histories, presented at the level at which they inevitably must be presented in general-science courses, will contribute much to the student's understanding of these conditions.

II

But however interesting and useful the accounts of how scientists came to make their discoveries may be, recognition of the "nonrational" elements in "private science" should not be bought at the price of ignoring the rational dimensions of the scientific enterprise. It would be a grave disservice to students to persuade them that the picture of science drawn by the New Dionysians is a sham, by minimizing the paramount importance of those "rational" activities in "public science" that are directed to assessing the validity of experimental and theoretical claims. It would be an equal disservice to students to have them conclude that because the conception of the logic of scientific inquiry advocated by the New Apollonians is an arbitrary invention, there are no principles for weighing evidence and no logical requirements that conclusion of inquiries must satisfy. For as Dr. Holton has noted, modern science is not simply a series of unrelated private activities, but is a social institution that involves certain distinctive habits and more or less explicit standards of workmanship. In particular, what is called "objectivity" in science is not just the product of individual intentions but is the outcome of the scientific community's ongoing criticism of claims to knowledge. Accordingly, it is not enough for students to learn that scientific investigation has a highly personal aspect or that certain conclusions about various sectors of nature have been reached. In my opinion they also ought to be made keenly aware of the evidential grounds on which those conclusions are held, of the logic involved in assessing the evidence, and of the character of those critical activities of "public science" that contribute to the successful pursuit of objective truth.

It is perhaps futile to debate whether or not becoming familiar with the intellectual methods employed for evaluating the cogency of cognitive claims in the sciences is a more significant contribution to a student's appreciation of the humanistic import of science than becoming familiar with the drama of private science. But in any case, although the importance of the former is often *formally* recognized, there appears to be relatively little effort in the actual teaching of science to make students aware of the problems involved in establishing claims to knowledge, or of any of the principles employed in appraising their validity. Indeed, even practicing scientists are often not *explicitly* aware that there are certain requirements of critical method that competent work in the sciences must satisfy, as the following anecdote illustrates.

About ten years ago, a number of natural scientists, historians, students of the fine arts, mathematicians, and philosophers at Columbia organized a university seminar to discuss a variety of educational issues raised by recent developments in technology. At one meeting of the seminar some of the physicists present denied that there is such a thing as scientific method, and maintained (as did the late P. W. Bridgman) that in the conduct of research everything goes and no holds are barred. However, they withdrew this claim when Dr. Dana Atchley, the distinguished internist at the Columbia Medical Center, illustrated the value of rules of scientific method for improving medical practice. He recalled that when he began his career, the approved therapy for treating typhus patients was to give them cold baths, even though no one had apparently systematically examined the question of whether the therapy was really effective. The practice was abandoned when the introduction of control groups showed that cold baths had no remedial value for the illness.

The use of control groups illustrates the application of a rule for *testing* (or validating) certain types of scientific hypotheses, not a rule for *inventing* them or for *discovering* causal connections in nature. It is not the only rule of scientific method, nor is it always relevant for assessing the validity of cognitive claims. Moreover, scientists commonly acquire sound habits of workmanship conforming to canons for such assessment but without becoming explicitly aware of any of the principles underlying those habits. It is nevertheless desirable that such principles be made explicit, so that the habits may then be subjected to critical examination more effectively and perhaps may be improved. Accordingly, it is no less desirable that courses in science, those intended for future scientists as well as for nonscientists, at least formulate the more frequently used principles of critical inquiry and exhibit their actual operation. And if science is not an enterprise carried on by isolated individuals, as Dr. Holton rightly emphasizes, it is also desirable that the social character of science be mentioned to students and that they learn something of the mechanisms built into the institutions of science for carrying on the task of critically evaluating cognitive claims and for achieving objectivity.

III

The logical method of the natural sciences has been regarded for centuries as the most effective way men have yet devised for acquiring competent knowledge of the nature of things. However, this belief has been put on the defensive by some recent thinkers, some of whom Dr. Holton discusses. One of the strangest challenges to this belief has come from the Nobel Laureate physicist Max Born. Born declared in the Preface to his collection of essays, *Physics in My Generation* (in which he described some of the remarkable achievements in physics to which he had himself also contributed), that when he began his career some thirty years ago science seemed to him to be incomparably superior to religion, metaphysics, and poetry as a way of gaining knowledge. He then went on to make the amazing confession that he now thought this belief was an illusion, because developments in physics showed science to be no more capable of obtaining "objective knowledge" of nature than those other disciplines. It is easy to recognize the inconsistency of using the *conclusions* of physics to cast doubt on the ability of physics to gain genuine knowledge. It is not so easy to understand why an outstanding physicist should have had such feelings of disillusion about his science. Part of the explanation no doubt lies in Born's unhappiness over the limited effectiveness of modern science in improving the state of mankind. But I suspect that part of it consists of his inadequate conceptualization and comparative analysis of the nature of the scientific method itself.

A more serious though related example of current skepticism concerning the cognitive achievements of science is an interpretation of those achievements expounded, curiously enough, by some of those Dr. Holton calls the New Apollonians. It is now widely recognized that no conclusion of scientific inquiry is established with the force of a logical demonstration, that all factual as well as theoretical claims are subject to criticism and revision that are, in principle, nonterminating, and that the scientific search for solutions to problems is therefore fallible. This doctrine of fallibilism was an essential component in the "critical commonsensism" of Charles Peirce, and was adopted by numerous American philosophers (including two of my own teachers, Morris R. Cohen and John Dewey) whom Peirce influenced. Like many others who were brought up on it, I found it to be a clarifying and liberating doctrine. For it showed us how it is possible to acknowledge that the sciences do achieve genuine knowledge of how things are organized (in the sense that the sciences provide reliable answers to many of the questions that inquiries seek to resolve), without having to assume that there is an absolutely foolproof criterion for the validity of cognitive claims. Thereby, one can avoid both a wholesale skepticism as well as the dogmatisms of atomistic empiricism and classical rationalism. However, the fact that observational reports and theoretical assertions are always corrigible in the light of further inquiry has been taken by some of the New Apollonians as the basis for maintaining that the sciences do not yield genuine knowledge after all and that the so-called "conclusions" of experimental as well as of theoretical research are simply "guesses" and "conjectures."

But this seems to me a perverse and absurd interpretation of the doctrine of fallibilism, and some effort should be made to give students of the sciences enough perspective for dealing critically with it. I suspect that one basis for this interpretation is a tacit commitment to the view that takes the certainty of demonstrative mathematics as the hallmark of genuine knowledge. In any case, students should recognize the fact that, though as a matter of general principle every cognitive claim is open to an endless process of criticism and revision, not all such claims have actually been found to be mistaken, that many problems which have been investigated have been correctly solved, and that the relevant standards for assessing the adequacy of proposed answers to problems in physics or biology are perfectly sound even though they are not the norms employed in mathematics. The history of science undoubtedly shows that many beliefs about the world once held to be true have had to be modified or abandoned. Nevertheless, students should also come to recognize that, at least in the natural sciences, there is a growing body of undisputed knowledge and that it is seriously misleading to characterize the findings of many inquiries as just tentative guesses and conjectures.

IV

There is one question that Dr. Holton does not touch upon in his discussion of a desirable general course in physics, and it is a question that deals with matters upon which thoughtful men have reflected since antiquity. It is a well-known feature of the history of physics that a theory developed initially for a certain limited class of phenomena (for example, Newtonian particle mechanics) may eventually be successfully employed to explain regularities found in quite different domains (as for example, the behavior of fluids, thermal phenomena, and so on). When this happens, one branch of physics is often said to be "absorbed by" or "reduced to" another branch; and there are even cases where the laws of a distinct science (such as chemistry or biology) have been reduced, or are thought to be capable of being reduced, to the laws of some allegedly more "basic" discipline (such as physics). But just what is taking place when one theory is reduced in this way to another? How are the theories and their corresponding domains related? In particular, when the familiar qualities of common experience (for example, the colors, sounds, smells of daily living) are explained in terms of assumptions about entities not directly observable (such as subatomic particles and processes) that do not possess those qualities, does this mean that the qualitative world of common sense is an illusion, as many scientists and philosophers continue to maintain? The belief that it does mean this is one basis for much of the traditional hostility toward natural science and seems to be the basis for the New Dionysians' attacks on science.

For this reason alone, the character of reductive explanations in the sciences, the requirements for successful reduction, and the import of reductions for a responsible view of the relations of man and nature are issues that should not be neglected in liberal-arts courses in the sciences. Indeed, my own guess is that a serious discussion of such issues is probably a more efficacious way of meeting the challenge of the New Dionysians, and is a more substantial contribution to a sound presentation of the humanistic dimensions of natural science, than is a heavy emphasis on the idiosyncracies of private science and the personal dramas of scientific research. But in what specific contexts and in what detail these issues might be discussed are matters that would require much consultation between those actually teaching a general course in physics.

The Uses and Limitations of Science Teaching

Michael Rabin
Hebrew University

I shall address myself to the question of what should be the guiding principle in the construction of a curriculum in the sciences for students on various levels.

We are living as teachers and researchers in a period of crisis in the teaching of science. We have witnessed in recent years a change in the attitudes of both public and students toward science, and I think that this changed attitude makes it incumbent upon us to rethink and reevaluate what we have been doing. The teaching of science in the universities in the last two decades or so was predicted essentially upon three generally held assumptions.

The first assumption was that we are in a period of ongoing progress, facilitated by science and, in particular, by basic scientific discoveries (as opposed to technology and the cumulative effect of technology). The second assumption was that our students came to us with an inherent desire for knowledge in the truest and deepest sense and that, whether they intended to become scientists or not, they felt it to be of the utmost importance to understand, among other things, the nature of science and scientific discoveries. The third, and perhaps less important, assumption was that whether or not the student was deeply interested in science, whether or not he intended to be a scientist, it was good for him to study science because it would develop his reasoning power, lessen his gullibility, and in general prepare him better for subsequent activities in life.

I believe that these three assumptions, though not proved completely erroneous by recent developments, do require a reevaluation. This reevaluation has significant consequences with respect to the question of *who* should be taught science, *what* science should be taught, and *how* science should be taught. There is no doubt that science is currently under siege. This is a worldwide phenomenon that is not confined to the United States. We have heard about reactions to these crucial questions in Russia and elsewhere. This siege has deep-rooted, intrinsic reasons that go beyond the conflict between rationality and irrationality. I think that the attack of the irrationalists is not the reason for the current troubled situation in science but is more a consequence of the vulnerable position of science in general today.

At the end of World War II many people heralded the advent of a number of new science- and technology-based revolutions that were expected to change, elevate, and liberate human lives. There was talk, in journalist-coined terms, of the space age, the atomic age, the computer age, and the wonder-drug age—to mention only a few. And we could add the promise of revolution in communications, in travel, and in other fields. It was widely believed at the time, following the example of what was achieved during World War II, that the developments in basic science and the fundamental discoveries of science were the key to a continuous and rapid progress that would move humanity very soon into an age almost matching the visions of science fiction, and completely changing our lives in very short order.

Now, after almost forty years of these hopes and expectations, I think the picture looks quite different. Perhaps the pharmaceutical revolution and the Green Revolution have exerted a significant and positive impact on the lives of the mass of humanity. I think, however, the fact that the United States and other parts of the world have an energy crisis, thirty years after the liberation of atomic energy, shows that those expectations for very rapid progress and change through fundamental discoveries in science were exaggerated. Further, anything that we could say about the reasons for the energy situation right now would be more in the nature of excuses than a shoring up of the position of science and its potential for producing rapid change.

This more recent and almost abrupt realization that we are not going to move into a science-fiction world through science and that changes are slower, more mundane, and less certain has brought an almost inescapable reevaluation of the role of science in society and education. When we assumed that we were going to march from triumph to triumph, that there was a need for an almost unlimited supply of scientists, we expanded our research and educational facilities at an almost exponential rate. That expansion lasted, as we know, for about two decades. But now we must ask what can be done with all the scientists we are producing and wonder about the willingness of society to support science and science education on that massive scale. And whether we like it or not, this has affected the desire of students to study science.

I think that a certain disenchantment has been a healthy thing. The somewhat exaggerated hopes we have had for the totally beneficial influence of science on our lives did distort the correct perspective with respect to science. Though for some of us who are scientists, the decline in the prestige of science is, of course, a painful occurrence, the relegation of science to its proper place in the total fabric of society is a healthy thing. Let me add parenthetically that the rush of students into science was not altogether beneficial. We had far too many students who had no business being in science courses or in the scientific community; they were lured into it by the existing prosperity. As a result we now have a number of inadequate researchers and teachers in research laboratories and universities.

While science was in the ascendancy, students could not but fail to be influenced by the general atmosphere. I think that they studied the sciences in a positive mood, which reflected the mood of society as a whole. Even if they were perhaps not inherently interested in the subject, they felt that extremely important, useful information was being conveyed to them and that they were studying a subject that seemed to dominate many of the other intellectual activities. Within this atmosphere of enthusiasm, the question whether most of the students were genuinely interested in the subject tended to get lost.

I would like to say at this point that my remarks are directed to the question of how to approach science and how to teach science throughout the educational system. I think that we cannot pretend that we are just going to teach students at Harvard, Yale, the University of Paris, Oxford, or Cambridge, or those students who do have within themselves a burning and inexpugnable desire to become scientists. During the great increase in science education there were hundreds of thousands of students quite different from members of those select groups. I do not think that we can approach the question of education in science meaningfully if we do not keep this total picture in mind. We should not be surprised therefore that with the recent decline of science into what I would call its proper place students now lose some of their enthusiasm and start raising questions they did not feel inclined to raise before. Their questions are predicated partially on certain sound philosophical considerations rather than upon the loose, vague, unformed considerations engendered by the irrational philosophies that are now common. And I think that this questioning also has a practical basis. If students feel that there are not many careers in science, that science is not going to be all-prevailing, then it is appropriate to ask: Why should we be forced to take, or why should we be offered, these courses in science when there are many other pursuits we find no less interesting than science?

It is, of course, essential for us to know how the physical and biological world operates. Here, I am in complete agreement with Professor Sidney Hook: that one cannot be fully educated unless one knows some highly significant basic facts, facts that now cover a rather large area in scientific fields. However, we cannot hold scientific information supreme over other useful, important, and liberating kinds of knowledge. To the average educated man the understanding of economics, psychology, and history is no less meaningful, no less important than the understanding of science. (To be sure, Dr. Hook mentioned these matters, too.) However, this means that science teachers probably cannot make excessive demands on their students. Some students will find science, its logical structure, the psychology of the people in science extremely exciting, perhaps more exciting than other fields of knowledge. Others, while recognizing the importance of knowing these facts, will remain rather cold, let us say, toward the basic epistemological assumptions that underlie physics or toward the psychology of invention in the mathematical field. They might consider, for example, the psychology of Bobby Fischer when he plays chess to be of more interest to them. One simply cannot argue with this attitude on any generalized absolute grounds.

As for the third assumption, about the usefulness of science in preparing students to think, I am afraid that this has been overrated. The irrationality of the discovery process notwithstanding, science is, of course, very logically ordered; it is a very precise domain. But, if we talk about that large mass of students who are not going to follow a scientific career, I do not think that learning the laws of physics or learning rules of evidence in science is really the best preparation for their lives and careers, whether they will be economists, or administrators, or insurance salesmen. There is too much of a disparity between the approach in science that strives to separate and isolate factors, that strives to reduce things to clear, precise formulations and what goes on in other fields of knowledge or everyday life. Anybody who has tried to arbitrate a dispute, let us say, between two professors or two rival factions in a department within his own institution knows that in real life there are few hard facts. You usually have a sort of Rashomon situation, where the facts depend upon who relates them and their point of view. There are, by and large, no fixed, infallible rules for dealing with human situations, or if there are such rules, we are still very far from their discovery. The methodology of science has very little bearing on the handling of these situations. Even if we try to take a somewhat more exact field like economics, one can certainly find two economists arguing about the question of whether the rise of interest rates will stop inflation or accelerate inflation. This is most unscientific. (But I am not saying that economics is not scientific in a very broad sense; in this context, I am using "science" in the sense of the exact natural sciences, including mathematics.) Outside of these disciplines we have nothing comparable in the way of methods that will give us valid statements of the same degree of certitude.

Let me recount very briefly a certain argument to which I was once a party. A man who was developing a new curriculum for high-school mathematics introduced a system for solving equations by iteration. You try a certain value, x_1, for the solution and if this does not work you take a second approximation, x_2, and continue with successive approximations until you find the right one. It was essentially Newton's rule for the solution of equations. When he tried to defend that as part of the high-school curriculum he said, "That is very useful because the students learn from this how to correct themselves." What he really meant was that if at first you don't succeed, then try and try again. That appeared to me to be an extremely esoteric and roundabout way to introduce this principle. In any event, I think that for any student who did not already have an intuitive grasp of that principle by the time the material was presented, it was too late for him to learn it by looking at these iteration methods for the solution of equations. The utility of science as a way of preparing the students for rational and precise discourse in other domains should therefore be reconsidered and put into a more modest perspective.

In view of the foregoing, we may ask what *is* the right place for science in our system of higher education? I would again concur with Professor Hook, who said that curricular requirements cannot be deduced from certain a priori axioms or assumptions about the nature of man, the needs of man, or other purely philosophical considerations. The construction of the curriculum has to be attuned to some extent to the needs of society and also to the opportunities that society offers, to the needs of the student, and of course, to the needs of the subject matter. With this in mind, I would like, in very rough outline, to talk about science as it might be taught to various groups of students.

First of all, science in general education. Science has a very important and essential but also a limited role in general education. A man cannot be educated, cannot be liberated through education unless he has a broad understanding—or knowledge, if the term "understanding" suggests an overstatement—of nature. I think that the main burden in this area should be carried by the high school. I believe that students should come to the university with much of their knowledge in physics, in biology, in chemistry, in meteorology, and so forth. What the nonscience student can be taught at the university (and the level at which he can be taught if we remove the mathematical aspects, for example, because those are certainly by and large too hard for too many of them) is not really worthy of the university. Of course, when students come to the university with deficiencies in science education, there is no way but to teach them at the university. But this requires that we put the emphasis on factual material. We must supplement and close up those holes in their science education that result from lack of proper preparation in high school. This does not mean that there cannot be courses in the history and psychology of discovery and about the methodology of science. But I think that these courses should be elective in nature. Unfortunately the student will leave the university still largely lost in a sea of ignorance, but we have to make choices. When we make choices, it is not at all clear to me that it is more important for the student to know how Einstein discovered the theory of relativity than to know some basic facts and principles of economics, because the pursuit of pure science, I think, will be limited to much smaller groups of people. It is, of course, interesting to know Einstein's thought processes but perhaps not everyone is interested; and it is important at most to a few.

Let us turn to another example.

We have more daily contact as a rule with physicians than with physicists, and it is certainly more important to us to know how a physician reaches his conclusions and how he works, because—it may be argued—we may then perhaps, if we know enough biology, test for ourselves his results, and somewhat control what he is prescribing. Now, I am not recommending this necessarily as a course in the curriculum, but I confess that I do not see much difference between this type of course and, let us say, the analysis of the way great scientists think, in terms of importance to students.

When it comes to the teaching of science proper let us bear in mind that science is a tool and prerequisite for various professions, whether engineering, applied science, medicine, systems analysis, or various fields of decision making. People who have to make policy decisions certainly need some knowledge of science as an indispensable tool. We should provide for those people an appropriate study of those various fields of science at the university level that have a direct bearing on the area of their future professional activity as well as the necessary theoretical underpinning. Although the main emphasis must be instrumental, we should keep a sharp eye open to discover and encourage those students who have manifested a marked interest, aptitude, and insight for theoretical science.

Of course, the most exciting area is the teaching of science to future scientists and researchers. Most of our discussions about the teaching of science within the university center around this area. All too often we fall into the trap of thinking that all of our students are going to be researchers and that they have dedicated themselves to science as a vocation. We therefore tend to overemphasize this aspect of science instruction in our discussion of the curriculum. Only those students who have the intellectual capacity and who have shown an appetite for science should be encouraged, but we should not prescribe even to them. If we prescribe to them, if we take those decisions completely into our own hands, then we are going to make large numbers of people quite unhappy later on, either when they find that they have no jobs or when they find they are very pedestrian practitioners in areas that require brilliance and excellence.

In the teaching of science to *possible* future scientists (I am talking about honors and graduate courses within the universities), there is really no single position valid or even advisable for all students and subject matters. I do not want to be doctrinaire about it and say that science majors *have* to study the methodology of science or the invention process in science. This is one possibility and an excellent one—if there is an inspired teacher who imparts knowledge best in this way. On the other hand, if there is a teacher who feels that he should teach the subject matter and show by his own example how discoveries are made, letting the students form their own impressions and approach to the question of creative work, that is also a possibility. I do not think that the process of invention will remain obscure forever. It is a very exciting field, somewhat touched upon of course by people who work with artificial intelligence; right now it is a somewhat disreputable field, but I think this may be true because there are as yet no solid results. But it is not altogether unlikely that significant and reliable findings will be made someday.

Until such a time, however, whatever we can say as teachers and active researchers about the process of invention is necessarily going to be somewhat personal. It is possible that research and analysis will show that the ways Einstein and Enrico Fermi worked are only particular cases appropriate to the special psychologies of these distinctive individuals. It is also quite possible that what these scientists themselves say about how they arrived at their discoveries is not accurate because the creator himself is not necessarily the best judge or even the best analyst of his own thought processes or procedures, despite his intimate knowledge and his very honest effort to give a true account of his discovery. But I think that students who are truly interested in science will find this aspect of their subject quite exciting and for those who are interested I would, by all means, recommend inclusion of inquiries of this sort in their course of study.

I would like to conclude by making a number of comments in response to some of the things that have been said at this symposium. With regard to Professor Hook's remark about the possibility of transferring the methodology and approaches of science to fields outside of science, I don't say that this is impossible. Certainly there are situations where one can get an idea or use an idea—acquired during scientific training—in nonscientific situations. But I still hold the belief that such situations are rather limited. Let us take, for example, the important device of controlled experiment, which is quite central in biology and medical science. Certainly a student who saw a controlled experiment in biology that involved two plants will use that idea, if he is at all intelligent, with respect to typhoid patients, for example. There is a transfer, but of course these two domains are not too far apart. But obviously there is almost no occasion to use a controlled experiment in human relations, though we can certainly find limited or sometimes artificial examples that seem to be to the contrary. By and large, however, there are no controlled experiments in human relations. Though there is a *possibility* of transfer, I think that in dealing with the complexity of human relations—which almost always involve conflict and emotions, because if they don't there is really no problem—it is much better to learn how to deal with such problems more or less directly, through the study—I don't like the word, but I will use it—of *relevant* subjects like sociology and psychology. There are some scholars who would debate the usefulness of these subjects, but I think they provide the best tools we have right now. Coming back to my earlier example, I think that to correct oneself on the basis of past experience is something that is more directly learned within a given situation than, say, within mathematics.

Still, if we disregard the possibility of transferring scientific experience and insight to other fields, I do consider science an essential part of general education. I would agree with Professors Holton and Hook that one cannot be a truly educated and liberated person if one does not know basic facts, of which there are now very many from physics, biology, and other fields. So therefore, even without the phenomenon of transfer, instruction in science is an essential part of the education of a liberal mind.

I come now to the question of what should be taught in the university and what in high school. If we are talking about the revision of our system of education, if we are going to make changes, why should we start at the level of the university? Professor Holton himself has been involved in curricular changes within the high school. If physics and chemistry and biology are essential, then why shouldn't we strive to use our influence to put these subjects back into the high school? There are great demands on the student's time when he comes to the university; he may already have certain specialized interests in other directions and may therefore consider the sciences as a burden. Consequently it seems preferable to have those subjects taught in high school. We should begin our reform there rather than at the university.

I would also like to make a comment on the remark that science has not done anything about the notion that man does not live by bread alone. That is, of course, a very common criticism leveled at science, but I think that disenchantment with science arises to a large degree because science promised and did not solve for humanity the problems of bread or energy or health, even though there have been large strides forward in the field of health. Of all the technical revolutions promised, the pharmaceutical revolution has perhaps been the most successful. It is rather easy to say, "Oh, we are rich, affluent, healthy, but what about the spirit?" Yet even in the developed countries, with the exception of very few, everybody is not rich, well-fed, well-clothed, and adequately housed. These problems have not yet been solved by science, certainly not for the underdeveloped countries, and certainly not for that very substantial part of humanity that is suffering from plain hunger. Let us recognize it. The important promise on which we have not yet delivered is the promise of the deliverance of humanity as a whole from certain kinds of misery. Once we do that we can start talking about the other things that are still missing.

Now, as to the area of discovery as a field of study. When I said that this field of inquiry is somewhat disreputable, I was referring to certain prevailing notions about it, not my own personal views. I would like to clear the record on that. I think that this field is intellectually perhaps the most exciting field open to present-day investigation. Having had some contact with it, I believe that the problems, although very formidable, are still amenable to our scientific methods, that we can hope to make progress, and should not be discouraged by the apparent lack of substantial progress thus far. If and when we make a breakthrough in the area of understanding our own processes of discovery or—and this is not the same thing—in learning how to construct machines that are intelligent, it will not be the same as understanding ourselves. It is not like solving problems in transportation. The transportation problem was solved by the invention of the wheel and not by the invention of cars. The mechanical solution is entirely different from the human solution; you can invent the wheel before you understand how the human joints and system of muscles and nerves work to make animal or human locomotion possible.

It is possible that, even it we do not understand how we discover things by means of artificial-intelligence machines, we will be able to do things in different ways by utilizing their enormous memory banks and their immense operating speeds. If that comes about, it will constitute a revolution of great significance to our lives. I don't think that the computer age—this is, in some sense, a promise on which science has not yet delivered—has thus far had a big impact on our lives. It doesn't really make much difference to you and me whether our bank statement is being processed by a computer or by a horde of clerks, or whether airline reservations are made by somebody sitting at a desk and making notes or by a computer system. These are behind-the-scenes operations that do not affect our immediate lives very much. But if we have a breakthrough in artificial intelligence—and I do consider that to be in the realm of the possible—it is going to be a significant quantum jump in what we can do. For example, if we understand how a computer—let's mention a frivolous example—can play mediocre chess, or can solve problems that are not the hardest but are still fairly hard, I am convinced that we won't be able to do so without knowing at the same time how to teach the machine to play chess excellently and how to do things that human beings cannot actually now do. I think that once we achieve a breakthrough it's going to be more or less complete. Therefore, if we are looking for frontiers, here is one of the most exciting frontiers open to science.

Multilevel Teaching of the Natural Sciences

Miro M. Todorovich
City University of New York,
Bronx Community College

In one of his thoughtful comments, Dr. Eugene Wigner summarized the dilemma presented by some symposium participants as follows: "If we look at a picture of Rubens, should we only look at the picture, or should we also explain how the picture was painted and what motivated it? If we listen to the music of Strauss, should we only listen to the melody or also try to understand what motivated it?" I am afraid, however, that the problem is much more involved than this dilemma would suggest. The teaching of science and the associated curricular formulation of the subject matter is a very complex undertaking. A satisfactory resolution of the problem requires a conscious effort toward multilevel teaching of the experiences and modes of understanding that have evolved in the natural sciences.

Some five hundred years ago, the scope of the scientific endeavor was naturally more restricted and thus its unfolding and dissemination was more tractable. Despite a continuous intertwining with manual activities—careful experimentation could not, after all, be delegated merely to hired hands but required the personal attention of the philosopher-scientist—scholarship in the natural sciences remained highly abstract and therefore akin to other existing branches of intellectual activity. In order to get a sense of the inherent elusiveness of the most fundamental scientific concepts, one need only remember the polemics concerning the definition of forces and masses in Newtonian mechanics that surfaced periodically among physicists. Recently we have witnessed a new attempt by David Bohm and his supporters to supply a deterministic interpretation of quantum mechanics, which, according to some of its principal creators, is intrinsically probabilistic.

At the same time, the results of experimentation are eminently pragmatic and thus suitable for extensive practical application. Our entire civilization has found itself permeated by the tangible products of scientific thinking. Its very existence has become almost totally dependent on the tens of thousands of technically trained persons who operate its power plants and mines, its transportation and communications, its food production and commerce, and its hospitals and pharmaceutical industry. This state of affairs demanded the establishment of an adequate educational system and, therefore, over the past century the expansion of educational enterprises proceeded at an explosive rate. To the universities of yesteryear was added an ever increasing number of polytechnic schools and colleges, institutes of technology, and Soviet-type semi-independent schools ("faculties") of physical, chemical, and biological sciences. In addition to schools of engineering sciences one finds an ever growing number of four-year institutions of engineering technology. Also, two-year colleges are offering a host of terminal technical, as well as transferable, engineering degrees. All of this has caused great stress in curricular philosophies and planning and has led, in the physical sciences for example, to numerous innovative pedagogical approaches by well-known schools and scholars (course sequences by Richard Feynman, the Berkeley group, the MIT group, and others). These efforts were aided by various specialized panels and commissions.

The feasibility of such a multitude of approaches can be recognized by comparing the ways in which various authors of scientific textbooks attempted to handle identical subject matter. Works dealing with the advanced aspects of classical electromagnetic theory are a good case in point. For many years the textbooks by Wolfgang Panofsky and Melba Phillips, William Smythe, J. D. Jackson, and the earlier classic by Abraham, Foeppl, and Becker—to name just a few—have been successfully used for the education of new generations of physicists. A quick comparison of their tables of contents shows that, in addition to a basic common core, each book has extended coverage of topics that are not discussed by the other authors. This situation is quite understandable if one bears in mind that the amount of existing accumulated knowledge is so extensive that no single textbook (and no associated course) could possibly cover within the required limitations of space and time all the topics of potential usefulness and possible interest. What makes a textbook satisfactory even to the point of elevating it to the status of a classic is the sufficiency of the selected subject matter. The material must be so structured that anyone who successfully masters its presentation can make independent progress in any desired direction in the field covered by the text. A comparison of the volumes mentioned shows that there is more than one sufficient and satisfactory selection and presentation of the material.

And so it seemed during the early part of this century that one could handle the problem of curricular flexibility with two basic lines of approach. First, as we have just seen, one could make different subselections from the overall body of knowledge, provided one did not violate the condition of sufficiency. Second, a single subject matter could stand various degrees of "dilution" to suit alternative clienteles. University physics minus the calculus became college physics; the elimination of trigonometry and quadratic equations from the latter yielded physics for the liberal-arts student. Of course, both ends of this spectrum were losing something: the engineering practitioners of science never really acquired a feeling for the philosophical and cultural implications of scientific discoveries. The liberal-arts student, on the other hand, often could not care less about the number of grams of ice left after a burst of steam entered a calorimeter. Still, one could hope that the professional would become wise by remaining and working long enough within his or her chosen specialty and that the demands imposed on the imagination of the liberal-arts citizen would be limited by the essential clarity and orderliness of classical pre-twentieth-century physics and other sciences.

This was the situation during the twenties and thirties, when a degree in physics could be obtained for work restricted to a fairly compartmentalized area. Even the renowned universities of Western Europe, for example, graduated specialists in mechanics or thermodynamics who did not know much outside their immediate sphere of interest or beyond what they learned in general courses. In France it was enough to master the four volumes of George Bruhat, in Germany the three volumes of Grimsehl-Tomaschek. A solid Nazi academic of the late thirties would perhaps stick to Philip Lenard's German Physics, in which the discoverer of Lenard's window thundered against the tricks of Einstein's Semitic theories. Georg Joos' Theoretical Physics was for the truly curious and advanced.

This scene changed dramatically during and after World War II. The work on the atomic bomb in the United States and radar research in Great Britain paved the way for a gigantic synthesis of all the previously semiautonomous branches of physics. This trend had an enormous impact on the teaching of the subject. Graduate courses and studies began to flourish everywhere, establishing an intricate edifice of prerequisites topped by tough PhD qualifying exams. This development had dramatic effects on the various traditional branches. For example, modern quantum physics affected the study of the material properties of solid objects to such an extent as to give rise to a completely new discipline, solid-state physics. The latter, in turn, by creating solid-state diodes and transistors influenced electronics and engineering to such a degree that students of electrical engineering, for example, are presently required to study elements of quantum mechanics. Similar revolutionary developments have swept through other physical subdisciplines like optics (in the wake of the advent of laser-spurred holography) and astronomy (via astrophysics).

These events in the physical sciences soon found their counterpart in other active branches of the natural sciences. Presently, this trend is most clearly discernible in the field of biology, where branches of the mathematical, physical, chemical, biological, and medical sciences have delineated a broad field for complex joint investigations.

The consequences for the curriculum and general education of these developments that affect the substance of our knowledge and the potential for practical application are enormous. In my judgment, they go far beyond the simple debate between those favoring the inductive approach and those partial to the deductive method, that is, between those who are interested in the picture and music per se and those who like to learn and understand the motivations at the root of creation, as well as the history from the inception of an idea to its fulfillment.

In spontaneous and numerous ways, the response to the deeper and broader problem of an adequate transmission of our scientific heritage has already been answered. We encounter courses in environmental physics and the physics of energy resources, physics of the stars as well as of waste disposal. There are physics courses for philosophers and physics for poets. Modules have been designed for technical physics and for the self-pacing of open-admission students. We can also buy such books as *Essentials of Physics, Principles of Physical Sciences, Physics for Engineering Technology, Basic Physics, Foundations of Physics, Introduction to the Science of Physics, Fundamentals of Physics, Concepts in Physics, Fundamental Laws of Physics, Elementary Physics,* and many other different books all called simply *Physics.*

Obviously, facts about the diversified approach are already there; what we apparently need is a theoretical understanding of what we are already doing. In physics, for example, we should appreciate that we may often teach:

- a class of hundreds of pre-engineers with the hope that a few of

these will be "salvaged" for the Parnassus of pure science;
- a mixture of premedical students, many of whom may become general practitioners and a few who may later use radiation markers for their research;
- future chemists predestined for industry, with a sprinkling of participants in mixed scientific-research teams;
- liberal-arts students of every conceivable inclination, from the historically minded to the most outspoken specimens of the "now" generation;
- students with an excellent intermediate background and open-admissions students who need a great deal of help;
- future trial lawyers, who should know the meaning of automobile deceleration prior to an accident, as well as future lawmakers, who will be asked to appropriate funds for elementary-particle research.
Similar stories can be told about other branches of science.

The recognition of the multilevel quality of the student audience leads necessarily to the suggestion for a conscious multilevel teaching of the subject matter. Such an approach, which takes into account the differences in the background, capacity, and interest of the audience, strives also to balance the need for pedagogic effectiveness with the maintenance of the intellectual integrity vis-à-vis the given discipline. An axiomatic presentation that may be a delight to the initiated may constitute the ultimate barrier for an otherwise interested outsider. It can be modulated—with great promise for successful teaching of poets and lawyers—by a judicious incorporation of historical narrative and anecdotal illustration. Such storytelling should, however, never become an end in itself at the expense of the precision and rigor of the particular discipline. There should always be a sufficient number of examples and problems clearly illustrating the features and precision of the scientific method. The mathematical shorthand should regularly be promoted to the absorption limit of the particular audience.

From this vantage point, the process of curricular packaging and effective educational presentation becomes one where, ideally, the wisdom of the scholar is symbiotically united with the skills of an orator. The teacher selects the essential elements for the understanding of the subject matter and channels it to the student, using the most suitable and effective means of cognitive communication. Within this scenario, parts of the initial dilemma become complementary elements of a synthesizing process. Rigorous presentations of scientific theorems and the precise calculation of predictive consequences are mixed with historical descriptions and discussions of analogies and parallels, which may be simultaneously enlightening and entertaining.

Within this context, the Rubens picture and the Strauss music may even contribute directly to the teaching of physics: a Rubens slide may serve as an image in geometrical optics labs (why should it always be a black or red arrow?), while the brilliance of Strauss waltzes (be they from the pen of Johann or Richard) is a living testimony to the importance of musical overtones.

PROBLEMS AND DILEMMAS
OF THE SOCIAL SCIENCES

The Social Sciences in Liberal Education

Nathan Glazer
Harvard University

When we consider the full range of the problems that afflict liberal education[1] in the colleges, the social sciences do not appear to be particularly at a disadvantage. These problems are well known, some have been discussed in other papers at this symposium, and I do not mean to devote much time to most of them. They include the conflict with vocational objectives; the overlap with the ever more ambitious offerings of high schools, which deprive the first college year of its impact as something new; the conflict with the organized departments, which tend to establish or to wish to establish their own sequences, and to give little support to general education; the ever present staffing problems that result from the fact that college teachers are trained as specialists and progress as specialists.

By saying that I will not discuss these issues, I do not suggest in the slightest that they are unimportant; they are all key issues that must be resolved if a strong liberal education is to flourish. But in my career as a teacher of the social sciences, one that has encompassed the teaching of courses that have reflected most of the popular approaches of the last decade to general education in the social sciences, I have become increasingly aware personally and increasingly troubled by what I would call the specifically *intellectual* problems of providing a general or liberal education based on the contemporary social sciences. To my mind, these specifically intellectual problems are more severe in the social sciences than in the humanities or the natural sciences. And apparently we cannot avoid them, whatever the type of approach we develop to introduce college students to the social sciences. As a teacher, I have participated in and helped organize courses that are explicitly interdisciplinary, courses that attempt to deal with great issues, and courses that are based on great or important books. I now teach a course on urban social policy that is explicitly problem-oriented and implicitly multidisciplinary. And I am convinced that our first problem as social scientists is not that students are seeking job training, or that they lust for the relevant and the sensational (after all, we should do best at providing that), or that the departments are unfriendly, or that the assistant professors are uninterested; rather, it is that we do not know, for reasons tied up with the development of the social sciences, what we should teach as a foundation required of any educated person.

Interestingly enough, whenever people get together and discuss the objectives of general education, first place—or at least a very important place—is always given to the social sciences. Thus, as Professor deBary points out, in the Carnegie Commission's report *The Purposes and the Performance of Higher Education in the United States* general education is defined only twice, once in the words, "acquiring a general understanding of society and the place of the individual within it, . . . [including] contact with history and the nature of other cultures" (p. 13) and "broad learning experiences—the provision of opportunities to survey the cultural heritage of mankind, to understand man and society" (p. 65).

Clearly this is a mandate for the social sciences to play a leading role in general education. But whereas we find that natural scientists have undertaken such great and apparently successful tasks as the reform of the teaching of physics, chemistry, and biology in the high schools and colleges and that humanists eagerly play leading roles in any effort to revive or revise general education, we will find that social scientists are almost always the most reluctant to engage themselves. Distinguished social scientists will not teach introductory courses (as will natural scientists and to a lesser degree humanists), the younger professors will evade general education, and leading lights in the field have had little to say about the subject. Of course we must also add that the single most valuable book on general education, to my mind, is Professor Daniel Bell's *The Reforming of General Education*, but I would hazard a guess that humanists would make as strong a claim that he is one of them as social scientists do, and his range of interests and knowledge makes him unique.

So, while on the one hand we are summoned by leaders in the

field of higher education to provide students with "a general understanding of society and the place of the individual within it," to provide opportunities "to survey the cultural heritage of mankind, to understand man and society," on the other hand, those who appear on the surface best qualified to do this, to whom this summons is addressed, seem most reluctant to answer.

One could give easy, but to my mind false, answers to explain this situation. One could say that social scientists are lazier than their colleagues and will not apply their minds to the problems of general education. Or one could say that social scientists are more ambitious and, fat with research grants, will not devote the necessary attention to the teaching of first- and second-year students. (As a social scientist, I will have to admit that research might well bear out these explanations; perhaps it will be found that social scientists *are* lazier, or more ambitious. But it is just this difficulty of making relatively well-established assertions that is one of our problems in the social sciences.) Other explanations however make better sense to me. I believe it was Seymour Martin Lipset who pointed out that natural scientists seem more willing to take up tasks in the field of general education—a position as dean, the development of a course, and so forth—because their major work is generally done while they are young. It may also be pointed out that opportunities for humanists to do research are more limited; that, in any case, the urgency of research—because of the character and nature of the fields involved—is not as marked for humanists as it is for the natural and social sciences; and that the concentration on a canon of given works means that whether one teaches novices or graduate students one may well be talking about the same thing, which makes the demands of shifting from one level to the other less severe in the humanities. But what appears to me most compelling in explaining the problem of incorporating the social sciences into general education is the simple fact that our foundations are insecure, we are uncertain what our foundations are, we cannot agree on what should be taught first and what should be taught second, and it is in the nature of most of the disciplines included in the social sciences that it is not likely that we will soon, or ever, overcome these problems.

In contrast to the uncertainty created by these shifting foundations, consider the situation of the natural sciences and the humanities. Whatever the problems in incorporating the natural sciences and humanities into liberal education—and they are certainly severe—for the most part, *the natural sciences and the humanities cannot be other than they are.* The natural sciences are based on a sequence or hierarchy of secure, if changing, laws, theories, concepts. Their relations to their own history and inner disputes must always be secondary to the teaching of the body of established (as of the time) knowledge. As Daniel Bell has written, "Science is a self-corrective system of disposing of useless facts."[2]

I would argue that the humanities are given a secure base because in the end they are based on a canon, on texts. The canon changes, the texts change, but whether in literature, philosophy, art, or music, there is some clear conception at any given time of what should be known, what should be understood, what should be pondered.

As one evidence of the security of the natural sciences and the humanities as compared with the social sciences, I would point out that when we see—as we have—a sudden increase in student interest in the natural sciences and humanities, it is *not* because they are suddenly teaching something different, or in a new way. It is because for various reasons—a new interest in a career, perhaps a new interest in the exotic and the nonrelevant—students turn to these fields, and when they do they find in them what they expect: rigor and sequential learning in the natural sciences; great works—however they may respond to them—in the humanities. I think too that teaching methods in these fields change less than in the social sciences, and in particular that what is taught in these fields changes less than in the social sciences. In the social sciences we can see the most radical shifts in a very short time in what is considered essential to learn. In part, these shifts are responses to the changing times, student interest, and the interests of social scientists themselves.

In the natural sciences and the humanities it is possible to respond to shifts of student interest only by considering how what is already definite and secure can be presented; one cannot, for example, abandon astronomy for astrology, the teaching of French literature for instruction in how to travel in France, despite the fact that one may suspect that astrology and travel are of greater interest to students than astronomy and French literature. (One can of course replace Shakespeare with the Beatles, but how often is that really done?) In the social sciences unfortunately it is possible, and even respectable, to respond to students' interests by changing what one teaches: to give up Max Weber for Frantz Fanon or a pluralistic approach to American society and politics for a Marxist one; to replace Western civilization with Eastern or African studies.

This chameleon-like character of the contemporary social sciences, one might think, should be highly popular with students. At times it is; at other times nothing quite seems to work. And the new and old, the conservative and the radical, the empirical and the theoretical, the relevant and the irrelevant, the disciplinary and the multidisciplinary, the committed and the uncommitted, the value-based and the value-free—are all equally in disfavor. I think we are passing through such a time now.

It is my understanding that it is not only at Harvard that we have seen a surprising drop in enrollments in various introductory and general-education courses in the social sciences, and an even more surprising loss of favor of certain newer efforts of the social sciences to respond to contemporary concerns—for example, Afro-American studies and urban studies. (Jewish studies seem to be flourishing, but because of their content—Hebrew, texts, history—they are closer to the humanities than to the social sciences, which bears out my general point.) More significant, to my mind, is the student judgment on courses in the social sciences. I have been studying an interesting report from the dean of Harvard College on the student evaluation of courses that enroll large numbers of freshmen. About half are general-education courses; the rest are introductory courses in various departments. The report summarizes questionnaires distributed to students in spring classes. They are asked to rate the courses along a number of axes, including "dull—stimulating," "clear—incoherent," "time well spent—time wasted." The survey included eleven courses in the social sciences, eleven in the natural sciences, and five in the humanities. The courses in the social sciences were almost uniformly rated more incoherent, duller, and time-wasting than the courses in the natural sciences and humanities. The very modest survey is, of course, not conclusive, but I report it because I believe it is representative of what we would find in universities and colleges around the country, and it conforms with my experience in a number of places.

I note too, with interest, that in a survey made of the college class of 1961 seven years after their graduation, when the respondents were asked "Are there any courses you wish you had taken which you did not take?" not a single social-science subject was listed. The subjects they were sorry they had not taken were foreign languages, literature, English, creative writing, science, philosophy, art, and art history.[3] While it is not easy to fully interpret this response, it is clear that whatever they had of the social sciences did not impel them to wish for any more.

Paradoxically, there is little the natural sciences and humanities can do about their unpopularity among students; yet at the moment they are relatively quite popular. There is much that the social sciences can and do, in fact, do; yet at the moment they are unpopular. But my point is not to argue that it is unfortunate that the social sciences are unpopular; it is rather to suggest that there is some basis for a student judgment of incoherence, and to set the stage for arguing that the problems of integrating the contemporary social sciences into a system of general or liberal education are primarily internal to the social sciences as intellectual enterprises.

II

Let me first specify the social sciences I have in mind when I argue that intellectual difficulties are at the base of their role in general education. Economics is of course a social science, but its development has been different from sociology, anthropology, and political science. Specifically, economics has developed to the point where it may be appropriately ordered from the elementary to the advanced; it may be presented sequentially; and it increasingly requires a base of mathematical competence. Thus, in these three key respects, as well as in others, it becomes divorced from sociology, anthropology, and political science.

One indication of both the problem of the social sciences in general and the unique role of economics is to apply the test: Can one conceive of the introductory course in these fields as being tracked, so that one is given to students who have had advanced work in the field in high school, another to those who want only as much of the field as is necessary for a liberal education, a third to those who plan to go on to advanced work, and a fourth perhaps to the specially gifted in this field? This kind of tracking is now quite common in mathematics, physics, and chemistry, and is recommended for other fields by Daniel Bell.[4] It is even to some modest extent possible in the humanities (though far more modest than for the sciences). But it is very hard to see how such tracking can be done in sociology, anthropology, and political science. We have a situation in which there is apparently no more elementary and less elementary form of these disciplines, no easy way of distinguishing what freshmen might be taught from what graduate students might be taught. If one studies theory, then Marx, Durkheim, Weber, Parsons, and Merton are as suitable at the beginning as at the end. If one studies specific subject matters, there is no reason why one should begin with stratification, or ethnicity, or marriage and the family, or socialization.

Political science may properly begin with political philosophy, or American government, or international relations, or even, I would guess, studies of voting behavior. Generally the political science or government department is a collection of subdepartments with these and other interests as primary, and it finds great difficulty in establishing what should be a proper introduction to all its semi-independent branches. A common solution these days is to demand three or four introductions, one to each subdepartment, thus carrying the division of the curriculum by the independent departmental powers one step further. We know that anthropology is the science of culture, and clearly the elementary course must deal with this large, elusive, and indeterminate concept. One will find however that the graduate-level course—insofar as anthropology tries to be theoretical—deals with it also. In contrast, it is possible to track the introductory course in economics, to have one for those who want only a general introduction to economics and to have another for those who want to specialize in it.

In distinguishing economics from the other social sciences, I have already pointed out what I believe to be a key problem for them: *There is no principle, no mechanism, no generally accepted set of concepts at the present time by which we can distinguish the elementary from the more advanced, no way in which we can order the subject.* If we cannot order it, we cannot determine what part of it belongs in the education of the citizen, what part belongs to general or liberal education. I do not suggest that we cannot so order these fields, or that we have not done so in the past. After all, general education at Columbia, the University of Chicago, perhaps in its early days at Harvard, was such an ordering. But any such effort today has about it something arbitrary. It is for this reason that the efforts to bring sociology, anthropology, and political science into the high-school curriculum strike some of us as a terrible idea. If we cannot decide on the introductory course in college, and on the contribution we should make to general education, how can we decide on a curriculum for high schools?

Daniel Bell points out that the pattern of learning in the natural sciences is sequential; in the social sciences the pattern is that of establishing linkages between one discipline, one field, or one set of concepts and another; in the humanities the pattern is concentric, in which one returns again and again to the same texts or materials with deeper and fuller understanding. Clearly there is no problem of ordering from elementary to advanced in the natural sciences (and in economics). But even in the humanities some kind of ordering, if not as organic as that of the natural sciences, is possible, and provides a frame. The ordering principle in the humanities is chronological, there is a before and an after, and it is meaningful. One may study a text or a work of art or a philosophy independently but one important way of studying it involves what came before and what came after. And even if one is original and begins history or literature with the moderns, it is always implied that one does so in order to work one's way back. In any case, there is an ordering frame, leading an independent and real existence. Every question in history involves knowledge of some preexisting condition, and any study of a work of art, or the development of a body of work, involves the notion of development, even if in short takes. Admittedly this may not be the only or the most important way of studying the work of art, but when it intrudes it is not completely arbitrary—it *is* meaningful, it is one way.

The behavioral sciences, I have said, cannot determine their sequences (admittedly this is open to argument, but it is my conclusion after twenty years of attempts to formulate introductory sequences). Nor do they have the "out" of the humanities. There is no chronological ordering frame that responds to their claim to be sciences, establishing generalizations, laws, governing concepts. As sciences, these generalizations should have an order, rather than the accidental order either of history or their own development as disciplines. Actually, one relatively satisfying way of ordering the social sciences *is* historically, in which case they become generalized history. Another way, which is scarcely satisfying, is to use their own history as an ordering principle—the history of their great minds, their great books. But as we know from the natural sciences and economics, the history of the discipline is only a minor branch of a developed field. In sociology, political science, and anthropology, there is the fear that in emphasizing the history of the discipline one abandons the claim to science, for science is a "corrective system of disposing of useless facts." Nevertheless, the temptation to simply teach the history of the discipline (Marx, Durkheim, Weber, and so forth) is always there, because as a matter of fact we have no way of deciding what facts—or theories—are really useless, once and for all. Just as we have no dominant ordering principle that determines what is elementary and what is advanced, we have no principle for determining *which historically generated theories should be set aside and which ones should become the basis for disciplinary work.*

In the fields I am considering, it seems that nothing is ever shoved under the rug forever. What, after all, seemed as dead a few years ago as genetic explanations of intelligence? What seemed as limited as Marxism in its various forms? The revival of interest in genetic interpretations of such matters as variations in intelligence, income, and occupation, and in Marxist theory, is not based, basically, on *internal* development in the disciplines. While there has been new work and important work in genetics, it is not that work but rather new social developments leading us back to old studies, and well-known data, that lead to the new prominence of genetic theories. It is harder to point to what kinds of developments provided any scientific reasons for the new prominence of Marxist theory. In both cases, clearly, external developments led to the return of what was earlier considered simply outmoded, inadequate, wrong. There is alas no final graveyard of social theory. This makes for another problem in determining what should be taught as part of a general or liberal education.

I do not want to be taken as having presented a purely nihilistic or skeptical attitude about some of the key disciplines of the social sciences. First of all, these disciplines provide us with data—that is, facts; and whatever the state of theory we apply to facts, the facts themselves are useful. They inform us of social conditions, political structures and processes, cultures in various parts of the world, and the like. Secondly, parts of all these disciplines have the lineaments of the better-developed sciences: bodies of theory, tested by experiment and data collection. Thus, demography in sociology, perhaps some of the generalizations of psephology in political science, and linguistics in anthropology are scientifically in somewhat better shape than other parts of the field. And finally, some theories seem to me more adequate than others. I prefer the complexity of Max Weber's views of social change to Karl Marx's; I find social explanations of phenomena more satisfying than racial, climatic, and others; I think pluralistic interpretations of the sources of American power and politics more adequate than monistic ones. And yet as I move from the areas of secure or relatively secure data and from well-organized and structured subfields to these larger questions, which we must include if we are to make general education in the social sciences serve for "acquiring a general understanding of society and the place of the individual within it," it is not easy to *establish* before a body of students, influenced by the ideas and tempers of the time, my preferences, which to me are fairly solidly based. Passion influences them; and I cannot deny that passion influences me too, in my preferences, even if they are founded on a broader base of knowledge, thought, and understanding.

Nor can we limit ourselves simply to the data and the more secure parts of our field. The parts of our disciplines in the best order may be, from the point of view of contemporary interests, marginal. We must deal with the large issues, whatever the limits of our scientific understanding of them. Unfortunately, when in presenting our fields to young minds we do choose such a subject as social change, the social preconditions of democracy or of political developments, or cultural change during economic development, our communication is often at the level of an ordered history, or a history of ideas, or a higher journalism. I would be the last to spurn such contributions; it is the one I believe I make in my own teaching, but then one must be ready to answer the student who asks: "What do you have to offer that I would not know if I had been reading newspapers and journals more regularly and consulting statistical abstracts?" Those of us in the field do not abandon the larger subjects in sociology, political science, and anthropology, and we often believe we can make a good case for one larger general theory as against another, but we must always be ready for ambushes from abandoned theories—genetic, economic determinist, climatic—that often put up a surprisingly strong case and leave us very uncertain over the status of our disciplines not only as sciences but as something we should proffer to the young as part of their general education.

I will not say we present illusion or falsehood or uncertain knowledge as truth (though many of us do); we *can* make a contribution to general education. But the fact that we cannot decide what, in our fields, is elementary and what is advanced, and we cannot decide what theories and general explanations we can finally discard, makes this task a very difficult one.

There is no question that our uncertainty about these matters is now much greater than it was ten or fifteen years ago. We have passed well beyond the heyday of expectations over the formation of a general behavioral science that would serve as the foundation of the policy sciences. The Center for Advanced Study in the Behavioral Sciences at Stanford still admits fifty scholars a year, but they are ever more divorced from each other, ever more wrapped up in specialist undertakings, and the hope embodied in the title of that institution has receded. The Department of Social Relations at Harvard, another symbol of the hope of a behavioral science, is now disbanded into its various parts. Parts of the newly developing behavioral science about which we were once most optimistic (for example, the new subdisciplines of economic development and of political development of new states, both of which, in their blend of materials from a variety of social sciences and their focus on great contemporary issues, offered ideal subject matters for general education in the social sciences) now seem to have weaker foundations than we thought. Who, twenty years ago, could have predicted that only Israel and India of the new postwar states would not be under military or one-party rule, or that Chile, Argentina, and Uruguay would be considered part of the economically underdeveloped world today? We can make explanations after the fact; the problem is, it is not clear to our students that our explanations are any better than those of the daily newspapers and weekly magazines—even though we are better funded to make them.

In *The Reforming of General Education* Daniel Bell writes that "the 'intellectual capital' of both courses [the Columbia Humanities and Contemporary Civilization courses] is being used up. This is a process at work in any intellectual enterprise, as the organization of ideas, once novel, becomes common coin, or, as new critical views develop, intellectual styles become altered and the analytical conceptions, the organizing principles of the course, become questioned."[5] The intellectual capital that Professor Bell refers to is in part an educational approach, in part "real" intellectual capital, a point of view, an approach that has become either common or questioned. There is little doubt in my mind that we have exhausted our intellectual capital in both respects.

We face a moment in the social sciences in which not only are old approaches questioned but satisfactory new ones have not been formulated. We are well past the enthusiasm for social planning and engineering of the New Deal period, past our self-confidence about reshaping a democratic and productive world with the aid of the social sciences in the post-World-War-II world. In the sixties there was a burst of enthusiasm over the use of the social sciences to reshape domestic society, over moving on from a more abstract and remote and explanatory social science to one that became directly involved in the shaping of policy. I think that was and is a most productive line of development, but we must report that early enthusiasms became rapidly sobered, both by the difficulty of actually developing policy sciences so they were relevant to policy making and by the subsidiary difficulty of structuring these new fields for education and training. Major new focuses of research and teaching—for example, urban studies or policy studies—have been difficult to incorporate into general education because their intellectual foundations were so diverse. Once again, in these new areas as in others, it was hard for us to determine what was elementary and what was advanced, and what our theoretical foundations were, if any.

Admittedly there are many social scientists who feel much more sanguine about our present condition than I do, who feel more confident about presenting our disciplines to young minds as a key part of their education in understanding the world about them. But on the whole, if we review the history of our disciplines since 1945, we will find that, while there has been progress, it is a modest progress and more in method than in ordered knowledge. In any case, we are faced with students today, and we must use the disciplines we work in as they are in their present condition, and even if we plead that we stand only where the natural sciences stood in 1550 or 1600, we are still called upon to give an account of ourselves in general education. It is easier undoubtedly to devote ourselves to research and graduate training for research in the hope that eventually we will give a better account of ourselves. The question is, what can we do now?

III

It is far easier to describe our problems than to prescribe solutions, but let me make three suggestions that I believe, on the basis of my experience as a teacher, might enable us to contribute more effectively to general and liberal education.

First: I believe we should think of social-science liberal education as based primarily on two disciplines, history and economics. It is these that I would like to see strengthened in the secondary schools and in the first year or two of college. History provides, to my mind, the best basis for the as-yet-undeveloped social sciences of sociology and political science. Daniel Bell believes that anthropology, too, is a good foundation for the other social sciences. I find ethnographic data and generalization either too special or too uncertain to be of great value. Nevertheless, I am impressed with the long-lived contribution of anthropology to the curriculum of even primary schools, where children year in and year out study Eskimos and jungle dwellers, and I could well admit some part of anthropology to general education. My fears for anthropology begin when it considers developed societies, where it arrives at the same uncertainties—in its attempt to describe structures, predominant values, national character—that I find in sociology.

The history I conceive of as being one of the two basic foundations for general education in social science is one that is informed—as history increasingly is—by the large general considerations that have been a contribution of the other social sciences. I think of history as including the development of urbanization, patterns of social mobility, the social characteristics of major revolutions, changes in the family and demographic change, in bureaucracy, in participation in government. In all these areas we have seen the ingenious use of reconstructed statistics in order to answer the kinds of questions that sociologists and political scientists have raised for contemporary society.

Economics is the most developed social science, and it permits us to introduce the student to the complex relations between theory building and data collection, to show how certain questions could only be answered after the development of a certain data-gathering technology, and how certain questions could only be asked when certain kinds of data become available. But most important, it shows us a social science built on clear and well-developed concepts, incorporated into theoretical schemes, and interacting with empirical investigation.

While the two foundations for general education in social science should be history and economics, certainly sociologists and political scientists can and should play a role in general education. After all, many sociologists and political scientists today train themselves in economics and work with historical materials. And even if they are without the full competence of those working in these disciplines, they can play a role in general education—to the benefit of their own work in their own proper fields, as well.

Second: Those parts of sociology, political science, and anthropology that are best developed as systems of generalizations interrelating with empirical data should also play a role in general education. Thus, leading candidates from these fields for general education in social science would be demography from sociology, electoral analysis from political science, sociolinguistics from anthropology. These may only brush some of the large issues that are so often the meat of general education in the social sciences. But they have a number of virtues. First, they introduce students to the use of numbers in social science; and to teach the social sciences without numbers and some numerical skills is a serious mistake. Secondly, they permit students to make some modest acquaintance with empirical work in the social sciences; to teach the social sciences—even in general education—without empirical work is, I believe, a serious mistake. Our danger is windy abstraction, and whatever we do to protect ourselves from it will be worthwhile. Small polls can be taken, small studies undertaken in the use of language, as well as exercises in the significance of certain changes for population growth. Admittedly these rather more modest essays will never solve the question of whether Marx or Weber was right. But then, what can?

Third: It is only on the basis of such a foundation—in a second year or a third year or, as Daniel Bell suggested, a synoptic fourth year —that I would want the large questions and the large abstractions to play a major role in general education. Here we would confront all the problems I, and others, have described; we would very often have to present our materials in the form of debates, some long and well established and not soon if ever to be resolved, others new and recently launched and conceivably to be settled in time by further research. [6]

It is on the basis of secure disciplines and preliminary essays into the scientific side of the social sciences that we would tell students whom we want to educate that they can enter as educated men and women into these controversies. The controversies inevitably lead a double life as part of the coin of everyday discussion and political conflict, and as part of the unfolding disciplines of the social sciences. We can neither indoctrinate—because we are teachers—nor can we provide more settled knowledge and understanding than we have. But in the context of a hope that human knowledge does develop, we can give an honest statement of where we are, after first requiring from students that they accept the responsibility of learning what limited knowledge and science we do have.

I am not happy with these tentative suggestions, and would thus add finally that we need leading social scientists to engage themselves, more than they have, with the problems of general education. Is our lack of achievement in developing new curricula, as the natural sciences have done, a final statement on the character of our fields and their possible contribution to an ordered education? It may be. Or is it possible to invest further effort in the creation of a sound and valuable general education on man in society? For the moment, I vote for the second alternative. We will not know if it is feasible until more of us try.

NOTES

1. While one can certainly make a distinction between general education and liberal education (the first term, as the special contribution of American undergraduate education, is easier to define), I use the two terms as synonyms in what follows. My concern is with the social sciences, not in their role as professional disciplines, but in their role as part of the education of the citizen, the informed person. Whether in liberal education or in general education, it is this role that the social sciences are called upon to fulfill.

2. Daniel Bell, *The Reforming of General Education* (New York: Columbia University Press, 1966), p. 175.

3. Joe L. Spaeth and Andrew M. Greeley, *Recent Alumni and Higher Education: A Survey of College Graduates* (New York: McGraw-Hill, 1970), cited in William Petersen, "What Remains of Liberal Education?" *Change*, Summer 1973, p. 47.

4. Bell, pp. 202-203, 251.

5. Bell, p. 211.

6. I am myself troubled about the modesty of these proposals. I realize that the large issues—the individual and society, the causes of social change, the shaping of consensus, the contradictions of democracy—are put aside for later. These are not only the large issues but the important ones. Is it possible to say to young people, "We propose to you a self-denying course in which we deal with the questions we can answer better, rather than those that are of the greatest importance?" I am further troubled by the fact that at the same time that I suggest a greater investment in the ordered, the empirical, the quantitative in the social sciences themselves—as Daniel Bell points out in a seminar on general education (unpublished notes for a talk to a Columbia University seminar, Oct. 11, 1973) —we find a new emphasis on normative questions. One thinks of the enormous impact of John Rawls' *Theory of Justice* and Christopher Jencks' *Inequality*, and sees in sociology, political science, and economics that the issues involved in the achievement of a just (regularly interpreted today as an equal) society play an ever more prominent role. Certainly a very different approach to general education in the social sciences from the one I have formulated could be presented and justified. But it is just because so much of general education has begun with the big issues and has turned out to be, to my mind, educationally and intellectually unsatisfying that I propose the sequence I do. Further, because I fear the effects of discussion that is undisciplined by fact and analysis, I suggest beginning with those facts and analyses that we can present with the greatest security, even if this procedure requires us to hold the larger questions for a later part of the college career.

The Economist Among the Social Scientists

Charles Issawi
Columbia University

Most unfortunately, I find myself basically in agreement with Professor Glazer's excellent essay. I say most unfortunately, since there are few spectacles more entertaining and educative than that of austere, unprejudiced, passionless scholars hissing and tearing away at each other like wildcats. What I do find a little surprising, however, is *his* surprise at his main conclusion, namely, that the study of the social sciences is less satisfying, intellectually and emotionally, than that of either the natural sciences or the humanities. Not only has that fact been obvious to me for a long time but the reason for it is plain. Natural scientists study God's handiwork, from the movements of the stars to the intricacies of the genetic code, and God is a tidy and competent craftsman who, to paraphrase Einstein, likes to puzzle and tease, but wicked he is not. The humanists concentrate on the works of the finest men and women in recorded history, produced during their divinely inspired moments—Plato and Gautama, Dante and Shakespeare, and Mozart and Wagner, and one has to be very dull indeed not to be warmed by the fire that consumed them, or not to see a little more clearly in the light they radiate.

But the unhappy social scientist is, essentially, studying the work of the Devil—if not the direct intervention of the Devil (which occurs only rarely), at least the result of man's fall at the hands of the Devil. For as medieval Schoolmen often pointed out, Work and Private Property, War and Conflict, the State and Social Stratification, and all the other subject matters of the social sciences are the result of Original Sin. Is it surprising, then, that these topics are less satisfying than the natural sciences and the humanities?

I would like to point out, however, two further handicaps under which the social scientist operates: the object of his study is more complex, and in a sense more opaque; and his vision tends to be dimmed by gusts of passion, the more violent for being suppressed. As regards complexity, let me remind you of the rather absurd but true anecdote about Max Planck: he originally intended to study economics, but he found that too difficult and switched to physics. Of course, physics calls for far higher mental powers than economics. And yet in some sense the natural sciences are less complex; they can concentrate on a smaller number of variables, can control the others more effectively, and can therefore carry out highly elaborate yet meaningful and conclusive manipulations. But it is the social scientist's curse that the abstractions he is forced to make result in a distortion of reality that deprives his conclusions of much of their meaning and relevance. I shall return to this subject later.

As for passion, the subjects we are studying impinge on our deepest interests, values, prejudices, and taboos, and arouse in us the fiercest emotions. This is sad but human, but what is really bad is that most of us keep on reminding our students that we are unbiased, objective searchers for the pure truth and that our conclusions are based on the findings of Absolute Reason itself.

Lastly, there is the question of style. In the humanities, style is usually part of the content itself. The natural scientists often (though by no means always) manage to convey their thoughts in clear, terse, and occasionally noble prose. But we social scientists excel at producing turgid, flatulent, pretentious paragraphs, full of jargon that, at least four times out of five, is quite unnecessary.

But when all this has been said, the fact remains that the social sciences are here to stay, and we just have to live with them. Greed, ambition, lust for power, and so on have constituted the warp and woof of human society. Someone has to study them and make sense of them, and everyone has to have at least some understanding of them. As Goethe reminded us, "Even Hell has its laws," and these laws are well worth investigating. Social problems are not going to disappear, and mischievous and dangerous nostrums for their solution abound. If the social scientist does not offer guidance, politicians and charlatans will. In many fields, the social scientists—even if we cut their claims to the most modest dimensions—have a certain amount of tested and applicable knowledge, and the size and quality of such knowledge is growing. And in the other fields, the social sciences can at least offer a methodical and disciplined approach which, if it cannot provide ready-made solutions, at least can give direction to thought and policy. As long as men are social, that is, human, they will continue to deal with such matters, and the social sciences will continue to have their place in the process of education.

Professor Glazer has some kind words to say about economics and history. I cannot quarrel with his choices: I was trained as an economist, and with every year that passes am more convinced that the only sensible approach to the study of society is through history. But if he can be a renegade sociologist, I can, with much less anguish, be a renegade economist. Economic behavior is more rational than social or political, and its study is therefore more satisfying. But I sense among students of economics the same malaise that he sees so clearly among sociologists and other social scientists. It is true that our discipline is more orderly and more sequential; we pass from micro- and macro-economics to money, international trade, econometrics, growth, public finance, and so on. We are also much more quantitative, statistical, and empirical, which is all to the good. And our style is, on the whole, distinctly better than that of other social scientists. In particular, we are less addicted to jargon: when we use technical terms we usually define them clearly and even formulate them mathematically. But we have made four mistakes that are beginning to irk the young.

First, we have spoken with more assurance than we had the right to; we have promised more than we could deliver; we have talked of "fine tuning," when we are jolly lucky if we can get the station at all; we have undertaken not only to explain the past but also to predict the future, and events have confounded the most eminent among us, including those foolish enough to give advice to American presidents.

Secondly, economists have, consciously or unconsciously, operated within an unduly narrow sociopolitical framework, which, to be precise, is the Western capitalist-democratic. Many of their assumptions are based, implicitly or explicitly, on the existence of a specific set of Western values, habits, and institutions, and many of their conclusions apply to Western, but not necessarily to other societies. In other words, they have regarded as parameters what may well be variables, and vice versa. Now, I too happen to believe that capitalist democracy is, on balance, the best of a bad lot, but it is certainly not the only system that has existed in the past, exists in the present, or is likely to exist in the future. And to base one's economics on it as heavily as we do is to commit the error made by Brittanus in Shaw's *Caesar and Cleopatra*, who thought that the customs of his tribe were the laws of the universe.

Thirdly, economists make the mistake described by the fourteenth-century Arab sociologist Ibn Khaldun of "constricting their gullets when pecking at the grains of truth." In their very legitimate anxiety not to trespass beyond the limits of their discipline, they have abandoned many adjacent fields to other social sciences. In doing this, they have—to change the metaphor abruptly—often thrown out the baby with the bath water and made it impossible for themselves to grasp the major factors affecting the process in question—for example, a land reform, or the nationalization of an industry, or a rise in petroleum prices, or even an inflation. In other words, they have rightly concentrated on certain variables but wrongly ignored other variables that are often even more important.

Lastly, as a result of our very legitimate concern with the quantifiable factors, we have often ignored those that could not be quantified, and therefore have once more omitted the major variables operating in certain situations.

Having said all this, I must confess that I have very few basic criticisms to make of the way economics is being taught. I wish we could imbue our students with more modesty and with a greater sense of the relativity and contingency of social phenomena. But, essentially, I think economics is on the right track, and the critique it is receiving from radical economists today may help it to correct some of its attitudes and assumptions without changing its essential and time-tested methods. [1]

A few words may be added about history. Of all the social sciences, it is the most inchoate and the one furthest removed, in method and approach, from the natural sciences. Unlike the other social sciences, it does not lend itself to the statistical testing of hypotheses—though of course it is constantly confronting various theories and hypotheses with the available evidence, usually with devastating results. Attempts to discover "historical laws" have been uniformly fruitless, and have been given up by professional historians, as distinct from amateur outsiders. Nor has the effort to find rhythms, cycles, and patterns fared much better. Of course, one can discover general trends and movements, but those who have tried to predict the future by extrapolating such trends have not been conspicuously successful; history seems to be about as closely related to futurology as astronomy is to astrology. Lastly, nothing seems to be more frustrating than the attempt to profit from the "lessons of history," since that usually consists in applying the conclusions drawn from the study of a past, and very imperfectly understood, situation to a present problem that is almost always different in some essential aspects. Thus it is said that Louis XVI, when confronted with his own revolution, judged that

Charles I of England had lost because of excessive obstinacy and inflexibility and then committed the opposite error. And recently, in Vietnam, we have seen an excellent example of the misapplication of the "lessons of Munich."

What history does offer, apart from the sheer excitement of the story of mankind, is an understanding of how social processes actually work—as distinct from how the utopian theorist or amateur politician thinks they work. It gives its students a picture of the complexity, variety, ponderousness, stubbornness, and internally contradictory nature of social reality, an insight into the social nature of man and an account of how men have in the past tried, according to their dim lights and in their fumbling way, to cope with the various problems that confronted them. That, by itself, is more than enough to justify its inclusion as an essential ingredient of human culture.

Lastly, a few words about curriculum. Professor Glazer picks history and economics as the two social sciences he would like to see strengthened in high schools and in the first year or two of college. I completely agree with his statement that "history provides . . . the best basis for the as-yet-undeveloped social sciences of sociology and political science." But I wonder whether geography—both physical and human—would not be a better choice, particularly at the high-school level, than economics. It is more concrete and more rounded and earthy (if one may use such words) and may therefore be more accessible and interesting to youngsters. And quite a bit of elementary economics can be introduced into it by way of economic geography. With a good grounding in history and geography and a solid foundation in algebra and calculus, I believe college students would be in a far better position to tackle both economics and the other social sciences.

What then should be given at the college level? A fundamental distinction must be made between those who intend to specialize in the discipline and the far larger number who do not. For the latter, I would suggest that a good social-science core could consist of European and American economic history, introductory economics, political theory, and sociology-anthropology. Economic history would show the actual evolution of the world's leading economic system from its earliest beginnings in the Middle Ages. Political theory would raise the main issues and introduce students to the clash of opinions that forms the Great Debate of the last twenty-five hundred years. Sociology-anthropology would give them an understanding of social structures and processes at different levels and of the variety and complexity of social forms. Lastly, economics would teach them rigorous method and quantification, and acquaint them with the findings of the discipline, while carefully stressing the limited applicability of such findings. Such a program might well constitute a nucleus around which the average, intelligent, educated man could continue to add and fit knowledge for the rest of his life.

NOTES

1. For a very thoroughgoing critique of the assumptions and methods of economics, see Oskar Morgenstern, "Thirteen Critical Points in Contemporary Economic Theory: An Interpretation," *Journal of Economic Literature*, X, No. 4 (Dec. 1972). No economist can read this article without feeling very uncomfortable.

Social Science and General Education

Thomas Sowell
*University of California,
Los Angeles*

Since I substantially agree with the paper by Nathan Glazer, I shall try to use Glazer's theory of social-science teaching as an entering wedge for a discussion of general education. The most heartening finding in Professor Glazer's paper is that there is *not* a trade-off between course popularity and analytical content, except perhaps in the very short run, when fads are at their peaks. This suggests that what students insistently demand at a given time ("relevance," subjective preference) is not what will ultimately satisfy them. It is therefore not a question of substituting faculty preferences for student preferences—which might be justifiable but is always uncomfortable—but rather it is a question of enforcing intellectual standards that students themselves ultimately come to respect. What they are seeking, apparently, is analytical structure and disciplined reasoning. These they do not find in general-education courses or in introductory or other social-science courses. The question is: Should they *expect* to find intellectual emphasis in either place?

Every field must have both descriptive information and analytical principles, and within each field some point is reached where analysis supersedes description. I would argue that this point is largely determined by how spontaneously interesting the purely descriptive material may be. Clearly, a mere description of the inanimate physical world has little interest; neither does a bare synopsis of events in a novel or a poem. Such areas must be analytical or reflective, almost from the outset, if they are to hold anyone's interest. But the social sciences focus on people, and people have a certain spontaneous interest for other people. Many aspects of human life remain interesting when merely described, or when the accompanying analysis consists only of surmises, suggestions, or even a dialogue of visceral opinions. This enables the social sciences to get away with a lower intellectual level of discourse than could be tolerated in the physical sciences or, to a lesser extent, the humanities. Moreover, the sheer volume of background information necessary for dealing with social-science complexities provides a legitimate reason for remaining at the descriptive level for a considerable time. In the natural sciences, the corresponding complexities are summarized in mathematical and statistical formulations that make it unnecessary for molecules or chromosomes to become a central preoccupation. In the more structured humanities, elaborate traditions of long standing limit current subjective input, much as mathematical-statistical formulas reduce it in the natural sciences.

Economics, as the "exceptional" social science, confirms this pattern. People are the subject matter of economics to a much lesser extent than in the other social sciences. *Things* are the proximate subject matter of economics—though ultimately it is in their relationship with people. The balance of payments, the interest rate, and the Gross National Product are not things that cause adrenalin to flow spontaneously. They can become interesting only within some intellectual framework, in the light of various hypotheses, and with some systematic procedure for analysis. Even introductory economics must introduce analysis or risk annihilation.

The comparisons of the various disciplines have thus far been in terms of a static picture as of a given time. But the disciplines differ enormously in age: mathematics, the natural sciences, and the humanities are many centuries older than the social sciences. Economics again is somewhat different from the other social sciences. It is more than two centuries old, or more than double the age of sociology. It may be that the disciplines will approach a similar pattern over time as the need for structural analysis increasingly permeates the thinking of the professions—and ultimately the lay public.

How does this relate to general education? The problems of the social sciences—notably diffuseness and dilettantism—are even more pronounced in "general education," as that is usually conceived and practiced. General-education courses in social science largely purvey information (including misinformation) and make minimal demands in the form of disciplined analysis, even if such courses do tax memory or patience. The avoidance of such courses by distinguished scholars in the social sciences may be more to their credit than a cause for blame or dismay. Even the so-called leading lights of the social sciences cannot possibly provide a sweeping "general understanding of society and the place of the individual in it." One of the ways in which the natural sciences are more mature is that they do not pretend to offer courses on "organic and inorganic matter in space and time." If such a course were somehow forced into the catalogue, it should not be a source of consternation if leading chemists, physicists, and biologists left it to be taught by the more reckless assistant professors.

When discussing general education, there is a tendency to pour out our fondest hopes and indeed to put forth a list of demands that would shame student radicals. These demands are often individually sound, and their goals urgently in need of realization, but collectively they are often impossible in the context of a four-year college and a twenty-four-hour day. There is no question that there will be compromise—whether rationally devised or forced upon us by intractable constraints. What can be sacrificed without sacrificing the essential goals?

If the history of social-science education has any lesson, it is that analytical methods are essential intellectually and—in the long run—are even required to maintain student interest and respect. These methods of course differ by field, so that the natural sciences, the social sciences, and the humanities should all be represented in general education. What will have to give then? The breadth we would like to see in each field will have to be sacrificed. It is undoubtedly desirable that a student know philosophy as it has evolved from Socrates to Camus, but it is infinitely more important that he know something about the analytical methods of philosophy. Even if these analytical methods are taught historically, a course devoted solely to William James has more chance of success than a course that sweeps across the centuries in a semester. Merely trying to understand one thinker is an education in the process of interpretation and criticism, beginning with initial misconceptions, which are virtually inevitable, and proceeding through uncritical acceptance, followed by the devastating criticisms of various opponents and the burden of empirical evidence. It may not be worth it to go through all this just to understand William James (or any other thinker or subject), but it is worth it to understand first what is meant by understanding, and second, to exercise discipline and judgment in evaluation. To me, that is what general education is all about—not breadth of subject matter but depth of analytical methods and breadth of applicability.

This kind of general education—in-depth studies in a wide range of subject areas—need not be adversely affected by the problem of faculty specialization or the problem of student choice of courses. It is precisely the specialist who can best lead a student through the intellectual labyrinths of his field to a narrowly circumscribed goal. A series of narrowly focused general-education courses in scattered fields can also allow the student to "do his own thing" *without doing it in his own way.* If he is charged up to study imperialism, then this visceral energy can be usefully employed to get him through a series of demanding theoretical and empirical investigations, beginning with a dissection of the theories of imperialism in Marx, Lenin, J. A. Hobson, and others, and proceeding to hypothesis testing with statistics. If racism is his interest, then he can get into the complexities of the IQ controversy or wrestle with the economics of discrimination. Some of these things can be done by an entering freshman, while others require special skills. This means only that general education cannot be localized in a particular span of time and regarded as a phase that passes, never to return. So much the better. This approach also means that general-education courses should not concentrate on "covering" a particular subject area, but rather on *uncovering* the complexities that lie beneath many apparently simple questions.

A Role for Social Science?

Robert L. Bartley
The Wall Street Journal

In pondering the question as to why I, a journalist, was invited to comment on the remarks of so distinguished a social scientist as Professor Glazer, I started with a formalistic approach. In assessing my credentials, I can say that I was once a social scientist myself, for eleven or twelve months at the University of Wisconsin. I must also report, though, that during this period I did no teaching. So while my credentials are scant enough to discuss social science, to discuss the teaching of it they are utterly nonexistent.

One thing I did learn during my year as a social scientist was that this formalistic approach is not often very useful. So I abandoned it for a functional approach. Obviously, here I am; so if I can discern what I am good at, it may answer the question. I began to ponder what it is I do. I find that one day I am advising the Pentagon on the strategic balance, the next day I am telling the Supreme Court how to rule on the Watergate-tapes issue, and the next day I am predicting the outcome—accurately, I might add—of the Billie Jean King—Bobby Riggs tennis match. Scutiny of this list makes it perfectly obvious that the reason I have been invited to comment on this subject—though I really don't know anything about it—is that I am an expert on commenting on subjects I don't know anything about.

What makes it particularly relevant is that I find the social sciences particularly useful in this endeavor. It may be the ultimate mission of the social sciences to teach people to comment on things they actually don't know anything about. Certainly that is the mission of general education, which is the broader subject of this conference.

I know social scientists who, if I sense their mood correctly, would think my assessment of their place in the scheme of things an optimistic one—"Thank God, there is *something* we are good for!" Certainly there is plenty of this in Professor Glazer's paper. The question he is really asking, or so it seems to me, is whether social scientists know anything worth teaching. He has a faith that they do, but he had difficulty specifying what it might be. He decides that economics is not too bad and that in other fields there may be isolated topics like demography or voting behavior that may also be worthwhile.

This mood is of course a reaction to the "overpromises" of the 1960s. During that decade, we learned that social scientists are no good at identifying key variables that can be adjusted to move whole social systems. That promise was the reason for the great popularity of social science during the 1960s, and disillusionment with it is the reason for the unpopularity Professor Glazer finds today.

Professor Issawi is also quite correct in saying that the same disillusionment extends to economics as well as to the "softer" social sciences, but I think that here the key variables are political ones. If economists had been philosopher-kings, their science might have been wise enough for economic policy to have been better managed than it has been.

In general, I think the current disillusionment with the social sciences is healthy, but there *is* a danger that it can be overdone. Social science should never have been asked to reform society in the first place, and the fact that it is not good at that task does not mean it has no role to play. I think that it continues to be important for a number of reasons.

One of these—one not to be underrated—is that social science is a characteristic expression of our times. Someone living in modern American society cannot understand his life and times without some understanding of social science, any more than an ancient Greek could understand his life and times without some understanding of comedy and tragedy. I am not saying that social science is as useful a guide as tragedy and comedy, but I think that we cannot understand our society unless we understand social science.

I find, for example, any number of people who distrust public-opinion polls. That is healthy enough, but they give the wrong reasons. Often they seize on the size of the sample, which is probably the *only* thing about the polls that is beyond question. These people are functionally illiterate in this day and age. You would be surprised at how many I meet. General education ought to do something about it.

But I think there is a second and even more important reason for studying social science. Professor Glazer took as his text Daniel Bell's *The Reforming of General Education.* I would like to borrow a couple of insights expressed in Professor Bell's *The Coming of Post-Industrial Society* (1973).

The first of these is that as society grows increasingly large and increasingly complex, a greater level of abstraction becomes necessary. Only by acting on large abstractions, for example, can a policy-maker have any effect on society. Professor Bell might deny this, but I detect in his book an enthusiasm about this state of affairs that I do not share. I think it is downright dangerous, and I feel that the problems of our last and troubled decade resulted directly from too great a trust in too large and too many abstractions. But I do not deny his point that even more such abstractions will be necessary in the future. I only hope that they will be tested analytically and used modestly. Social sciences will necessarily provide both the source of the abstractions and the methods of testing them.

This is all the more important because of a second of Professor Bell's insights. He remarks on the vast expansion of higher education. Just as the political and cultural battles of the last fifty years have centered on working out the place and status of the industrial proletariat, the next fifty years, he predicts, will be spent working out the place and status of the new class created by mass higher education—a class comprised, if you will, of the recipients of general education.

It is clear already that as this new class asserts its claims, one of its weapons will be social science. I do not think this is any great danger to society; social science is not all that powerful a weapon. But I do think it is a great danger to social science. I can easily conceive of a time when social science will be even more powerfully discredited than it was by the 1960s, and for much the same reason.

Also, I think there is a danger that this new class will use social science as an excuse to delude itself. I think this is the point of Daniel P. Moynihan's *Maximum Feasible Misunderstanding* (1974). When I first read this book I understood it, as I think it is popularly understood, as a story about how people were misled by fallible social science. Upon reflection, I understand it as something more profound: a story about how those who organized the community-action programs convinced themselves they were following social science, when in fact they were following something else, an inner *Geist.*

With all this in mind, I would propose that the introductory course in social science be entitled "The Limits of Social Science." I suppose this is an heretical idea and an unrealistic one. Even so I would propose that any introductory course include a lot of debunking. There is a book called *How To Lie with Statistics* that is an excellent introduction to statistics for journalists and other slow people. I think we could use something similar with respect to the social sciences.

To do this, though, I think social scientists will have to face up to certain problems more squarely than they have in my experience. One of these is the simple problem of quantification. Professor Thomas Sowell suggests that when sociology is as old as economics it will perhaps exhibit the same methodological state. I very much doubt it. The fact is that the essential data of economics are readily quantifiable. The data of sociology are not, and I guess never will be.

Therefore, I have certain doubts about Professor Glazer's suggestion to emphasize economics as an introduction to the social sciences. I do think that it would be socially useful if more people who have suffered general education understood economics. And I sympathize with Professor Glazer's desire to latch onto something real and something useful.

But I would disagree with any suggestion that economics be taught as a methodology for social science, as something the other sciences could approach with time, or even as something they ought to aspire to. The same goes for other methodologically advanced portions of the social sciences. I think it fundamentally misleading to suggest that the other social sciences will be able to, or even ought to, approach this rigor.

The second problem is that of values. I think values ought somehow to be introduced more explicitly into the social sciences. Take, for example, the question that currently agitates the field of genetics. There are, of course, important empirical questions, and I suppose these will have to be debated now that they have been brought up. But there is a powerful tendency to debate questions of value disguised as questions of fact.

Assume for a moment that Arthur Jensen is right, and ask the value question: If you have two gene pools, and there is some difference in the median IQs, what does this imply for the treatment of an individual from one gene pool or another? I would think it perfectly clear that the answer is: absolutely nothing.

Or, take the concern that agitates partisans on the other side of the debate. Assume that Professor Jensen is wrong, and that the medians are identical. Does that justify racial quotas among college faculty? Or does it mean that if the medians in income or education are not equal twenty years after a society has started to disavow its admittedly racist past, that it is irredeemably racist today, even though statistics also show substantial progress toward equality in key variables such as young husband-wife families? Again, I think the answer is clearly no. And I think that if both sides were trained to face value questions squarely, empirical questions would be seen in far better perspective.

Even though I think a lot of debunking appropriate, I would by no means write off the positive values of social science. As the new class of graduates of mass higher education evolves and grows in importance, one of its great problems will be to remain in some touch with the rest of society. To put the matter in a political framework, I am impressed by the ability of Richard M. Scammon and Ben J. Wattenberg, who paid close attention to public-opinion polls, to maintain a sense of what was happening in the larger society, while the McGovern movement, which I take as the political embodiment of the new class, could not. As this new class grows in size, importance, and power, the proper use of the social sciences may help it to remain in touch with the society around it.

To summarize: I think the current disillusionment with social science can be overdone. Social science cannot solve all the problems of society, but it can give its students a language, some methods of thought, a data base, a source of speculations, and a method of testing them. None of this will produce any Rosetta stones, but it will enlighten and elevate the quality of public debate. That should be contribution enough.

REFLECTIONS ON THE CURRICULUM

Experiential Education
and Revitalization of the Liberal Arts

John B. Stephenson and Robert F. Sexton
University of Kentucky

Our purpose is to explore the relationship between two aspects of higher education: the liberal arts and experiential learning. On the one hand, we are dealing with that aspect of education which is rooted most in tradition and is the university's strongest link with the past; on the other hand, we have an educational method that is, in some respects, a latecomer. Our suggestion is that a marriage of liberal-arts objectives with the methods of experiential education can result in a strengthening of liberal education at a time when circumstances severely threaten its future. The first part of this essay deals with the nature of these problems for the liberal arts, the second part, with the potential of experiential education.

THE CONCEPT OF LIBERAL ARTS

For most of the twentieth century the term "liberal arts" has been used to connote the learning that led to the creation of the "educated" person. This part of the curriculum, in the form of distribution requirements, general requirements, and a major, contained the basics of the university's nonvocational program. When combined with a major, which presumably would prepare the student for a career, the liberal-arts requirements were to contribute to the totality of the educated person.

The goals of the liberal-arts curriculum remain about the same today, despite efforts in recent years at refurbishment through name changes, and the validity of these goals continues. Basically, the liberal arts provide a means for the individual to understand his or her relationship to the larger environment. Traditionally, we have considered the tools for this understanding to be a knowledge of the heritage of Western and/or Eastern civilization, an exposure to the nature of man and the nature of historical and social forces, and the ability to analyze information independently and with the broadest possible vision. In essence, the goal is to help individuals control events or, failing this, to understand rather than be baffled and influenced by the whim of circumstance. In this context, history, literature, and philosophy are to give the student the knowledge of his heritage and of human nature. Sciences and languages are to provide experience in the rigor of intellectual discipline and the nature of logical thought. The social sciences fill the need for systematic analyses and the testing of hypotheses on the nature of group process and actions, for understanding both self and others. And the arts provide awareness of and sensitivity toward individual expressiveness and an understanding of the interrelatedness of beauty and functionalism; and, some would contend, they form the cathedral where man's ultimate achievement may be observed.

In sum, the liberal arts have sought to awaken the intelligence and open the doors of self-awareness, and to create the ability and desire for self-renewal through self-awareness and self-education. In the extreme, the lack of a relationship between the liberal arts on the one hand and vocations and careers on the other has been typified by John Stuart Mill's statement that "men are men before they are lawyers or physicians, or manufacturers; and if you make them capable and sensible men they will make themselves capable and sensible lawyers or physicians."[1]

But in fact, the goals of liberal education have never been completely divorced from the goals of society. It has always been assumed both explicitly and implicitly, for example, that this breadth of vision, this perspective, and these tools of analysis and reflection are needed by people who will successfully attack society's problems. In the sixties, when universities were polarized around the question of how far their commitment to the world outside academia should extend, the claim that academics should not take sides nor become involved was never consistent with the broader rhetoric supporting higher education. Sidney Hook, for example, makes a strong plea for the use of creative intelligence inspired by the humanities to perform the primary function of "taming power." As for utility, he contends that "the [educational institutions] must teach not merely the facts, but how to test them, how to relate them to problems, and how they bear upon relevant alternatives." [2]

But this vision of the liberal arts has come upon difficulties in the last few years. These difficulties may not have been perceived clearly by those within the system, and in many cases may be expressed only as problems of personal identity, but they are nonetheless real. At least five circumstances can be identified to explain this malaise: the so-called new vocationalism [3] and its relationship to a highly technological society; the influx of new learners with new needs into an old system; the ethical dilemma posed for the nation by political events surrounding the Watergate miasma; the growth of the management and accountability movements in higher education; and the confusion of identity and purpose among liberal-arts faculty themselves.

INCREASED VOCATIONALISM

Much has been written lately about the so-called new vocationalism. There seems to be little doubt that today's students are more concerned with identifying and training themselves for satisfying careers than was the case in the 1960s. This trend can be seen in the general thrust of federally sponsored commission reports and of federal programs based on such concepts as career education. It is also reflected in student attitudes and choices of academic majors, which show that students are turning away from the more esoteric academic fields and toward those that are more marketable in a tight economy.

This shift in national policy and consumer attitudes finds its expression in such starkly utilitarian pronouncements as one official's, to the effect that "if learning cannot be useful, then it is not learning," [4] and in such critiques of the liberal arts as Marvin Feldman's in the *Conference Board Record.*

> Our reverence for "liberal arts" is rooted in myth. It is graduates of technical or vocational colleges who create the options that make our society civilized. Without them life would be ugly, empty, and drab.
>
> Without artisans, the concept of liberal arts is sterile and vapid. We are often told that liberal arts serve to liberate the artisan from the necessary narrowness of his special skill. But it is also true that the liberal arts need the nourishment of practical expression, and thus the practical arts are the basis of liberal values. [5]

Kingman Brewster's response to the growth of vocationalism is particularly vivid.

> There is an almost frightening avalanche towards law schools and medical schools. And the country doesn't have that many good law schools

and medical schools. So that this is a kind of bottleneck, which does mean that college, instead of being a place to discover yourself, and to take some exploratory trips in fields of knowledge that may not be related to your career, now is kind of pre-professional, and slightly grim in its professionalism, because of this bottleneck into law schools and medical schools.

And that bothers me because I think a general education, a liberal education, is still the best way to develop between the ages of seventeen and twenty-two. And it would be too bad if that were squeezed into a professional groove of some kind. 6

The colleges and universities with the strongest commitment to liberal-arts education have not yet responded creatively to this development. As President Landrum Bolling of Earlham College has said, liberal-arts colleges have not yet "come to grips with the dilemma between abstract knowledge and vocational competence."7 Sidney Hook made the same point almost thirty years ago in *Education for Modern Man*.8

THE NEW LEARNERS

Education in the liberal arts has also been affected by expanding enrollment since the early 1960s and by the resulting change in the nature of the college undergraduate population. It is one matter for the president of an Ivy League school to speak fondly of the humanizing objectives of the college experience to a group of students attuned by their social backgrounds to the value of learning; it is quite another matter when the subject is addressed in the open-admissions university of the 1970s with a student body composed of new learners, minority students, older students, and lower-income students, unaccustomed to these traditions. To the new student a degree means a job and increased income; practical and career-related courses are most important. Although, at least to us, it is beyond dispute that the humanities remain important, it is also obvious that new motivations are necessary to encourage many students to pursue these subjects.

ETHICS IN PUBLIC LIFE

A less tangible impact on the liberal arts, but perhaps the most distressing one, has come as a result of the ethical questions posed by the Watergate episodes. Media coverage of hearings and trials probably created an uneasiness among some academics about the nature of their ethical obligation. Political commentators were quick to point this out. Tom Braden, for example, in a nationally syndicated column entitled "What Was Wrong with Their Education?" mentioned the obvious doubts that legal educators were experiencing, but went on to emphasize the need for undergraduate education to consider right and wrong behavior. "But by the time anybody enters law school, he ought to have had some acquaintance with moral questions. In four years of undergraduate study, some professor, some course, some reading should cause him to ask himself whether a thing is right rather than whether a thing can be done."[9]

While it would be absurd for academicians to assume that they are totally responsible for the sins of their students or that they are accountable for the ethical behavior of all college graduates, many professors nevertheless feel that one of their jobs is, indeed, to profess. The academy by and large holds that no one set of values should be advocated by the liberal-arts curriculum, but it is at the same time committed to creating persons who will make the right decisions. This seems an uneasy resolution to the profound question of whether higher education should or should not—perhaps we should say "can or cannot"—be value free. This is an ancient dilemma, but it has been brought more sharply into focus in our times, largely because of events in public life.

NEW FORMS OF MANAGEMENT AND ACCOUNTABILITY

The drive for greater efficiency in the use of scarce resources has created what Earl Cheit calls the management movement in higher education. Elaborate models are now available for the analysis of faculty activity, the measurement of productivity, the attainment of carefully specified management objectives, the impact of resources on curricular change, and the flow of students and faculty through institutions. Such management devices, once found only among business corporations and some government agencies, are increasingly being adopted by planners and managers of educational institutions searching for means to adapt to the new "steady state" of the seventies.

This movement is encouraged in no small degree by pressures from vital elements in the external environment: parents, taxpayers, donors, higher-education coordinating boards and systems officers and legislators. All seek answers to the central question: Are we getting our money's worth from higher education? The question will no doubt become sharper as inflation continues throughout the decade.

When the money's-worth question is turned on the liberal arts, the answers are not easily forthcoming, especially in terms that humanists find agreeable. What, for example, are the measurable outcomes of a liberal education? What can be cited as evidence of value obtained (either by society or the individual) that will make liberal education compete successfully in the minds of legislators who must divide the education dollar between professional programs and liberal-arts disciplines? What competencies can be promised from a study of the *Aeneid* that compare well with those promised by studies of human anatomy, soil science, or constitutional law? What have the humanities to offer that pays off in knowable, countable, consumable, or spendable units?

Clearly it is a time when advocates and purveyors of the liberal arts should be raising their own issues about learning objectives and desired impacts, rejecting the notion that discussion of the aims of education in our time can only lead to stale platitudes. The alternative is to leave to business-minded managers and accountants inside and outside institutions of higher education the task of redefining the uses of the liberal arts, through such practical measures as the rate of successful entry into the job market.

CONFUSION OF PURPOSE

Irving Kristol recently observed that "the question of the relevance of the humanities to young people only arises today because so many professors of humanities don't really believe in them. They don't believe they are teaching [all the] important or even the most important things." [10]

The hesitation about the profession of values makes its own contribution to the crisis of the liberal arts. The question of whether the humanities should be value free may have arisen naturally in response to the radical challenge to values on which there was assumed to be wide consensus. A retreat to the supposedly high ground of ethical neutrality is a normal response to value confrontation. It does, however, leave us with the question of what is left that is humane about the humanities and what is liberal about the liberal arts.

To this dilemma we can add the almost certain anxiety and confusion with which some faculty must react to the threat of declining enrollments. A few may choose to weave a cocoon out of the status quo, hoping that the current bad market conditions will eventually go away; most faculty, we would imagine, are wondering whether they have been doing the right thing, and wondering what, indeed, that right thing is.

These self-doubts among faculty members who should be the key advocates and interpreters of liberal education are recognized in Charles Hitchcock's observation: "There is a widespread conviction in the universities that liberal arts education has failed and needs to make way for something else, whatever that might be." [11]

Whether the liberal arts will survive intact in their present form is not the question, for they almost certainly will not. The pressures for accountability and evidence of improved management are more likely to grow than diminish. Unless the thrust of federal policy in the direction of career education subsides and unless students and parents return to an unquestioning faith in the nonvocational values of higher education, there will continue to be unrelenting demands on the liberal arts to "make learning useful." To the extent that new learners are responsible for the shift toward a career-oriented clientele, that orientation is likely to grow rather than weaken as we make progress toward equality of access to higher education. And finally, the current anxieties and dilemmas of identity and ideology among liberal-arts faculty do not seem likely to undergo spontaneous remission. These circumstances are enough to define the situation of the liberal arts as problematic; what defines it as a crisis is the fact that at the very time the liberal arts are weak and disoriented, the consequences of living in a utilitarian, virtually nonethical and nonhumanistic society are becoming clear, particularly in our public life.

MODES OF TEACHING AND LEARNING IN THE LIBERAL ARTS

Turning from the concept of a liberal-arts education and a consideration of its current traumas to the teaching of the liberal arts will lead us to a consideration of the potential role of experiential education in the learning process.

The lecture, of course, continues to be the device most often used to reach undergraduates in the arts and sciences, partly on the assumption that a person of learning can convey knowledge orally in large doses and that students will retain it. A somewhat more personal and dynamic approach is the seminar or discussion section, with an increase in readings and papers and interaction with the knowledgeable faculty member. Both lecture and seminar rest on the premise that the student's mind is a willing receptacle for information, which will then be turned by hard work and study into genuine learning and understanding.

A step closer to the concept of student involvement in the teaching-learning process is the independent-study project, which is sometimes used to structure field research academically but most often involves library research done at the student's initiative. In the sciences, the laboratory is in some ways comparable to independent study, because it confronts the learner directly with research material.

The student may spend more time outside the classroom in the social sciences, where a period of observation—in some cases, field trips—is widely used. Under close supervision, the student's observation of a policy-making board or a social worker in action, for example, is expected to help him or her relate to the "real" material, that is, that which is presented in the classroom. In other areas, such as geology, forestry, anthropology, and archaeology, the laboratory is actually somewhere in the field, as might also be the case when language students travel and study in the country whose language they are mastering.

What is represented in these examples of settings for teaching and learning appears to be a kind of continuum involving such dimensions as (1) dependence on the use of the classroom; (2) dependence on oral transmission of information; (3) dependence on the instructor as the source of knowledge; (4) dependence on the student as the generator of integrative principles; (5) degree of opportunity for application of theory to practice, abstract to concrete, general to particular; and (6) need to assume student motivation and self-direction for effective learning. [12]

As we define experiential education, it would come at one end of this continuum of teaching devices. The student in the experiential learning situation ideally would be expected to spend fairly large amounts of time on a regular basis outside the classroom. The location of the work, whether in a formalized institution or a less structured situation, should permit the student to become an integral part of the institution or learning environment, hopefully performing real work with real value in a manner similar to other nonstudent participants in that environment. This immersion is important, because simple observation—that is, from the periphery of the environment—might not be enough to help the learner understand the inner or hidden meanings, the cues that reflect real versus superficial activity. [13]

In this learning environment, the learner is expected to apply the same analysis and reflection demanded by other learning approaches. (It is important that academic credit is usually not given for the work or activity itself but rather for the reflection upon it.) It is here that the student's relationship with the instructor is crucial. For it is through the interjection of outside stimuli—conversation with the instructor, reading, and the integration of both into verbalized reflection—that the learner sees how action and reflection are combined in the total intellectual process. In some cases, this process may be extended over a long period of time, with intense structured preparation for the fieldwork (preseminars) and follow-up. Or, the preparation and reflection may be integrated into the same time span. No matter what the method, the goal is the integration of facts, ideas, and experience into a synthesis of understanding.

EXPERIENTIAL EDUCATION AND LIBERAL ARTS

Rather than further defining experiential education in general terms, it should be more fruitful to examine in depth its specific relationship to the liberal arts.

At the outset, we should deal with a commonly held assumption that experiential learning, internships, practica, and so forth are basically professional or vocational. There is, of course, no doubt that there are career advantages in experiential situations. In some fields (for example, medicine, education, and social work) it is a pedagogical truism that field experience is an integral part of professional training. There is also little doubt that the internship, when employed by any student, provides the opportunity for career exploration and gives a potential employer the opportunity to recruit an employee. In addition, several disciplines, including some in the humanities, are beginning to realize that the student with a real work situation on his or her résumé ("assistant to a legislator," "public relations specialist," "management intern") is more competitive in a tight job market. As a college degree becomes more and more commonplace, these advantages will become more important.

But it is our assumption that it is not just career advantages that support, or in some cases justify, experiential education as a component of a student's general studies or liberal-arts curriculum. On the contrary, what does justify experiential learning is its relationship to the reflective objectives of liberal-arts higher education.

We suggest, for example, that one of the goals of the humanities curriculum is to help the student understand the nature of man and his environment through the study of history, literature, and philosophy. At the same time, instructors in these fields have probably wondered whether their students, who may have little concern for the disciplinary methodology that beclouds the presentation of this general understanding or who may have little aesthetic appreciation or sense of identity with past personalities, are learning materials by rote for the purpose of passing examinations and never reflecting on the broader implications of that material.

For several years, for example, one of the writers has tried to interest students of American history in Southern politics by suggesting T. Harry Williams' biography of Huey Long. In the beginning, the book was a disaster, partly because its length and detail were oppressive to most students, who had a limited understanding of the relationship between politics and administrative manipulation. Quite logically, they questioned why they needed to read nine hundred pages to get the information they thought the book contained; the understanding the book could have provided was simply unavailable to all but a few.

But a breakthrough occurred when the writer developed seminars for full-time undergraduate interns in state-government settings. All the interns were located in situations where they did real work for administrators of government agencies that related directly to the governor. The interns were aware, in a routine fashion, of the implications of practical gubernatorial power through their internship assignment, not their seminar. When the seminar reached the point of reflecting on the role of the contemporary governor, *Huey Long* was assigned. The book took on new relevance and meaning for the students. They could identify immediately with both Huey Long and his administrative environment. "My agency would have reacted differently in that situation!" "The Governor pulled that maneuver on our department" were their reactions, indications that each student had a peg on which to hang the information. Moreover, the wealth of detail and analysis in the book, formerly a hindrance, now became an advantage; a thorough analysis of the milieu of one governor and one state political and administrative structure, in the context of practical experience, brought understanding.

The interns, therefore, each had a personal experience with historical understanding; they placed themselves and their agencies in the context of historical experience. And this was not, we should note, a matter of their relating theory to reality. They realized that this book, this "history," was in fact reality; historical consciousness dawned upon them when Huey Long became as real as their current governor; the only difference was that they read about one and observed the other personally.

This anecdotal example draws us toward a larger question. According to Ralph Tyler, a dean of American educational theorists, the belief that the mental process of abstraction comes before application is a middle-class belief related to social-class or employment differences. From this it followed that all persons, despite intellectual differences, were to be taught abstractions in the mode of training potential professionals. He argues that the notion is faulty, especially when applied to persons whose socioeconomic background is not middle class but oriented toward pragmatic vocationalism. (Our experience suggests that the middle class have difficulties as well.) This suggests that we will not reach the new college student with our standard approach, if indeed we are now reaching the old. Abstract curricula are meaningless to many of today's students unless we provide them with some reason, some motivating factor to appreciate and use the abstraction. This motivation can be a field experience.

But experience can be chaotic and meaningless unless the mind puts it into meaningful order. Reading *Huey Long* caused the student to reflect on his experience and added the "order" of historical context. The college learning experience should simultaneously provide the means of generalizing upon one experience to come up with a myriad of experiences and a conceptual framework for those generalizations. Another way of stating this is that the idea, the abstraction provides the individual with a reason to explore an experience, and when the idea and experience are thus observed they both have meaning. Having meaning, they will be remembered, used again and again, interact with other ideas and experiences that have been generalized, and finally enter the total being of the individual.

We have argued that an experience becomes more meaningful when combined with abstraction. In experiential learning situations, the reverse can just as easily be the case. The abstraction (the theory, the generality) can be tested in a nontheoretical environment, its validity can be assessed in a concrete instance, its extension to this particularity examined, and the practical applications determined. One would hope that the theory, when merged with experience, will also be remembered better and used in the future.

It is one thing, for example, to read in Max Weber of the distinction between charismatic and rational-legal authority and quite another to see, as an intern, the exercise of leadership in the rule-bound process of lawmaking in a legislature. In fact, it is one thing to read about the application of Weber's ideal types to reality and quite another to attempt that application oneself. While Kant's observation that nothing is more practical than a good theory cannot be disputed, it can also be said that nothing reinforces a good theory and cements it to a mind like a living application of it. The best teachers, from Socrates and Christ to the present, have understood this principle and have imported their applications into their "classrooms" as analogy, illustration, parable, case study, and simulation, all of which are techniques only one step away from using live experience as the "casebook." As Paul Freund says of teaching about abstractions such as values in context, "They become part of a whole, to be apprehended kinesthetically, as you learn to play a composition on the piano. In context—not by dogmatic repetition but by working through problems with values in mind."[14]

The field experience designed to relate theory to practice has its risks and pitfalls, of course. Chief among them is that the theory, which may be sound, may be thrown out completely by the student because the observed real world does not confirm it. The marketplace, in other words, does not guarantee the purchase of a high-quality academic abstraction. Colleges of architecture, for example, are attempting to create in their students an appreciation for the total environment of man in his created landscape, as well as a sensitivity toward long-term aesthetic needs. However, when this appreciation and sensitivity are tested in the real world, economic, political, and social factors may demand that architectural firms set such considerations aside in favor of plans that contribute toward further pollution of the man-made landscape. One suspects, furthermore, that in schools with cooperative education programs for architects the student sometimes returns to the campus determined to challenge the validity of the abstraction and to demand that functionalism and profit be the foremost ingredients emphasized in the academic program. What is to prevent students from returning to the academic cloister with disillusionment, cynicism, and exclusive regard for the world of practical affairs when they test theories of peace against the facts of war, theories of democracy against the facts of unequal distribution of power in public life, theories of economic development in a world of cutthroat international rivalry, theories of truth in a world of propaganda, and theories of justice in a world of injustice?

There is no reassuring answer to this question, but it must be pointed out that the same dangers exist when students leave the college or university after four years, degrees in hand, to confront those same realities. But because these students will never return, there is no way to reinforce (or restore) their faith in the original concepts and principles. We suggest, therefore, that from the educator's point of view it may be more advisable to have the theory tested under supervised field conditions, in which the instructor and the student can rebuild, defend, or refurbish it, than to have the theory destroyed forever as a result of one bout with a hostile, nontheoretical situation.

There are other relationships between experiential learning and the liberal arts. One of these concerns the purposes related to moral choice, ethical decision, and citizenship in a participatory system. Sidney Hook, for example, maintains that making a choice among alternatives, all of which may be somewhat unattractive, is the constant dilemma of man. He argues as follows: "As I understand the philosophical bequest of the humanities to the modern world, it reinforces our awareness of the indispensability of human choice in every moral situation, and the dignity of human choice as constituting the glory and tragedy of man. Indeed, the operating effectiveness of human choice is what we mean by freedom. In the end, power can be tamed, if at all, by the human spirit which alone is the carrier of cosmic value, and by the use of intelligence in the service of human freedom."[15] Hook argues further that the responsibility of an individual with an educated intelligence demands that he analyze the information coming to him and perhaps swaying him by "sophisms, propaganda and brass bands." "And it is precisely here that the educational agencies of a democracy have an enormous responsibility. They must teach not merely the facts, but how to test them, how to relate them to problems, and how they bear upon relevant alternatives. They must also stir imagination and sensibility in envisaging the effects of proposed modes of conduct on the human situation." [16] The same argument was put as a truism by Whitney Griswold: "The liberal arts inform and enlighten the independent citizens of a democracy in the use of their own resources." [17]

Of course neither Hook nor Griswold is arguing for the use of experiential learning as such. But it is our contention that the moral choice, the relationship of intelligence to problems and to the impact on people, and the ethical virtue Hook ascribes to the humanities, are those that Americans currently feel are unrepresented in our college programs. And this may be because of inadequate pedagogy used to relay these virtues. In essence, the making of intelligent choices cannot be learned in a vacuum, for no decisions are made in the context of an ideal value-oriented environment. Decisions—the determination and solution of problems—are made in the context of dynamics influencing the individual in the most graphic and personal ways. Decisions have potential for negative impact on home, family, career, and life itself. Of course, it is the academic hope that the "context" will be provided by the understanding gained through the humanities and sciences; these will provide the framework for taking in information and basing decisions on it. But, as we have seen dramatically, there is no guarantee that the abstract context will hold up, or that it will be remembered, or that the intellectual value orientation will not be thrown out at the first confrontation with hostile circumstances.

We therefore return to our earlier argument: that the integrated context of learning and experience may provide not only the means of remembering the learned abstractions but also a way of reinforcing them during and even after the time in which they are being tested by the hostile condition. We contend further that the values Hook advocates fall largely into the areas of appreciation and sensitivity, which cannot be adequately tested in the mind of the undergraduate learner as he sits through a lecture on Plato or the abuse of power. They may be tested, however, outside the classroom in a supervised experiential situation in which the learner forces a personal confrontation between his or her values and decisions (an intellectual and internal confrontation), assesses the results, and returns intellectually to the abstraction either for new insights, for reinforcement, or to modify the abstraction so as not to change its essence but to see how he or she can work within its general limitations while making the hard choice.

Using Hook's position that the goal of education is to be able to understand the relationship between ideas and problems and their impact on man, we also suggest that these relationships cannot be questioned through traditional teaching. Despite the importance of historical awareness, we have seen that the new learner, without an inherent attraction to abstraction, may have to be confronted by the problem before the abstraction becomes germane and can be used to make the decision. Therefore, a field experience, where the problem is explored in a controlled but real environment, should be preferable to a situation in which the same person makes the same choice ten years later as a presidential assistant.

LIBERAL SKILLS AND THE TECHNOLOGICAL SOCIETY

In discussing the nature of the liberal arts earlier, we mentioned the necessity for controlling technological as well as political power. One of the central challenges is to discover new methods for the training of technicians and professionals—and even ordinary educated citizens— that do not produce "minds in a groove," to use Whitehead's phrase. A demanding economic environment and the historical development of a technocratic society have brought the realization that skills, as well as concepts and perspectives, must be produced by the educational process. Some would suggest that higher education in the 1970s faces a choice between abandoning the liberal-arts curriculum in favor of vocationalism or reaffirming the liberal arts in hopes of interrupting the ascendent curve of "blind" technology.

But perhaps the choice is not so extreme. It would be interesting to explore the possibility of developing "liberal skills," in addition to the "liberal knowledge" that dominates current curricula. It may turn out that these skills are best approached through nontraditional means, such as field experience.

Let us dwell for a moment on the notion of liberal skills. A case can be made, we believe, for the proposition that, although the traditional concepts of liberal education are valid for our time, these classical concepts require reinterpretation, recasting, and perhaps a new vocabulary in order to address contemporary needs and understandings. We might profitably ask ourselves what competencies are likely to be required of educated persons approaching the last quarter of this century. The answers will vary according to the ways individuals read the near future. One set of answers has been suggested by H. Bradley Sagen in his provocative discussion of the "professional model of undergraduate education."[18]

Sagen argues that while it remains true that knowledge is a proper end in itself, educators must understand that there are proper uses to which systematic knowledge can be put and that adding the practical component to pure knowledge, as in the professions, is a key to revitalizing undergraduate education.

He observes that "if we continue to teach only the scholar's conception of knowledge to undergraduates and fail to convey the importance of perspective and consequences, we may well also fail to control complex technologies and social systems."[19]

Among the "task-oriented competencies" that Sagen argues should be sought through undergraduate education are these:

1. Professional problem solving; that is, coping with "the kind of problem for which the solution does not begin with a review of the literature." Application to real problems will require multidisciplinary approaches, dealing with conflicting values, working under the pressure of time with inadequate resources and information, and so on.

2. Organizational and interpersonal skills of the kind needed to cope with corporate, governmental, and urban settings in which most of us will spend our lives. Component skills in this area would include leadership training, empathic skills, and self-developmental competencies.

3. A related skill is "the ability to interpret complex information to those less well educated," or, in other words, learning how to teach others.

4. Other skills mentioned include decision making, dealing with large quantities of complex information (for example, by use of the computer), the process of design, and legal reasoning.

Sagen does not intend that his list of competencies be taken as fully developed; each of us would offer our revisions, additions, and perhaps deletions.[20] But this list does serve to illustrate a basic point: that we are capable of making guesses about what skills will be required for us to face the future as educated persons. These skills are anything but alien to the time-honored and still-valid aims of liberal education, without which, "the results will be first, a nation of technicians who lack the capacity to predict the potential implications of their actions; and second, a nation of citizens and leaders who lack the wisdom to judge wisely the proposals of technicians."[21]

Sagen's treatment underscores, furthermore, what we and others have suggested about more effective learning of such skills: that the liberal arts might learn something from professional education, that is, the latter's greater emphasis on learning through the application of knowledge to practice.[22]

Shelton Williams, in describing the policy-research field program at Austin College, points out this merger of skills and knowledge by explaining that the program is to "assist students in applying techniques acquired in liberal arts education to the study of contemporary social issues. These techniques include not only modern research skills but the analysis of the ethical bases on which policy is or should be based."[23] Daniel Bell explains the process in broader terms, emphasizing the need to "uncover the underlying intellectual structure in which one's work is embedded." He adds, "In this way, the context of specialism can be enlarged, and becomes an aspect of the liberal education itself."[24]

SOME THOUGHTS ON IMPLEMENTION

Thus far we have generalized about the liberal arts and experiential learning. A few examples of the possible ways such experiences might be incorporated into the curriculum are now appropriate. The examples are presented with certain disclaimers. First, we are assuming that certain important advantages of field experience are sufficiently obvious not to need elaboration here. These advantages might include help in career choice for the students, financial assistance, a sense of the real world, or a commitment to service. Secondly, because most readers will be familiar with such instances of out-of-class teaching and learning as government-intern programs, intern placements in business or architectual firms, and independent field study, we will turn our attention to less ordinary examples. Finally, it should be clear that these are illustrative examples, not proposals, and that the list is by no means comprehensive.

One possibility for tying a modest amount of field experience into a program such as English might be to relate a field experience directly to the content of a specific area of literature. This might require some course restructuring, but today it is not uncommon to structure upper-level courses by social characteristics of the literature. We might, for example, work with a course entitled, "Social Literature of the 20th Century." The reading list for this course might include *The Jungle, The Grapes of Wrath, Cannery Row,* and several of Richard Wright's novels.

The objectives of such a course, in keeping with the aims of the humanities generally, would be to use the insights of the best writers in this area of literature to illuminate real human problems in the present, and vice versa, and to illuminate the insightfulness of certain writers through confrontation with actual human problems.

One plan might be to extend this course over two semesters. During the first semester the student would work in a setting similar to that of the setting of the literature: a migrant-labor camp or an agency serving migrants, another laboring situation, or in an inner-city setting similar to those in Wright's books. The student would, of course, be expected to do more than observe behavior in these environments and therefore would have to spend a considerable amount of time in them, perhaps a minimum of twenty hours a week.

Credit would be awarded, not for the field experience itself but for the total experience. The student would enroll, for example, for nine hours of credit for the total package, and might complete part of a reading list while working twenty hours a week in the fall term, and then he or she would move in the spring semester into a seminar on the same subject with more reading and papers. A diary or log kept during the work experience might also be the subject of considerable discussion in the seminar.

The same model might apply to students in courses in recent political history. In this case students might be placed in a political campaign, a lobby, a labor union, or a bureaucratic structure. The student's responsibilities might be more related to research for the sponsoring agency, especially if the internship had to be carried out on a part-time basis. The related seminar in this case would be an effort to reflect on the specific machinations of the placement environment, as they were reflected in historical data.

The academic emphasis would be on comparison and generalization. Not designed to impart specific historical information, the total process (field placement and seminar) would be planned to help the student "read" his environment in its historical context. An alternative model appropriate for English or history might be field research, including the collection of oral history or oral data. Such a project could be tied to the specific research interests of the instructor. This approach has been used and discussed widely enough not to need extensive treatment here.

These examples propose modest programs of fieldwork. A more substantial amount might be included in a field-based course that would investigate the ethical basis of decision making in business or government. This course might be scheduled as a full-time field involvement for all or part of a semester and would be interdisciplinary. Students would be placed with persons in positions of management or supervisory authority. These executive supervisors would be carefully selected and told of the nature of the assignment in advance and could even be defined as a community-based "field faculty." The students would also participate in an intensive seminar, with a teaching staff comprised of an experienced business or government executive, a professor of philosophy, and a professor of administration. The student's specific academic assignment would be to identify and analyze a number of critical incidents where decisions were made and to test that analysis in the seminar setting. The specific program would, of course, be broader than it might seem (that is, meaningful not just in terms of ethical considerations) in that the student would be contributing real and constructive work and therefore would be getting practical experience; he would be examining the organization in terms of its total structure; and he would be developing skills of analysis more akin to those practiced in everyday life.

A much discussed but little used field-experience approach for the liberal arts might be a policy-research institute staffed by students under faculty supervision, such as the Austin College program mentioned earlier. A team of faculty members would supervise a task force of students in a contract relationship with a public agency. The contract would call for a thorough analysis of the applicability of a particular policy; the subject matter might range from the feasibility and desirability of a proposed highway extension to the legalization of off-track betting.

The policy-research approach could be designed specifically to give students the opportunity to delve deeply into the technical ramifications of planning, surveying, and forecasting. It could also give the students the opportunity to formulate, with some hope of implementation, their own rationale for the ethical base on which decisions affecting the entire community could be made. The model has the further advantage of not being tied to a specific place (that is, office space in an agency); research could be conducted in the community and reflection exercised in the classroom. An obvious disadvantage might be the unpredictability, from semester to semester, of community needs for policy-research projects.

Although these are modest sketches, they do point out the range of applications of field experience to the liberal arts. To repeat, there are numerous experiences already in existence or placements available for individual students that would also be of use in the liberal arts. These include not only the established government-intern programs but also opportunities to do field research and practical writing in archives.

The main point, however, is that the field experience could be useful in the liberal arts, that it has not yet been exploited, and that the range of options are as wide as geography and the imagination will permit.

CONCLUSION

We have tried to show that, while the aims of education in the liberal arts retain their validity, their vitality is critically threatened by forms of anomie and environmental threat peculiar to our times, and that one means for seeking their revitalization lies in the use of that family of devices for teaching and learning that we have called experiential education. Exclusive concern with experiential education in this paper should not be taken as evidence of naive preoccupation on our part with narrow pedagogical gimmickery for its own sake. We merely wish to present the case that such devices should be tried in furtherance of liberal-arts aims.

We can go no further than to suggest what appears to be a promising direction, and we would not dare guarantee success. So much depends on the quality of imagination, the willingness of faculty members to work through the problems of concept and execution, the administrative assessments of costs and benefits, and the readiness of students to make the most of such opportunities—to name but the most obvious problems—that one would be foolish to peddle experiential education as the "perfect product." Indeed, the proper training of the intellect, as Cardinal Newman pointed out in 1852, can be guaranteed by *no* particular method. He wrote: ". . . it is not mere application, however exemplary, which introduces the mind to truth, nor the reading of many books, nor the getting up of many subjects, nor the witnessing of many experiments, nor the attending of many lectures. All this is short of enough; a man may have done it all, yet be lingering in the vestibule of knowledge. . ." [25]

The objective for all of us, we trust, is to get beyond the vestibule of knowledge, by whatever means.

NOTES

1. Quoted in Alfred Whitney Griswold, *Essays on Education* (New Haven: Yale University Press, 1954), p. 150.
2. Sidney Hook, *Education and the Taming of Power* (La Salle, Ill.: Open Court, 1973), p. 30.
3. This phrase is taken from Charles Hitchcock, "The New Vocationalism," *Change*, April 1973. Also see John B. Stephenson, "Efficiency and Vocationalism—Renewed Threats to Liberal Education," *Liberal Education*, Oct. 1974.
4. This statement was actually an attempt by Sidney Marland to use A. N. Whitehead's words to support career education. The source is an Office of Education film, *Career Education* (Maryland State Board of Education, through Olympus Research Corp., n.d.).

5. Marvin J. Feldman, "The Relevance Gap in American Education," *Conference Board Record,* June 1972.

6. Quoted on "The Reasoner Report," ABC News, March 23, 1974.

7. Bolling's comment, made in 1973, was quoted in the *Louisville Courier-Journal*, July 8, 1974.

8. Sidney Hook, *Education for Modern Man* (New York: Dial Press, 1946), especially Chapter 8.

9. *Louisville Courier-Journal*, April 17, 1974.

10. "Values in Contemporary Society," typescript of a conference held by the Rockefeller Foundation, March 1974, p. 21.

11. Hitchcock, "The New Vocationalism."

12. Ideas relating to this continuum of learning are discussed in Daniel S. Arnold, "Differentiating Concepts of Experiential Learning," contained in John B. Stephenson, *et al.,* "Experiential Education: A New Direction for an Old Concept," ERIC Clearinghouse on Higher Education Document No. ED 086079. These papers were initially presented at the 81st annual convention of the American Psychological Association, Montreal, August 1973.

13. Here, we are not including discussion of experiential education as it relates to learning prior to enrollment in an educational institution or "prior experience."

14. "Values in Contemporary Society."

15. Hook, *Education and the Taming of Power*, p. 200.

16. Ibid.

17. Griswold, p. 7.

18. H. Bradley Sagen, "The Professions: A Neglected Model for Undergraduate Education," a paper presented at AAHE Regional Conferences, 1972-1973.

19. Sagen, p. 2.

20. In fairness to Sagen, it should be mentioned that we have taken the liberty of re-ordering his treatment of competencies.

21. Sagen, p. 9.

22. Robert Nisbet also seems to support the general view that the liberal arts may be rejuvenated by joining with professional education in new ways. He has recently stated: "The prosperity of the liberal arts will be far greater if they are woven into those professional fields central to the university's history, rather than being treated as they now so commonly are as a kind of museum of interesting exhibits which one should pass through on his way to chosen interest." *Change*, Summer 1974, p. 30.

23. Shelton L. Williams, "Policy Research in Undergraduate Learning," *Journal of Higher Education*, April 1974, pp. 296-304.

24. Daniel Bell, *The Reforming of General Education* (New York: Columbia University Press, 1966), pp. 286-287.

25. John Henry Newman, *The Idea of a University Defined and Illustrated* (London: Longmans, Green, 1910), pp. 151-152.

Education for the Future: The Liberating Arts

Paul Kurtz

*State University of New York
at Buffalo*

I

We have heard a great deal in the past about the need for general education. The traditional arguments in favor of the liberal arts are no doubt familiar and persuasive. They were embodied in the rationale for the Great Books program, courses or curricula in Western civilization, and the study of the classics. Many of us believe that the reaction against such studies in the sixties—reactions that often denuded or abandoned the liberal-arts curriculum entirely—were narrow and intemperate. Although many students and younger faculty claimed that such studies were "irrelevant" to their interests or to those of the social context, their responses were fundamentally unreflective. For the situation that higher education will face in the decades ahead is such that we need to renew our commitment to the ideals of general education.

However, we cannot go back to the older forms without modifying them. Much of the liberal-arts curriculum was too historical in character and will not meet many of the genuine needs of the future. Thus, general education takes on a new dimension: that is, education must in some way equip both the student and the social polity to deal with the new kinds of problems emerging. The old parameters and guidelines of the past—though they need to be studied and appreciated—are not a be-all and end-all and surely do not suffice by themselves. For example, it is apparent that we can no longer teach courses in Western civilization alone, for the new focus must be on world civilization, not simply on the history of the West, but the future of all humankind. Accordingly, the real question we face is how will education enable students and society to adapt to the rapidly changing world of the future.

Many students, in their boredom with traditional liberal-arts subjects (which we found so exasperating), have turned to vocationalism. "What does one do with a B.A. degree?" we are asked. "It bakes no bread!" Therefore, many students have rejected the liberal arts and the humanities with disdain. Many have also discovered that the completely unstructured, self-actualizing curricula did not enable them to develop a career or function in the outside world. The need to develop skills for a vocation, which the self-actualizing programs overlooked, is important. But one lesson to be learned is that vocationalism or careerism by itself, without supplemental nourishment by general education, is woefully inadequate; the continuing need is for some exposure to what I shall call the liberating arts.

II

The continuing problems that we will continue to face in the decades ahead are the disruptions and opportunities caused by intense social change. We are, in my judgment, living through a new Renaissance, which is expressed by a tremendous burst of creative energy; it is characterized by innovation, dynamism, experimentalism. The most direct expression of this can be found in the explosion in technology and science. The rate of technological invention and application is accelerating very rapidly and will continue to do so in the future. With each new scientific discovery, there are new possibilities and powers, as well as unforeseen by-products and fallouts. In the twentieth century, the automobile, air travel, radar, the Green Revolution, new medical technology, electronics, computers, and space travel have all had their impact. The same scientific and technological growth forces will no doubt continue in the future with powerful implications.

In consequence, we may expect social dislocation and fundamental changes in institutions, structures, and values. Indeed, at the present in this country—and in a good part of the world—we are experiencing a moral revolution, which involves a basic transformation of our values; our very notions of life, work, love, and sex are being radically altered. Given the tempo of technological change, this was inescapable.

The technological explosion and the consequent shift in values places a strain upon both the individual and the social fabric. The old order gives way to the new; all too few of the guidelines of the past seem adaptable to the present, and even less so to the future. The individual is often wrenched from a tranquil background and thrown on his own. Psychological distress and existential despair may overtake him. In a quandary, he looks for sustenance and support. He is often prey to every cult and fad, which feed on his gullibility and promise to answer his quest for security. Given these changing social conditions, rapid political and economic transformations also occur; here, too, most of the traditional parameters break down. Political movements seek both to respond to and to direct the vast technological and social changes going on. On all sides people ask: How shall we act? What should our goals be? What kind of world do we want to bring into being?

If we attempt to forecast the future, we discover that the number of problems we shall have to face as individuals, as a society, indeed as a world community staggers the imagination. On the bleak side are threatening clouds we are familiar with: resource depletion, the scarcity crisis, ecological destruction, the population explosion, political conflict, and—over all—the possibility of nuclear war. The individual faces a loss of values and an increase in his or her sense of alienation and meaninglessness in an increasingly dehumanizing technological society. On the positive side are a number of promises: new explorations and adventures, opportunities for unparalleled technological development, a world of abundance and affluence, the cure of disease and poverty, increase in life-span, increased creative enjoyment and freedom for the individual, and the building of a genuine world community.

There is one possible scenario for the individual, which is already happening and seems likely to continue in the future. First, with increased mobility and travel, the historic rootedness in one place—the commitment to the local community—will be eroded. Narrow parochialism will be overcome. Although this will no doubt expand the horizons of the individual even beyond the nation to the world community, it may also lead to severe trauma, a loss of the sense of belonging.

Second, people will need to change careers, occupations, and jobs more frequently, perhaps several times in a lifetime. New technologies will make some occupations outmoded and residual. The iceman was replaced by the refrigerator repairman, the seamstress by the sewing-machine operator, the bookkeeper by the computer technician. This process will continue. Even seemingly well-established professions —law, medicine, engineering, teaching—will be faced constantly with new demands and methods, often so innovative that they will sweep away and make obsolescent the best-trained but superannuated professionals of the previous decade. Thus the ability to change careers and vocations in midstream becomes a prerequisite of survival, especially the ability to adjust one's skills. If we wish to lead satisfying lives, we must be willing to adapt to new demands.

Third, the old moral values and religious traditions are becoming increasingly difficult to apply to the urgent needs of a new cultural reality: the rules governing marriage, divorce, family, and the role of women in society are being transformed. Breakthroughs in biology lead to new moral dilemmas: cloning, biogenetic engineering, euthanasia, voluntary sterilization, group cohabitation, changing sex roles, and behavioral control are only some of the new adventures in experimental living. The orthodox religions, as defenders of absolute values, have to compete with a number of alternative systems. They are hard pressed and must either stretch and change or become irrelevant. The individual discovers that he must create his own values and personal goals; there are no easy guidelines, and only his own conscience and conviction can help him.

III

It is in this situation that general education inevitably will play a vital role. Indeed, the entire educative process is crucial; the so-called "knowledge industry" will be the growth industry of the future, the pivotal institution of society. Whether we can meet the needs and challenges of the future as individuals and as a society will depend upon the kinds of educative processes that we undergo.

What do I mean distinctively by education? The learning process, the process of expanding the dimensions of experience and intelligence, the increase in imagination and understanding, the ability to adapt and adjust.

Now let me make it clear that although schools are essential to this educative process they are not the only institutions that should be charged with that mission. Moreover, education is not a commodity to be supplied only to the young, from elementary school through college. As I view it, it is a continuing process for all age groups and at all levels. It is never ending. Perhaps the greatest crisis of the generation ahead will not concern the young but will arise from the necessity of adults adjusting and responding to new and challenging horizons.

Classically, education was the task of the schools, whose chief function was to inculcate the beliefs, values, and basic skills of a society and to train for vocations and professions. It was, as it were, the transmission belt for the traditions of the past. Today, the perennial truths of history no longer seem adequate. The growth of knowledge is intense, and one cannot hope to obtain a degree in a specific field and then rest on one's laurels; there is the ongoing need to keep learning and growing. Virtually all of the institutions of society must have an educative function. The family, churches, labor unions, corporations, business, and industry need to incorporate work-study programs. But perhaps most vitally today the electronic mass media—TV and radio—and magazines, newspapers, and other publications have a role to play. Indeed, the greatest single need that we have, I submit, will be to develop new forms of adult education in society at large.

However, the colleges and universities will no doubt continue to make as their main contribution to society the fulfillment of the tasks of general education; they can do this *best* by providing a rich curriculum in the liberating arts—scientific and humanistic. These studies will help to fulfill one of the chief functions of education: enabling individuals to adapt to the changing future, to withstand future uncertainties and novelties, and hopefully to enjoy them.

It is clear that the curriculum of the future will need to undergo a rather drastic alteration that older forms of general education are unlikely to undergo. It should, in my view, involve several components, many of them familiar: training in the basic skills—reading, writing, computation, for example—professional and occupational preparation, understanding of the nature and practice of democracy, and an appreciation of history and the arts. Yet, the vital element is to increase, by means of the sciences, our understanding of the rapidly changing world in which we live so that *we can develop the ability to make reflective value judgments.*

These later emphases help to realize the ideals of a general education and of the liberal arts that many of our schools have recently abandoned for vocational training or programs in individual self-expression. I believe that we need to return to generalist endeavors but, in a new sense, by explorations in the liberating arts. The chief goal of this kind of education is to clarify our ability to formulate value judgments so that individuals can creatively expand and realize their potentialities in a changing world.

It is curious that in the United States, perhaps the most innovative scientific and technological civilization in history, a drastic critique of science and technology is now under way. Science is blamed for many of our current problems. There is in some circles a neo-romantic flight into anti-intellectualism. This points to a failure in education. For we have not adequately explained science as a great adventure in learning; nor have we succeeded in developing an appreciation for the scientific method: the appeal to evidence and logical criteria in judging hypotheses, the tentative and hypothetical character of knowing, the use of reflective intelligence as a way of solving problems. Given the rapidly changing character of the postmodern world, we cannot retreat from the use of technology and science.

Today, some are overwhelmed by a failure of nerve. If people are to adapt to the future, then education in the sciences—physical, biological, behavioral and social—must be a required part of every course of study, along with other courses in the liberal arts. But the emphasis must not be simply upon science as a static form of knowledge but rather as an instrument for control: science as a method of modifying the natural and cultural world. It is not scientific discovery that is to be feared but the misuses of scientific applications, their abuses by dehumanizing social and political forces.

Concomitant with this cultivation of scientific imagination is the urgent need for moral education, a continual process of value examination. By moral education, I do *not* mean indoctrination, inculcation, behavioral conditioning, but rather, as the psychologist Lawrence Kohlberg labels it, the process of cognitive moral growth.

Moral values, in the best sense, are the product of a process of evaluation that human beings engage in as they respond to the challenges in the environment: an appeal to traditional standards is never enough, though they be enshrined in religion, law, or custom. Rather, we need to learn how to deliberate about the things that we hold to be good, bad, right, and wrong, worth cherishing and appreciating. Mere emotion or passion is not enough; we need to learn how to deal with our values cognitively, by means of critical intelligence. According to Dewey, values should be treated as hypotheses upon which we act; they grow out of concrete situations and are most wisely grounded when they are fashioned in terms of the needs of the situation and their consequences in the world.

Given the strains of modern life, we cannot always provide young people with ready-made answers, and certainly not ready-made professions, careers, or occupations. No one can anticipate fully the future course of an individual's or society's existence; the best that we can provide is some resiliency, some help in developing cognitive moral awareness, as a way of life, a means by which the person can respond effectively to life in light of a deeper understanding of it. We need a whole new curriculum, one that deals not simply with what is or has been but with what is likely to be, given our effort and persistence.

Thus, surely one of the basic goals of education of the future—perhaps the most important—is the need to develop resourceful people, self-reliant, resilient, capable of critical and responsible thinking, able to adjust and adapt, hopefully with some sense of wisdom, some understanding of their own capabilities and power but also aware of constraints and limitations. Individuals especially need to know how to judge truth claims objectively, how to be skeptical, how to avoid gullibility, nincompoopery, fraudulent, and counterfeit promises, how to live with ambiguities and uncertainties. But if we are to cope with the future we also need some audacity and courage—a willingness to introduce new and daring departures. We must dare to dream, to create new visions of what can be. In a sense, we may become what we wish— if the wish is informed and implemented by a firm will, patience, and energy. As we face new problems, we need to introduce new means and new alternatives. Thus, creative imagination as well as deliberation are essential prerequisites for coping.

IV

In talking about education for the future, I am not unmindful of the need for the schools and teachers to deal with the individual learner. There ought to be electives; affective education is important, and we need to develop in students an appreciation for learning. It is not merely dead subject matter that we want to transmit; we want to deal with live human beings who need to be motivated.

But I fear that the recent movement for affective education— sometimes called "humanistic" and which is exemplified by Paul Goodman, John Holt, Edgar Friedenberg, and others—has emphasized the immediate experiences of the individual student to the detriment of his cognitive skills. There has been a tendency to depart from the hard and vigorous cultivation of the arts of intelligence—the difficult effort of mastery and achievement. We need to use our intelligence to judge claims about the world, to describe and explain what we encounter, and to develop normative judgments that will guide our decisions and conduct.

The task of education of the future is to enable us to cope with new and unexpected situations and challenges. But this can be done only if we liberate individuals from repression, discipline, and habits, and encourage impulse, creativity, and exploration. We need to draw forth and nourish innate spontaneity and curiosity, to satisfy a hierarchy of needs and drives. But part of human development and growth involves moral growth. This is not, I reiterate, obedience to dicta or law but a reflective process of deliberation, a recognition and appreciation, not only of our own mature needs but also those of others. Thus disciplined thinking, self-regulating and demanding, is required.

Moral education, as I conceive it, must begin in elementary school, continue in high school, reach fruition in college, but still be part of the ongoing life of a man or woman. Moral education cannot be left solely to religion or the home, as in the past; nor is it solely the task of philosophy departments, but it should permeate the curriculum. In the best sense, value education involves freedom and autonomy, the capacity to think critically and creatively about life's problems, about options, alternatives, and choices. Among the frontiers of moral concern will be the definition and evaluation of the ethics of freedom and equal rights, the implications of scientific discovery, and the creation of a world community in which our commitment to humankind as a whole, over and beyond narrow loyalties and parochial allegiances, is possible.

Freedom from authority, dogmas, ideology, or tradition in the area of morality need not mean subjective caprice, promiscuity, or anarchism in taste. It can lead to objectively relative and responsible judgments, based on human experience and reflection, value judgments worked out in shared experience. But if this is to occur, then it is essential that the *method* of critical valuation be cultivated, not only in the schools, but in all of the institutions of society.

In summary, possibly the most important needs for education in the liberating arts in the future will be to develop at all levels, including the area of adult education, the ability to adapt to a changing world; to expand our understanding of our own world, particularly by means of the sciences; to cultivate the skills of intelligence, especially as they bear on moral judgment and decision; and, finally, to develop autonomous individuals capable of withstanding the shock of rapid change and social conflict. The challenges to education have never been greater.

The Desirability of Pulling in One's Horns

Mortimer R. Kadish

Case Western Reserve University

If curriculum problems are to be manageable, educators must lower their expectations of what formal education can accomplish. In particular, those of us in higher education ought to get a better grip on our professional presumption. Such at least is the possibility I should like to present, along with some of its consequences.

The logical heart of our excessive expectations and our presumption, I would suggest, consists in a failure to distinguish adequately the ends-in-view of our educational strategies from the measures of utility (the principles of evaluation), in virtue of which we appraise the success of those strategies. Sometimes we take measures of utility as terminal points of action rather than as standards for judging action. Then, when those measures appear justified, we formulate educational ends radically disproportionate to the resources available for achieving them. We tend to act quite as though, in educating, we faced a known and fixed population under constant conditions and enjoyed, as in a game, the resources of knowledge and the opportunity to create in that population the qualities we favor, if only we devise the right rules.

Professor Sidney Hook talks in his paper about the "minimum indispensables that constitute the curricular core of general education." I take it that a "minimum indispensable" is of necessity an end-in-view. Yet granting that Professor Hook's "indispensables" are not vacuous simply because they are vague, it must surely be obvious that to number them among the proper ends of a general education in the sense that they are significantly approachable (say with a C+) through the available means of formal education represents what Samuel Johnson, in another context, called the triumph of hope over experience. Consider, for example, the "intelligent awareness of the great historical, economic, and social forces shaping our society" to which Professor Hook commends our attention. When one considers oneself and at least the majority of one's colleagues, the presumption of higher educators professing to provide such an awareness becomes almost too much to credit. Nor do "significant facts and theories about the conflicts of values and ideals in our times" constitute a less improbable burden for ourselves and our students. Even "methodological sophistication," measured in relation to the demands to be placed upon it (which in the contemporary world become increasingly grave), appears a very chancy thing, whatever the value of courses in logic and scientific method. For, clearly, such a "sophistication" does not designate a universal tool or key, but constitutes a class name for a very great variety of perceptions and approaches that we simply do not come by en bloc. Such "ends" as the above do not comprise objectives that are literally "minimal indispensables," or there is no such thing as a liberal education; they are at best a partial list of criteria by which to measure the success or failure of educational strategies, and among which, indeed, we might have to make choices in concrete situations.

To put the matter more bluntly, sensitive, civilized, intelligent men are not created in the classrooms even of higher educators, anymore than are statesmen or imaginative artists. In the abstract, of course, everybody knows that. The trick is to act upon that knowledge in formulating curricula, given the conceptual slide from measure of utility (or principal of evaluation) to end-in-view. It is only by making major assumptions concerning the efficacy of institutional procedures on actual populations that we are encouraged to look with much hope upon the advantages of breaking out of the first two years of a general education into the *Lebensraum* of continuing education. Only by forgetting our own limitations and the limitations of our students do we ignore the fact that interdisciplinary education of the sort contemplated in "general education" is actually many times more demanding than the traditional disciplinary education, since it assumes those traditional disciplines. And perhaps a similar diagnosis applies to educators seeking methodological sophistication through an ever renewed emphasis on redesigning science instruction, as though they had never heard of the limitations of the transfer of training or considered the pervasive naivete of so many of their science-trained colleagues. Such are the tactics of desperation; so at least they seem, if we take as a real possibility the desirability of pulling in our horns.

Is it indeed the case that continuing and interdisciplinary education and increased sophistication in the teaching of science and social science are intended merely to provide just a little bit of sophistication, just a few possible "facts" relevant to the society in which we live, just the bare possibility of a rational view of the universe, just a small advance on the often monumental deficiency in communication skills of the average, or indeed, above-average, high-school student? Not merely the language of "minimal indispensables" but much of the tenor of the recent discussion at this symposium on the philosophy of the curriculum suggests otherwise. The explicit failure to make focal in the evaluation of instrumentalities the particular world in which these instrumentalities are to be employed suggests a massive self-deception. The very abstractness of the discussion suggests not only that too many of us are seeking not merely to make some small contribution to the realization of certain values, but suggests that we seek, however unconsciously, if not a royal road to knowledge, at least a middle-class road: a road smoothed, straightened and cleared, requiring for its traversal only that the student put forward a reasonable effort.

In a word, the "philosophy of the curriculum" seems to slide full tilt into the old affliction of a utopianism that attempts to solve present and envisageable problems through strategies exclusively determined by the value of the end they are supposed to achieve and independently of the costs and probabilities of achieving that end. Max Weber would have spoken of an ethics of ultimate ends rather than of an ethic of responsibility in characterizing our behavior. Dewey might have referred to a failure to grasp the fundamental connections between ends and means. However one interprets or explains the phenomenon, the consequences are serious.

The most immediate consequence, particularly among persons unaware of the presumption of their expectations, is to substitute a sense of guilt for an appraisal of circumstances in determining action. The perception that we have failed to achieve the ends for which we hold ourselves responsible, impels a never-ending quest for new means for achieving those ends. Repeated failure, even with newly devised means, only serves to increase the sense of guilt. There follows a tendency to push aside another major objective of institutions of higher learning: the education of the educators themselves. For, after all, although the acknowledgment is no longer popular, most educators in institutions of higher learning realize that such institutions exist also for the sake of the educators, insofar as they participate in the processes of advancing and celebrating human culture. That purpose comes to be dispraised, subordinated in the quest for new devices, new gimmicks. Were the ends we formulated for ourselves more realistic—were they in effect ends-in-view which, achieved, would lead to still further explorations—educators might very well find it unnecessary to displace their obligation to what has been called the "community of scholars" for the sake of an improbable vow. Recognizing that even the curricula of universities constitute only one factor in the construction of a liberal education, we might even be able to fix for ourselves such ends that their pursuit would be of greater use to our students than our pursuit, unqualified by modesty, of ultimate ends.

Consider, for example, the current emphasis upon interdisciplinary education as a way to achieve the ends of liberal education in, say, the first two years of college. If curricular reorganization in an interdisciplinary direction, in the interest of generality and synthesis, spreads the undergraduate's education thin, one risks not merely the failure of still another experiment to accomplish much, but the actual nourishing in student populations of an attitude that already gives good cause to fear. Having, in effect if not in intention, been led to think that a relatively limited expenditure of time and effort might reasonably be expected to yield the basic intellectual and aesthetic equipment of a civilized man, the student predictably concludes that that which is difficult, subtle, or in any way beyond his individual capacities is either superfluous or insulting—in a word, elitist. Presumption on the part of educators has met its fitting response in presumption on the part of students. A general education has defeated the ends of general education.

On the other hand, there is at least the significant chance that another tactic with more modest ends—intensive inquiry into limited subject matters, inquiry aimed at distinguishing the complex structure and problematic intricacy of those subject matters—might encourage a respect for the knowledge or art that the student himself lacks and may in fact only be able to dimly appreciate. Let no one interested in the furtherance of civilized values in society condemn the awareness of limitations as an end-in-view of liberal education.

Observe one last consequence of that combination of goodwill and excessive expectations in higher education that induces us to take our standards of evaluation as our ends-in-view. Since all those standards are legitimately defensible, we are led to seek educational strategies that will satisfy them all—not one or two of the ends of a liberal or general education, but each and every one of them. Indeed, is one "minimum indispensable" less a "minimum indispensable" than another? Still, barring a prior commitment to utopianism in education, it seems hardly self-evident that a rational strategy might not prefer to concentrate its resources on strategies valuable in terms of one or two such "minimum indispensables" rather than in terms of all of them. Utopianism relinquished, to accept such a strategy requires only the realization that it is in the very nature of the educator's predicament to be working with limited resources against the greatest odds. Utopianism, therefore, does not simply fail; it leads us to dodge the undodgable problem, which is to order our priorities.

In sum, I would suggest that presumption on the part of educators —utopianism—has led to a radical misunderstanding of the problem of organizing a curriculum. The task of organizing a curriculum can best be understood, I would suggest, as the careful and infinitely complicated adjustment of means to ends in a world we never made, over which we have but slight control. The task of the "philosophy of the curriculum," then, becomes the task of examining the general conditions of such an adjustment.

On Sharpening the Horns

Sidney Hook
New York University

I am frankly puzzled by Professor Kadish's comments on my paper. It may be that some of his difficulties with it arise from the fact that he is reacting to a summary of my views rather than to the full text. However, the drift of his paper is clear enough, in that he believes that my conception of general liberal-arts education is too ambitious and too abstract and utopian to be effective with any except some highly gifted students. I do not believe such a conclusion is warranted except on the basis of empirical evidence. To the extent that historical educational practices approached my recommendations at Columbia College, Washington Square College of New York University (the Unified Study Curriculum), Amherst, and Dartmouth a generation or two ago, the educational results were not at all disheartening although they pointed to the need for improvement, especially in the techniques of teaching and individual guidance. Concern with the latter during that period was almost uniformly subordinated within the faculties to an interest in productive scholarship. One of the factors that contributed to the decline of the general-education movement was the failure to appreciate the central importance of gifted and dedicated teachers in its operation.

The test of my curricular proposals, I grant, will ultimately be found in the consequences of the educational practices based upon them. My paper is essentially an argument in behalf of adopting them in an experimental spirit. This seems to me to have been overlooked or ignored by Professor Kadish. His contention that I have failed to distinguish adequately between "the ends-in-view of our educational strategies" and "the principles of evaluation" in terms of which "we appraise the success of these strategies" is unsupported by argument or evidence. Obviously, unless we believe that anything goes, we must have some educational ends-in-view to build a curriculum. These ends-in-view must be justified by some underlying conception of what a liberal education is or what it is desirable that educated men and women in modern times should know. How we measure the extent to which students progress in acquiring the knowledge, the skills, and the sensitivities we seek to impart through the studies designed to implement our educational ends-in-view is a technical matter, the details of which vary from field to field. We need not expect students to acquire a complete mastery of a discipline—we need not even be conceptually clear about what constitutes complete mastery—to be able to determine whether progress has been made. What constitutes success or failure, adequate or inadequate performance is still another question that depends upon a number of variables that need not be explored here.

But emphatically it does not follow, as Professor Kadish seems to believe, that we cannot establish norms that are "significantly approachable," whether for purposes of grading or certification. The belief that we should permit universal *access* to higher education is utopian only if we fail to specify that not all doors to it open *in*, and if we are unwilling to recognize failures. The right to an education, and to the formal schooling necessary to implement that right, does not entail that everyone has a right to the same kind of education or schooling at the same time, place, and rate. If we avoid invidious racial, sexual, religious, or national discriminations, there is no ethical objection to making relevant *educational* discriminations. In his effort to avoid utopianism, Professor Kadish seems to me to be unduly cynical about the possibility of establishing goals that are "significantly approachable."

More pointed and questionable are Kadish's specific criticisms of some of the ends-in-view I listed as integral to a liberal general education. In justifying areas of required studies against those who argue for a complete elective system in which students should be free at the very outset of their higher education to study what they please, and as a guide to curriculum building, I wrote: "Every student has a need to become intelligently aware of how his society functions, of the great historical, economic, and social forces shaping its future, of the alternatives of development still open to us, of the problems, predicaments, and programs he and his fellow citizens must face."

To which Professor Kadish responds: "When one considers oneself and at least the majority of one's colleagues, the presumption of higher educators professing to provide such an awareness becomes almost too much to credit." Professor Kadish's modesty here may be too excessive. However, even if we accept his assessment about his own capacities as objectively justified, I find his skepticism about the majority of his colleagues "almost too much to credit." Can't they make their students intelligently aware of what they themselves are studying in the area of social studies? If they cannot, they should not be teaching undergraduates but doing research. Surely Professor Kadish does not interpret me as implying that either he or I or the majority of his colleagues know the answers to our current problems or what the shape of the future will be. We don't know the answers, but have we no idea of what the relevant problems are? Whatever the future of our society will be, it certainly will be influenced in part by the pressure of population, the development of technology, the nationalisms of the Third World, the growing scarcity of natural resources, the threats of nuclear weaponry, and a number of other phenomena whose priority and weight it is not necessary to determine to justify including them in the course of study in this field.

I went on to add that "Every student needs to be informed, not only of significant facts and theories about nature, society, and the human psyche, but also of the conflict of values and ideals in our time, of the great maps of life, the paths to salvation or damnation under which human beings are enrolled." Professor Kadish drily observes that such study does not "constitute a less improbable burden for ourselves and our students." Why should such study be burdensome to serious teachers? The logic and ethics of democracy, the challenges to it running all the way from Plato to modern forms of totalitarianism, the nature of capitalism, socialism, and the welfare state, the role of ideologies—all are themes that are intellectually important and deserve study in depth. A teacher would have to be almost a genius of a bore to make the study of these themes burdensome to students.

Professor Kadish is even dissatisfied with my proposal to offer studies that would help students "acquire some methodological sophistication that should sharpen their sense for evidence, relevance, and canons of validity." Although he admits the increasing and grave necessity for such sophistication in the contemporary world, Professor Kadish seems to reject the proposal on the ground that its achievement "appears a very chancy thing." But would he not grant that studies of logic in action, of statistical fallacies, of types and kinds of misleading rhetoric would make the achievement of methodological sophistication less chancy? There is always the difficulty about transference of training from one field to another, but the assumption justifying the study I propose is that it would make students less vulnerable to various kinds of buncombe than if they were given no training in logical analysis and intensive reading of texts.

The gravamens of Professor Kadish's criticism would be clearer if he had indicated in some detail what he would offer in place of liberal general education or in what way his curricular proposals for liberal general education would differ from mine. He seems to be under the impression that all education contemplated when the term "general education" is used must be "interdisciplinary." I make no such assumption except with reference to areas of study in the social and historical disciplines; but even here, whether "courses" offered in different fields are to be interdisciplinary or restricted to one discipline depends upon local conditions—the character of the teachers available and the special interests and capacities of students. What he does not appear to appreciate sufficiently is the variety of ways or courses through which the required areas of study may be taught.

Professor Kadish makes several observations with which one can agree without drawing the implications he derives from them. "To put the matter bluntly, sensitive, civilized, intelligent men are not created in the classrooms even of higher educators any more than are statesmen or imaginative artists." Granted, and one should add "any more than are good physicians, jurists, engineers, journalists, teachers, businessmen, labor leaders, legislators—or even parents." Because we cannot do everything in the classroom it does not follow that we cannot do much or that the possible range of achievement is unimportant. It may even be true that students do not learn how to read, write, and figure exclusively through classroom instruction. But the kind of classroom instruction they get can make a great deal of difference. If higher or tertiary education is conceived as something more inclusive than merely vocational or professional training, it does assume that a liberal general education will make it more likely that men and women who have experienced it will become more "sensitive, civilized, and intelligent persons" than if they were denied it. It does not assume that liberal general education pays off in money or social mobility or prestige. Even when it does, these are purely extrinsic effects. It is the quality of the educational experience itself that justifies it and its consequences in enriching the meaning of life.

Professor Kadish is mistaken in interpreting the educational ends-in-view of liberal general education as if they were abstract, timeless ideals comparable to Max Weber's ultimate ethical ends. This would not be true even of the values that influence our choice of educational goals. They are, like all ethical values, penultimate not ultimate, related to the nature of men and women in this time and in this society, with its promises and threats of change. Nor is it true that the educational ends-in-view have been formulated "independently of the costs and probabilities" of striving for them. Not only have these been taken into account, subject to corrections that further experiences will suggest, but the costs and probabilities of *not* striving for them, of continuing the chaotic pattern of the educational status quo, have also been considered. It is not utopian to believe that we can do better than we have been doing, even if it turns out that despite everything enlightened and dedicated teachers do, the upshot is unsatisfactory. The consequences of the educational means we use will certainly affect our educational ends, but the educational means used must be sought in the light of the educational ends we have reflectively endorsed. The normative character of the philosophy of the curriculum is no less normative because it is modified by the facts of experience and educational experiment.

I do not believe that, with reference to my curricular proposals for liberal general education, John Dewey "might have referred to a failure to grasp the fundamental connection between ends and means." For these proposals, with unessential modifications that reflected the problems of a different decade, were contained in my *Education for Modern Man*, which received John Dewey's public approval.

The Humanities as Scholarship and a Branch of Knowledge

Paul Oskar Kristeller
Columbia University

In my opinion, we have taken the concept and meaning of the humanities pretty much for granted but have failed to stress a very essential aspect of the matter. The term "humanities" carries with it a number of connotations and overtones that are hard to avoid and for many people are very pleasant but thoroughly misleading; it points to a kind of genteel education, but also to a "humanist" philosophy or religion that stresses the autonomy of human values, and finally to humanitarianism and all the good causes it includes. But for better or for worse, during the last two centuries a large body of knowledge has been accumulated in the historical, philological, and philosophical disciplines and has acquired a considerable place in research and in university instruction as well as in scholarly publications. This body of scholarly disciplines has, in recent decades, been designated as the humanities, as distinct from the natural sciences and from the social sciences.

This area includes not only history proper in its political, economic, social, and ecclesiastic aspects, but also the history and general theory of law and religion, of languages and literatures, of arts and music, of the sciences and philosophy, and of many more aspects of human civilization. This large area of knowledge includes a good many solid and well-established facts and insights, and it has developed fairly rigorous rules of evidence and methods of verification, where the certain and the probable may be clearly distinguished from the possible and improbable or false, and where the area of what is known is being steadily expanded as against the area of what remains unknown or controversial. We should be quite justified if we decided to recognize these disciplines as sciences, as all modern languages with the exception of English actually do.

This large and important body of knowledge must be steadily increased through further research, for which we need research institutions; it must be made available, for which we need scholarly publications; and it must be transmitted through the training of younger scholars, for which we need graduate instruction.

At the present time, further progress in these fields is threatened in this country and also elsewhere by several factors. Each field until recently has pursued its course pretty much in isolation, and the notion of interdisciplinary research and instruction has been developing but slowly. Historical scholars have not yet developed a conscious or common methodology, and most philosophers have not been of much help to them. We need a philosophy of historical scholarship and of the humanities to match the philosophy of the sciences that has made so much progress in recent years. Such a philosophy of the humanities should study the actual procedures and accomplishments of historical scholarship, instead of trying to insist on certain specific problems, such as historical explanation, that are at best marginal, or of imposing on the historian the task of discovering general laws, a task for which he is evidently not equipped. As I see it, it is not the task of the historian to explain facts directly known to him, or to make generalizations about them, but rather to infer specific or general facts from the data that are given directly to him. These data are artifacts, documents, and texts. A document is not explained; it is used as evidence for facts or events or developments that may be inferred from it. A text is explained or interpreted, not in terms of causes or general laws, but in terms of its intellectual meaning and in relation to other texts, documents, or facts. What we need is a methodology and a philosophy of the humanities, as it has been attempted by several historians from J. G. Droysen to Max Weber and Marrou, and by historically minded philosophers such as Wilhelm Dilthey, Heinrich Rickert, and Ernst Cassirer, Benedetto Croce, Giovanni Gentile, and R. G. Collingwood. We also need a general philosophy that assigns to history its proper place in the intellectual universe, as Vico, Hegel, and Heidegger tried to do. I leave it open whether and to what extent philosophy itself should be treated as a part of the humanities, except for the history of philosophy and the philosophy of history, which obviously have their place among or with the humanities.

Moreover, we are confronted with an almost complete lack of

public understanding for the humanistic disciplines, their methods, and goals. This lack of understanding, which in some instances is accompanied by outright hostility, pervades large areas of the general public, as well as the world of politics and of the news media; it also extends into the world of literature and the arts and even into the natural and social sciences, and hence even into the very institutions that should be obliged to sustain the humanities, such as colleges and universities (not to speak of secondary schools), libraries, and foundations. The scholarly community has been notoriously unsuccessful in overcoming this public indifference, and has even shown signs of yielding to irrelevant demands and pressures. This unfortunate situation was tolerable apparently as long as the humanities were allowed to lead a sheltered existence in the universities or under private patronage. But this same situation has become outright dangerous at the present time, when everything seems to depend on public funds and when everything we plan and do must be explained not only to university and foundation officials but also to journalists and politicians, if we want to gain the material support needed to carry on our work. The public cry for relevance, or in earlier years for actuality and usefulness, has never been countered by a public statement about the intrinsic and lasting value of scholarship, as it should have been. In the face of the current insistence on the contemporary as against the past, I venture to go one step further: the more historical scholarship turns to the recent past and to the present, the more difficult it is to maintain standards of critical and objective scholarship and the easier it becomes to slip into journalism and partisan argument.

In trying to explain our cause to the public, we should not make any false claims, which are often associated with the humanities. We cannot solve the political, economic, or social problems of the contemporary world. We do not make anybody happy and we do not bring about a moral or material improvement of the world. We do not even attain our own happiness in our work all of the time, for this work involves a good deal of boredom and drudgery, as every work does. We merely face this drudgery with the hope and expectation that we may find out something that interests us and attain some valid knowledge.

Our work can reach the general public, as distinct from other scholars, only insofar as it is being diffused and popularized. On this issue, a few points ought to be made clear. Scholarship and popularization are not the same thing, and the widespread confusion between them should be rejected, as should all attempts, most of them not disinterested, to substitute popularization for scholarship. On the other hand, we should welcome popularization, and even participate in it—not because it is the same thing, but because the valid results of scholarship, as those of the sciences, should be made available to the general public in a form in which they can be understood. For this reason, the popular books and textbooks on our subjects should be written by good and well-trained scholars and not by journalists or other professional popularizers. And all instruction, from the colleges down to the secondary and elementary schools, should reflect the valid results of the latest and best scholarship, and the basic elements of its method, on a level that is understandable to the student. In other words, we need an educational system where the student on each level receives a clear and forceful introduction to the humanistic disciplines, their results and methods, and where the available body of valid information is not replaced by cheap surrogates or altogether omitted, as is now so often the case.

To conclude, we need a careful definition of the humanities as a cycle of scholarly disciplines and a body of knowledge, separating original research and advanced instruction from the various levels of popularization (which are necessary and important) and eliminating the illusion that the humanities have anything to do with "genteel" talk, with "humanist" philosophy, or with humanitarian causes. A failure to do so will not only perpetuate and compound our intellectual confusion; under the present circumstances, it will bring about the actual loss to the humanities (and the misuse for other purposes) of institutions, of jobs, and of funds that were intended and reserved for our enterprise. In failing to preserve our standards, our goals, and also our privileges, we shall betray our students and all younger scholars, who will be called upon to continue our work and who will suffer severely if we fail to defend and transmit the tradition and the heritage that is properly theirs.

Questions of Viability
in Nontraditional Education

Herbert I. London
New York University

Before I attempt to discuss some of the conditions for the viability of nontraditional programs let me start my remarks with a brief parable.

> A starving grasshopper ran into a very healthy tiger and asked, "How can I be as healthy as you?" "It's easy," the tiger replied, "find an unwary antelope, kill it, and eat the meat around the carcass." Incredulously the grasshopper inquired, "How can I possibly kill an antelope?" The tiger looked at him for a moment and said, "I gave you the idea. Now you take care of the details."

The moral of the story is that spokesmen with general solutions should be distrusted.

Despite the fact that I am committed to experimental programs, I do not believe they can be viable until some aspects of traditional education are incorporated into nontraditional study. Philosophically I am committed to a set of transcendent values associated with Western and Eastern traditions. Although we might disagree on some of the sources that constitute this tradition, I think there is a body of thought that an educated man should be exposed to. In the last decade we have pushed pragmatism so far, particularly in so-called nontraditional studies, that if a student can do something or change something he is deemed worthy of a degree whether or not he is an educated man. The liberal-arts tradition has been so maligned that for me to use the phrase "great books" or "an educated man" at a conference on nontraditional study seems incongruous at best and finally bizarre, if you've been raised on a pablum called "progressive education." But from what I have observed, the experiments that work are precisely those that do not lose sight of historical antecedents and a vision of the "educated man."

Education is not existential. Whether we like it or not we are tied organically to the past. To neglect that, means that in every class or alternative-learning session we merely reinvent the wheel. Either we recognize and use the past or we are caught in the seamless web of enigmas and relativism. Dewey notwithstanding, I believe that Aristotle was right: education of either traditional or nontraditional character must pass on the previous contributions of human thought.

Invariably experimental programs ignore this tradition. In the name of all that is new or relevant, Plato and Confucius become the flotsam and jetsam of history and Malcolm X and Hermann Hesse the only heroes. In the name of egalitarianism, academics ignore their roles and let students decide what is worth reading. And in the name of self-actualization an encounter session leads to personal growth while an evening reading *The City of God* is considered an exercise in futility.

Curiously some of the most exciting experiments are occurring at relatively "straight" institutions. At Columbia University and at the Claremont Colleges an effort is being made to combine in some coherent way career objectives with those social and philosophical values implicit in every discipline. That seems to me an experiment too long in coming and too often ignored by the very experimenters who can apply its lessons.

But just as nontraditional studies disavow tradition, they often simultaneously dismiss traditional standards. I am, of course, not referring to a grading system that lost its legitimacy some time ago, but to requirements such as research and papers, and skills such as the tools of analysis and communication. It seems to me that while it is desirable to do things other than sit in a lecture hall, it is undesirable to ignore academic proprieties. There is, for example, no reason to believe that because a student engages in field study he has necessarily had a learning experience. The fact is that without sufficient preparation many field experiences are useless. George Bernard Shaw once said, "You can take an ass around the world and he won't become a horse." And you can take a student on every conceivable field trip, but without some perspective he too will remain an ass. Similarly, credit for life experience is an idea whose time has come but whose legitimacy is questionable. No one, I think, questions the validity of offering advanced standing to self-taught scholars, to an Eric Hoffer, for example. But most students I've encountered do not have Hoffer's study regimen. Do we categorically give credit to someone who has travelled, or is married, or has children, or is a good cook? The only rule of thumb that gives this practice justification is when the experience translates into the desired outcomes of a course.

Perhaps the most flawed assumption that experimenters often have is an unmitigated faith in freedom. "If he wants to do it, he'll learn," is a refrain I hear so often I do not even bother to challenge its illogic. What I have encountered is so much freedom in experimental programs that students spend all their time deciding what to do and as a consequence are even more inert than their counterparts in traditional institutions. Let me cite a recent case in point.

A twenty-two-year-old student from California stopped by my office quite unexpectedly and said he wanted to rap. Since I spend half of my waking hours talking to students I found his request not at all unusual. However, despite an inclination to rap he had nothing to say. "Why are you in the East?" I inquired. "Oh, just bumming. You see I'm a playwright and I've got to get my thing together." "Well, I'd be happy to discuss drama with you or read your plays. I am interested in Brecht, Pinter, and Grotowski." "Oh man, I don't even know those cats," he volunteered, "and I haven't written anything yet. I've got to see the world before I write." "But don't you think you should at least study your craft and read other playwrights?" I naively asked. "Oh no, that would just screw up my head," he replied. "I've got to keep myself open." Of one thing I was quite assured: his head was very open. He was probably not representative of students in experimental programs, but neither was he atypical. Freedom for him and for many with his world view means no constraints, no regimen, no serious study. André Gide wrote, "Art is born of discipline and dies of freedom."

When Sidney Hook wrote his book *The Paradoxes of Freedom* (1962), he noted that a freedom cult can develop an orthodoxy so rigid that it inhibits the very action it was designed to promote. How, it might be asked, can students write novels when they have never read novels? Do we produce filmmakers by merely giving our students cameras? And do we determine who our social scientists will be by how well meaning they are? The test of experimentation should be the same as in traditional programs: How knowledgeable are students and how well can they use scholarly tools? It would naturally be desirable if they also matured, developed, actualized (you can insert your own cliché), but these are the unanticipated consequences of an education. The fact is, despite everything written by adherents of the human-potential movement, psychologists do not know how to plan for self-actualization.

It also seems equally obvious to me that a professor who presumably knows his discipline can offer a student some counsel. Student initiative should be a goal of nontraditional programs, but this does not happen by willing it or by leaving students to their own devices. Students must be nurtured, advised, criticized until they are prepared for independent study. Independence suggests a divorce from the professor, a state of confidence engendered by the mastery of skills. That does not happen so easily. Students should earn independence in the same way a tadpole works to leave the pond and separate himself from the limitations of his youth. He works to be free.

What is the BA for experimenters? Is it nothing more than a student declaration of self-awareness? Is it a one-project certificate conferred on the student because he writes a satisfactory twenty-five page paper? It seems to me that without a reliance on some traditional standards—for example, competencies, knowledge, and skills—there is no way to measure performance except by intuition. And that is an article of faith, not scholarship. If judgments are to be that arbitrary, I would just as soon rely on the *I Ching* or random selection for a graduating class. I am not being facetious. At several recent conferences I have been told that my "uptight standards" do not distinguish those who are good. Since I am often unable to distinguish between good and not-so-good except at the extremes and since I am not sure how goodness relates to degree recipients, I asked my critics to tell me how their judgments are made. One fellow looked at me incredulously and said, "Man, you know, you just know." You can see why I need the *I Ching*.

Since I am an inveterate cynic, it is not at all coincidental that I associate the rise of alternative educational systems with the financial crunch in higher education. Although this is by no means the only reason for its rather sudden rise or the reason that its disciples honor, I am convinced that in many institutions, including my own, it was the overriding reason for the acceptance of nontraditional programs. I should also add that if I am right, most of these experimental programs will last only so long as their costs are minimal and their ability to produce income formidable. But is this sufficient reason to experiment, and if it is, can an experiment last when it is established on this basis? Educational experimentation should have a logic of its own, a logic unrelated to financial vicissitudes or even student demand. And despite some notable efforts in this direction—for example, the Carnegie Commission Report and the Newman Report—I remain unconvinced by the arguments. So, might I add, are most of my colleagues in this field and many of the students I meet.

Now that I have told you why I think many nontraditional programs are not viable, please indulge me while I speculate on how I think they can be. Any system that has legitimacy depends on a shared-

value orientation. Before 1960 most colleges shared a view of the baccalaureate degree that included the accumulation of credit, the satisfaction of a major requirement, a final project or dissertation, and an
oral exam or its equivalent. There were of course exceptions to this
rule, but this was the pattern. A degree meant something. Whether you
accepted it or admired the standard is irrelevant; it did have common
coinage.

This is obviously no longer the case. And to complicate the issue,
each degree from an experimental college has a special meaning all its
own. Even within programs supposedly sharing a philosophy, it is obvious that no two institutions share similar degree requirements. I
should point out that as a pluralist, I am not advocating national and
homogeneous standards; I am merely suggesting that experimental
programs that presumably share some common goals have some common degree standards. But the fact is, if there is an alternative-educa-
tion movement in this country, it suffers from incurable entropy. What
it translates into, of course, is an additional burden on students. A law-
school admissions officer recently told me that he ignores college
transcripts and undergraduate records. When there are so many idio-
syncratic record systems and when each college has a different value
orientation, the only thing that counts is the LSAT scores. At least that
has the advantage of some general meaning. I find this conclusion understandable, but still depressing. I also realize that with the prolifer-
ation of many new programs, each with its own philosophy, the trend
toward standardized testing will increase. Here is the ultimate paradox: in order to accommodate a variety of needs, we have been forced
to rely on a national standard.

The answer—and it is certainly chimerical at this point—is to develop a shared-value system about the goals and characteristics of a
degree program as distinguished from a nontraditional program. The
particulars of the model, which might include such issues as credits or
another system of evaluating achievement, how to allocate life-experi-
ence credit, the utility of field experience, a minimal liberal-arts background, the qualifications and expectations of a faculty, still do not
result in a philosophical harmony on the meaning of nontraditional
study. But the resolution of these particulars is the route to greater
understanding.

I am convinced that in the effort to merge work and formal study
lies the philosophical framework for experimental programs. But the
leaders of this movement should know why work is critical in the educational amalgam. They must be precise about what it can do and they
must find a way to measure its effect. I think we share some disenchantment when the liberal-arts student describes his degree as an

aggregate of one hundred and twenty-eight points. Yet, however specious its meaning, that *is* a description. What, I ask, are the assumptions in a nontraditional program and how are its degrees conferred? Until such time as nontraditional study has common assumptions—not attitudes, I might add—it is absurd to discuss its viability. Napoleon once said, "A form of government that is not the result of a long sequence of shared experiences, efforts, and endeavors can never take root." So it is with experimental programs.

Acknowledgment is gratefully made to the *College Student Journal* for permission to reprint "Questions of Viability in Nontraditional Education" by Herbert I. London.

On Interdisciplinary Education

Howard B. Radest
Ramapo College

I

Talk about education is, traditionally, afflicted by the use of faddist and uncritical rhetoric. And so these days, the word "interdisciplinary" becomes one to conjure with. To be "relevant" and "with it" is to intone "interdisciplinary" along with a select group of other magical formulas. It seems to make no difference what these kinds of words mean so long as they are used with proper reverence and grammatical nicety. Unfortunately, when they are taken seriously, as in seeking in them a basis for educational change or curricular experiment, this ritualism becomes costly. Since no one wants to admit to the use of empty language, what follows is not a confession of error but a complex dance of "interpretation" and "negotiation," masking the fact that the emperor really wears no clothes.

Were this use of signal words only an academic's game, we could remain indifferent and even a bit amused at our continuing folly. Since we do in fact have doubts about what it is we ought to be learning and teaching and doubts about whether our educational habits for doing these are any longer useful, we cannot afford to indulge our academicism while going on with business as usual. And I suspect that behind the signal "interdisciplinary" there just might be a reality worth probing. That means, of course, that we dare not presume to take its meaning for granted or regard it as a self-evident term.

II

I hear a good deal of talk about "interdisciplinary" study at Ramapo College, since it was founded with the "mission" of developing "interdisciplinary" and "innovative" undergraduate education. In all the talk, I can locate at least three primary meanings for the term. The first is an additive conception and merely labels traditional educational practices in a new way. Interdisciplinarity means only that the experience of a student shall consist in "exposure" to several bounded fields of study. Catalogue devices like "distribution" requirements are intended to give content to this definition. Once it is so defined, those who hold this meaning can believe that they have implemented the policy it contains in good faith. When they grow a bit more daring— even reformist—they may insist on a somewhat wider net of "requirements." Ultimately, they may even begin to talk "general education" language, by which they tend to mean that the net has a certain essential and sanctioned configuration.

This first meaning contains an implicit pedagogy, a rather naive psychology, and an irresponsible academic ethic. The concept of "exposure" identifies the entire province of learning as some form of benign infection. Were "exposure" really an adequate pedagog, then we could simply resign all educational institutions to the ubiquitous media, insuring only that they were sufficiently content-filled and adequate to the job of creating educational epidemics. That is, of course, nonsense, but when masked by the cloak of modernism (as in "teaching machines") or the sancta of tradition, we do not realize it. But nonsense it is! Why, for example, should we presume that "exposure" under our tender academic care will be more effective than that provided by the mass media? Most of us are far less adequate in the arts of "exposing" than the professional actor, commentator, and storyteller. Whatever our pretensions, commercial television is far more entertaining and effective than educational TV. So if we really mean "exposure," we ought, in good conscience, to close our doors and work toward the achievement of the most literate possible soap operas.

The psychology of exposure harks back to eighteenth-century "tabula rasa" views of human nature—enough said! Most disastrous of all, an additive conception of interdisciplinarity leaves the essential problem it poses—the problem of the integration and coherence of inquiry—in the hands of those who by definition are least prepared to undertake it, that is, the students. Indeed, one might say that the degree of coherence expected varies inversely with the amount of learning allegedly completed. Why else do we preserve our pyramidal model of education—broadness at the bottom, increasing narrowness at the top—a model that tells more about our educational practices than does our rhetoric. Those who adopt an "additive" policy reincarnate in academic form the dream that a "little child shall lead them." This sentimentality—for that is what it is under the guise of fostering hard, disciplined study—simply does not work out. We wind up with generations of degree possessors and a few brilliant illiterates. The latest instance of "interdisciplinarity" as addition is the proposal—in response to the Watergate trauma for the legal profession—to add "ethics" courses to the law-school curriculum.

III

A second meaning for "interdisciplinarity" arises when we hear of proposals for the specific interaction of two or several (but always a specified number) related disciplines to each other. Examples of this are numerous, and we can cite such relatively typical exercises as the marriage of disciplines in the sciences or the team-taught advanced seminar in political economy or urban architecture. Here, at least, we resolve the problem of integration by a method that forces the named disciplines to interact through their separate practitioners. Note, however, that this demands a relatively sophisticated constituency. The participants—students and teachers alike—must have both expertise in a discipline and some knowledge of the "other" for the process to work at all. The characteristic formulation of policy arising from this definition includes an entry-level apprenticeship in a specific field and, only subsequently, an attempt to foster the interaction.

Interdisciplinary study, in this view, is best left to the graduate school or, in some precocious educational environments, to the "advanced" student. Ideally, a true interdisciplinarity would be reserved to the "masters" in each field. If this interpretation of "interdisciplinary" should turn out to be normative, we might recapture meaning for now meaningless "degrees" by identifying postgraduate competence with the ability to achieve effective interdisciplinary inquiry. For the educational institution, this implies that interdisciplinary study is reserved to its higher reaches. By implication, then, disciplinary study should be the proper task of the undergraduate and other sub-institutions, and let us banish all this talk of general education and so forth.

On analysis, therefore, our second primary meaning for interdisciplinary education contradicts the first—something that was not initially evident. This second meaning contains radical import for the design of high-school and collegiate curricula and a directive to examine the pedagogical possibilities of a truly disciplinary education for the young. Simultaneously, it threatens the comfortable specialism of our graduate programs and thereby some rather powerful vested interests and psychological securities among the established professoriat.

Before accepting this interpretation, however, it is well to probe some of its more problematic dimensions. For example, it presumes that a "discipline" can be effectively defined and bounded. Stated as an explicit requirement, we become aware of the fact that it is precisely because this is decreasingly possible that interdisciplinary talk gets raised. The disappearance of boundaries—except in university departments and budgets—is precisely our experience of intelligence in the contemporary world. As biology, for example, becomes a species of chemistry (and vice versa), we begin to get biological hypotheses of a genuinely predictive character. As politics, economics, and sociology interact we begin to develop hypotheses of policy, that is, effective decision making around the uses of power and so forth. We inherit the names and prerogatives of the disciplines and enshrine them in our institutions, but we have trouble working with them the moment we leave their history and move into their praxis.

Lest I be suspected of trying to convert the academy to polytechnics, I do not intend to limit intelligence and inquiry to the opportunistic or even to the merely instrumental. Research is a form of praxis too, as is the dialogic interaction of ideas and idea holders. Praxis then stands for the operations of knowledge in a social framework that includes non-noetic elements—for example, resistant opponents, "objective" (nonmalleable) events and so forth. The efforts of the social sciences to "scientize" themselves by adopting quantitative models is a latent recognition of the need for new boundaries and a gradual emptying of traditionalist definitions of the "discipline." Hence, to adopt the second meaning of "interdisciplinary" is to demand that the "disciplinarians" attend to the proper naming of their activity and not just to the political and economic defense of their departments.

Another problematic issue of this notion of "interdisciplinarity" must be noted. Is it conceivable that those who have immersed themselves in a given discipline will be able to break its boundaries when the "proper" time arrives? One thinks here of the deepest commitments of the scholar and researcher to his field as models of this problem. Analogically, we have here a puzzle similar to the one in social policy that tells the "minor" to obey until he reaches his majority, when suddenly he is to be regarded as a free agent, that is, as a citizen. Put as baldly as that (and it never is), it becomes clear that some processes of coherent entry into the interdisciplinary world are indicated. But how is this to be achieved using the assumptions exhibited by the second meaning, that is, the assumption that disciplinary competence is a prerequisite for interdisciplinary activity?

Perhaps a reinvigorated classicism is indicated. Can we identify certain "disciplines" that are by nature nondisciplinary or even amateurish and that might be expected to serve a mediating role? As a guess we might turn toward history, languages, philosophy, and even mathematics as possibilities (though for purposes of mediation, mathematics might better be treated as a species of language). But then we run up against all the trouble that led us to abandon "general education" programs as superficial. Alternatively, we might examine any existing discipline for its possibilities as a mediating agent, that is, a discipline might be approached qua discipline and also qua mediator. For example, economics is both a technical inquiry and a locus of human behaviors entailing political, valuational, and behavioral knowledges. The dangers of an uncritical adoption of this solution includes the reintroduction of the unlamented deadly "survey" course or the fostering of intellectual superficiality (educational populism, perhaps) in the name of mediation. I am, in other words, proposing a puzzle but am not yet able to offer a solution.

IV

A third primary definition of interdisciplinary study arises when we shift our perception from the notion of discipline to the notion of the presented problems. This requires identification of those areas of experience that threaten, puzzle, or discomfort any person or group of persons—as for example, the nature of democratic polity in large-scale populations does, or the systemic interaction of industrial activity does. One historic model of this third meaning is the art of medicine. Though it is not always formulated this way and though recent developments have tended to technicize the profession, the presenting problem is that of ill health guided by some intuitive and normative notion of health. To the response of curing we bring, in the first instance, certain traditionalist disciplines, for example, psychology. And more recently (against the technicist trend) we broaden our normative notions of health and are forced to attend to issues of sociology and politics in order to meet requirements of prevention, of class injustice, of social epidemiology, of dietary deprivation, and so forth. Along the way, we find ourselves inventing new disciplines by marrying old ones and adding something that was previously not considered germane, for example, "social" medicine, or the as yet untitled inquiries that surround questions of demography in consequence of agricultural, marketing, and other social policies.

This third meaning is the most fascinating and puzzling of all. On the one hand it seems to presume an existing set of relevant disciplines. On the other, it achieves its reality by demanding that they be transcended. I wonder, for example, if our inherited set of disciplines can long survive their transcendence. For instance, the medical model feeds upon the work of nonmedical inquiries and would be impossible without them. It is therefore irresponsible to call, as some do, for dispensing with all disciplinary inquiry in the name of innovation, novelty, and relevance. To do so is to insure, somewhere down the line, the impoverishment of this third type of interdisciplinary study. While it is not very neat, this suggests a dualistic educational philosophy in which the second and third meanings of "interdisciplinarity" occur. In the other words, a curricular structure must emerge that is both problem-centered and disciplinary in order for interdisciplinarity to have a useful content.

This dual conception may also hold some hope of solving the question of vocationalism and specialism that so afflicts educational discussion these days. Insofar as the "problem" is the center of the third meaning of "interdisciplinarity," it may be presented either as a "pure" exercise or as a "field" experience. Insofar as it is the latter, it can become the nub of vocational education in a way that moves us past questions of mere economic opportunism or exploitative social policies. Parenthetically, vocation as "problem" can find a legitimate place in "liberal" education too, and avoid a foolish polarization between useful and consummatory experience. And, insofar as the "discipline" appears as a condition of appropriate interdisciplinary interaction, we have a clue to the dissolution of mindless specialism.

This has been all too brief a description of a highly complicated process and is more a statement of agenda than a solution. But at least it offers, I believe, a usable agenda in place of linguistic rituals and fruitless warfare.

V

I would like to add a few footnotes to these possibilities of approaching interdisciplinarity as the philosophy of the curriculum. Clearly, we are talking about a process that is expensive and inevitably error-filled. On the other hand, we notice that the issue of interdisciplinarity cannot even arise until a complex social system comes into being to force its problems on human consciousness. Putting this affirmatively, it is precisely such a social system that creates the resources for its solution; putting it negatively, failure to use the resources for such purposes is simultaneously to propose the failure of that system. Concretely, this tells us, in ways that are not merely matters of momentary political preference, that a modern society had better be an educationally investing society in far greater proportion than is the case when we use traditional criteria of social investment.

To cite one implication of this agenda: the Carnegie Commission recommendations for fiscal conservatism in education are suicidal. The advice to educators to "tighten their belts" and not expect more—whatever the satisfaction this may give to those who want to put the academy back in its place—is in principle a policy of social dissolution. Reducing the alleged "teacher surplus," like the alleged "PhD surplus," with concomitant directives to reduce the "production" of both, is effective only in the short run, but is ultimately disastrous. Precisely because there are or could be a sufficiency of skilled people around can we hope to achieve an entry into interdisciplinarity. And this achievement is urgent if the process of developing and using intelligence is not to be left to some saving remnant retreating into educational monasticism in order to preserve the values of the past by isolating itself from the crisis of the present. Interdisciplinarity, carefully examined, therefore forces us into a stance vis-a-vis educational social policy and provides us with a philosophic justification for challenging its present directions. It enables us, too, to defend our demands without being accused—too often justifiably—of special pleading for our own pet projects. As we suspect, issues of curricula, insofar as they are genuine, are ultimately issues of society. Change of curricula implies social action. The academy cannot solve its problems by itself any more than the society can survive in the absence of an effective academy.

The Logic of the Social Sciences:
To Be, To Do, or To Describe?

Henry R. Novotny
California State College,
Bakersfield

I wish to offer two rather simple propositions. First, I believe it has been unwise to exclude the discipline of psychology from our curricular considerations. Second, I suggest that many of the difficulties that Professor Glazer seems to have encountered when teaching sociology at Harvard are explainable as the natural consequences of the unrealistic ambitions of some social scientists, perhaps maintained by unrealistic expectations on the part of the general public.

I

As a clinical psychologist I must admit I have felt rather left out at this symposium. To my knowledge, psychology has been mentioned only once and then in passing and in connection with crime. Since psychology clearly belongs neither in the natural sciences nor in the humanities, I seem to have no option but to make a determined plea that it be admitted to the third and last category of disciplines discussed here: that of the social sciences. At the risk of being immodest, I extend my plea even to include what some may feel to be a rather specialized field, the field of clinical psychology.

Professor Glazer's exclusive preoccupation with sociology, anthropology, and political science notwithstanding, I submit that even clinical psychology has earned its rightful place both within the family of social sciences and among the contributors to what goes under the term of general education (certainly if the latter's goal is to "understand man and society"). Its contributions to the understanding and misunderstanding of man and his social characteristics include, for instance, the models of psychoanalytic man, behavioristic man, and humanistic man. If one were facetious, one could say that its "storytellers" (I believe it was H. J. Eysenck who first called Freud "a great storyteller") compare quite favorably with those of any of the other social sciences, and so do its proponents of social action. It is true that, much to the regret of Herbert Marcuse and his followers, psychoanalytic interpretations of human conduct have not yet precipitated large-scale social convulsions. On the other hand, the social consequences of psychodynamic abstractions seem to be just as widespread as those of Marxism. While Freud may not have disciplined cadres spreading his views on the nature of man by the sword on the battlefields of the world, he does not lack fervent followers and proselytizers. His teachings, for instance, have what amounts to a tacit endorsement—if not by the American Medical Association—then by what appears to be an overwhelming majority of psychiatrists.

On a more serious note, the involvement of clinical psychology—perhaps in the shadow of psychiatry, especially forensic psychiatry—in the regulation and design of social, cultural, and personal practices of the average citizen is well known and constitutes another good reason for including it among the social sciences. Having defined many of their basic concepts, such as "mental health" and "mental illness," in terms of the prevailing (or presumably prevailing) cultural norms and values, clinicians have created what is basically an ethical perspective, even though it is often employed as a medical one. I believe it would be preeminently within the purview of the social sciences to examine the presumably scientific basis of this clinical perspective and to investigate the social consequences of its employment in the psychiatric enforcement of social compliance and conformity. The ever increasing acceptance of a shift from moral values to health values and the resulting short-circuiting of constitutional guarantees of "due process of law" (both extensively discussed by Thomas Szasz) only seem to make the enlistment of clinical psychologists into the ranks of social scientists more urgent. I invite the uninitiated to visit some of the correctional institutions or hospitals for the "criminally insane" to observe how easily an aversive treatment may be administered to a refractory "patient" over his vigorous objections, not as an ethically questionable punishment, but as "medication" provided by a thoughtful and compassionate society.

My final argument for admitting psychology to full-fledged mem-

bership in the social sciences concerns the teachings, research activities, and clinical practices of the behaviorists, who of course include
Professor Glazer's renowned colleague, B. F. Skinner. It seems rather
unwise and arbitrary to exclude from the domain of social sciences
theoretical efforts and formulations that, according to some, not only
explain man's behavior but also provide blueprints for changing his nature and for redesigning his social existence.

II

To provide a frame of reference for my comments concerning the present state of the social sciences, their potential contribution to general
education, and Professor Glazer's difficulties, let me recall several
statements that he makes in his paper. He suggests that "the crisis of
general education, seen as an educational and intellectual problem, is
preeminently the crisis of the social sciences." He points out that he is
concerned primarily about "the specifically *intellectual* problems of
providing a general or liberal education based on the contemporary
social sciences" [italics in original] and concludes that "these specifically intellectual problems are more severe in the social sciences than
in the humanities or the natural sciences." In particular, he deplores
the "chameleon-like character of the contemporary social sciences"
and states that "as a matter of fact we have no way of deciding what
facts (or theories) are really useless, once and for all. Just as we have no
dominant ordering principle that determines what is elementary and
what is advanced, we have no principle for determining *what historically generated theories should be set aside and what ones should become the basis for disciplinary work.*" [Italics in original.] Recognizing that "our danger is windy abstraction," Glazer takes a look at
research efforts in the social sciences and concludes: "Admittedly
these rather modest essays will never solve the question of whether
Marx or Weber was right." He then poses a startling question: "But
then, what can?" Elsewhere he states: "There is alas no final graveyard
of social theory."

I sympathize with Professor Glazer's frustrations even though I
cannot quite identify with the situation he depicts. In his description,
social science not only seems to have no beginning and no end but
also is unable to discriminate between what makes sense and what is
nonsense. (Come to think of it, that might explain why there has been
"a surprising drop in enrollments in various introductory and general-
education courses in the social sciences" at Harvard and why social-
science courses were found to be "almost uniformly rated more incoherent, duller, and time wasting than the courses in the natural sci-

ences and humanities.") Although I cannot believe the situation is as hopeless as Professor Glazer paints it, I agree wholeheartedly that much improvement is overdue. I would even say that some of the necessary changes may be more drastic than some would like them to be.

Let us reflect for a moment on Glazer's resigned conclusion that it may be impossible to establish "whether Marx or Weber was right." If that is true and if "there is alas no final graveyard of social theory," one may properly inquire by what criteria those various competing explanatory systems in the social sciences are classified as "social theories." What kind of "theories" are they if they can be neither confirmed nor refuted?

The social sciences share a common legacy of unscientific, but enthusiastic and unrestrained, armchair philosophizing. They also show a common propensity for formulating their intellectual productions in a manner that renders their propositions at once untestable but endowed with social urgency that transforms them into moral imperatives. These productions are characterized by extravagant claims and all-inclusive, cosmic pretentions to the understanding of the human phenomenon, rather than by scientific restraint and methodological soundness. It seems alarming that these speculations and moralizations, cloaked in academic regalia, are still sought after and accepted by the general public—or at least by many of their influential representatives. Few seem to care that, in the process, scientists cease to act as scientists, and deliberate scholars become hot-eyed preachers and social prophets. I think the time has come for the social sciences to formulate their scholarly undertakings so that these do not exceed their methodological capabilities, and to sort out the subjects and topics their science can handle from those it cannot. As sciences, these disciplines should follow the rules of scientific modesty even when outside authorities or pressing social developments demand immediate global answers. My suggestion is not that research should be discontinued in *any* of the areas within their domain; in simple language, I only ask that they do not bite off more than their methodology can chew—or, to put it differently, that they obey the simple rule of truth in labeling.

To give a particular example, consider Professor Glazer's reference to the Carnegie Commission's report, *The Purpose and the Performance of Higher Education in the United States,* and to the implicit definitions of general education that it contains ("acquiring a general understanding of society and the place of the individual within it . . . to understand man and society"). Glazer concludes that such definitions clearly give "a mandate for the social sciences to play a leading role in general education." What is astonishing, he seems to accept the offered leadership without giving a second thought to its propriety.

It seems imperative to ask, in case Glazer's evaluation of the present situation in the social sciences is basically correct: How can we possibly entertain in all seriousness the idea of accepting the mandate he speaks of? How shameless and insensitive to intellectual integrity have we become when we seem ready to accept a leading role in educational programs to which we believe we have little of substance to contribute? Obviously, both common sense and intellectual honesty demand that whether or not a discipline should play "a leading role" should be decided on the basis of what it has to offer rather than by what others expect, or even demand, from it. It would be totally absurd if the social sciences should interpret the goal of general education ("to understand man and society") as an invitation for relaxing the scientific framework within which they are chartered to operate and accepting as "theories" some scientifically dubious and untestable, story-like interpretations of human existence (even though they might be morally exciting)—interpretations that would be easily "influenced by the ideas and tempers of the time." Fortunately, I believe Professor Glazer is unduly pessimistic about the general state of the social sciences. Nevertheless, the problem remains.

I acknowledge that Karl R. Popper's propositions regarding the social sciences may be overly restrictive and overly simplified. For instance, I would disagree with his implication that, unless demonstrably impossible, all future social and political developments carry, for all practical purposes, the same probability of occurrence. On the other hand, I do not think it should be beneath the dignity of social scientists to reflect on his criticisms. I believe, for instance, there is a great deal of truth in his contention that it is not "the task of the social sciences to propound historical prophecies" and that such "historicism" is "the relic of an ancient superstition even though the people who believe in it are usually convinced that it is a very new, progressive, revolutionary, and scientific theory."[1] Perhaps Popper is also right in suggesting that "the idea of a law which determines the direction and character of evolution is a typical nineteenth century mistake, arising out of the general tendency to ascribe to the 'Natural Law' the functions traditionally ascribed to God."[2]

In any case, I believe that social scientists should consider with some seriousness his proposition that the *"main task of the theoretical social sciences . . . is to trace the unintended social repercussions of intentional human actions."*[3] [Italics in original.] At the least, such an orientation would help the social sciences to gain some of the scientific respectability they seem to lack now.

Having based their theories on the authority of factual evidence, logical analysis, and empirical verification, the natural sciences have managed to purge their equations from the capricious forces that used to animate objects and lie always in wait, ready to thwart human undertakings. Natural scientists have given up trying to find out what the material universe "is" in some absolute, essential sense and have concentrated instead on finding descriptions of objective reality that possess power of prediction and hence make purposeful and intelligent behavior possible. In the process they even had to abandon the Newtonian concept of absolute time and space, which have become attributes of matter.

III

In psychology, even in clinical psychology, I hope we have turned the corner as well. I think that psychology is being put irreversibly on a scientific basis, and many of us regret the slowness of the process. We are beginning to distinguish between what makes sense and what does not and can usually even agree on where to start and where to finish. Again, I think that psychology has managed to progress because its theoreticians, following the lead of the natural scientists, have decided to stop trying to discover what man "is" and instead have focused their energies on finding solutions to his "problems in living," to use Szasz's phrase. Many modern clinicians now prefer functional analysis of behavior to chasing elusive "mental illnesses" by examining archetypes and the collective unconscious or by undertaking psychoanalytic excavations into repressed childhood memories of events that in fact rarely happened. We are slowly learning that labeling patients and pigeonholing them into obscure categories does not really help us to understand their behavior. By learning how to shed the outdated, the superfluous, and the mythological, one hopes psychology will become the "self-corrective system of disposing of useless facts" that Daniel Bell suggests science is. What is more, using Occam's razor has made none of us a eunuch; I urge my colleagues in the other social sciences not to fear the surgery. By staying with observable phenomena and testable propositions and by limiting research hypotheses to social events and processes that existing methodological tools can handle, the social sciences will gain more than they will lose.

Incidentally, it is not just old, venerable speculations that have to be challenged. Let me mention for instance the social propositions and calls for "cultural designs" made and publicized by Skinner. Having confused science with metascience and shifted from the scientific "as if" to the absolute "is" (from "science treats man *as if* he were deterministic" to "man *is* deterministic"), Skinner has created another "ism," another *Weltanschauung*, which in many ways resembles Marx's dialectics. Having replaced the unpredictive dialectical triad by the unpredictive (unless by analogy or extrapolation, to use Verplanck's terms) reinforcement triad, Skinner has constructed another ultimate, all-explaining description of social existence and its evolution. Skinner obliterated the crucial distinction between the universe of objective facts and the universe of human values. To reconcile the two, he disposed of all human content as an autonomous entity except for the imperative of cultural survival that somehow survived the purge. The Skinnerian man is disembodied and mechanistic. Having been completely preprogramed, he is also infallible and amoral: "When all relevant variables have been arranged, an organism will or will not respond. If it does not, it cannot. If it can, it will."[4] The question of ethics has been replaced by the question of control. In Skinnerism, social scientists represent the elite vanguard called upon to perform as cosmic midwives. Presumably armed with superior insight into the workings of the universe, a relative handful of select individuals (followed closely by excited college sophomores) will guide and supervise the social conduct and daily labor of their less enlightened fellowmen so as to perfect their manners and create a blissful society in which the original planners and caretakers, and their authoritarian bureaucracies, have forever faded away.

The present ongoing and unceasing epistemological battle against oracular "theories" in clinical psycholo / is perhaps best summarized in the self-explanatory title of a recent article by Lee Birk: "Psychoanalytic Omniscience and Behavioral Omnipotence: Current Trends in Psychotherapy" (*Seminars in Psychiatry*, 4, No. 2, 1972, pp. 113-120).

IV

Having come to pessimistic conclusions about the present condition of the social sciences, Glazer proposes that "we should think of social-science liberal education as based primarily on two disciplines, history and economics." While I respect Glazer's reasons for selecting history and economics, I do not agree that the other social sciences should be excluded, certainly not on the basis of performance. To start with, I do not believe that one should feel an exaggerated admiration for the complex mathematical structures often employed by economists. There is little doubt that the extensive employment of mathematical models and the use of computer data-processing have helped to increase the conceptual clarity and internal consistency of economic theories and to specify more clearly the logical interdependence between the various subareas and theoretical constructs of economics.

This much, the rest of the social sciences can only envy. But there are other important aspects to consider. One may inquire, for instance: How representative are the theoretical models of economic realities? How empirically corroborated are the presumed conceptual ties between economic theoretical constructs and their objective referents? How reliable are the economic predictions?

Without pretending to be more than an interested layman, I suggest that the apparent accomplishments of economics seem to be less than overwhelming. Perhaps the years I spent as a physicist have taught me to give less respect to the niceties of mathematical sophistications and more to the accurate descriptions of observable processes —descriptions that possess a demonstrable power of prediction. Assuming that leading economists are not conspirators who keep their best theories and predictions secret, it would seem that they fare no better than the rest of the social scientists. They give us conflicting predictions of events to come and they give us conflicting explanations of past events. When in a bind, they resort to blaming unexpected—usually calamitous—outcomes on various devious economic devils. I submit that, as an explanatory concept, the infamous gnomes of Zurich are a scientifically unsatisfactory construct.

Consider for instance the present condition of economic forecasting as once reported in *Business Week*: "Passing the midpoint of the year, the forecasters are scrambling to revise the projections they made so bravely last November and December. . . . They disagree not only about the prospects for the economy in 1975, but also about the outlook for the remainder of 1974. They cannot decide whether the U.S. is going into a recession. They cannot even agree on the trend of production, income, and employment at the end of the second quarter."[5] The unnamed authors come to the inevitable conclusion: "For a forecast, essentially, is the statement of a theory with specific values instead of abstractions. When the forecast goes seriously wrong, it suggests that something is wrong with the theory. And when all forecasts miss the mark, it suggests that the entire body of economic thinking . . . is inadequate to describe and analyze the problems of our times."[6] Later in the article they suggest that "economists no longer know what to make of figures that they once thought they could interpret with confidence."[7] In another issue, *Business Week* carried an article that stated: "Businessmen who once eagerly studied the data from Sindlinger & Co., the Conference Board, the University of Michigan, and elsewhere are now questioning their value."[8] The article gives an example of an inaccurate prediction and mentions several "explanations" that only seem to demonstrate how flexible the economic terms and statements may be: " 'There is just too large a gap between consumer buying patterns and consumer intentions,' says one major retailer;" and "Pollsters defend their data by claiming that this was 'hedge buying' and say that in real, adjusted dollars, the buying trend was flat." Perhaps the best remark concludes the article: " 'The problem was that they were right 50% of the time—but they didn't know which 50%.' " [9]

Intricate mathematical models can be only as valid as they are representative of the objective phenomena they are supposed to simulate. We have tried the mathematical approach in psychology, and I believe the present consensus is that, in most instances, such attempts at this time resemble the building of skyscrapers on sand.

It is tempting to suggest that, at least in part, the explanation of the forecasters' difficulties lies in the fact that (perhaps following the lead of other social sciences) economics seems to be undergoing a subtle but fundamental shift in focus: from aiming to discover the preferences of the economic man, conceived as a free and autonomous agent, to designing procedures by which he can be molded and coerced to behave in ways that would promote what the economists in power consider to be desirable economic and social goals. Economists seem to be on their way to joining other social scientists who believe that their primary professional mission is not to examine, to catalogue, and to understand social reality but to change it. I believe that "free" feedback from economic reality has been seriously attenuated by an ever stronger intervention by the government and its economists in our lives, and the power of unbiased prediction undermined by what can perhaps best be described as the emasculation of the economic man. Various levels of government are now taking control over our spending and saving, and have just about managed to destroy all of the stable, universal, and independent measures of personal wealth that in a way are measures of our freedoms. (I believe it was Voltaire who said that the true charter of liberty is independence maintained by force. Personal property is such a force that helps us to stay free of governmental and other coercion.) Until recently, American citizens, for instance, were not allowed to buy or sell gold: My feeling is that Americans are now to be allowed to purchase and sell gold only because the governing powers need them to do so. Once they have served their function, either the privilege will be taken away from them again or the price of gold will be manipulated so as to extract unauthorized taxes from the American population.

Instead of a monetary measure that is relatively independent of governmental interference, we are now given governmental promises and promissory notes based on revocable agreements and paper definitions. With the government frequently defining in a very real sense how much what we have is worth at any particular time and place, and with the labor-industrial complex regulating our working and leisure habits, as individuals we represent only a shrinking fraction of the forces that determine the actual economic outcome. Ultimately, when governmental and other social controls over our economic behavior become complete, the power of prediction in the traditional sense will have become as obsolete a concept as in Skinner's *Walden Two*. In both instances, the relevant variable will be social control. Economic studies will then become studies of the means and ethics of economic coercion.

V

In summary, then, I believe that *all* social sciences have *some* respectable knowledge to contribute to general education but that it is imperative to temper their presentation with intellectual modesty and an explicit recognition of existing methodological limitations. The critical question is not so much *what* specific subject matter to include but *how* to present it.

The mark of a viable, "self-correcting" scientific discipline is its effective and systematically planned utilization of corrective feedback from objective reality. It is the kind, the extent, and the quality of such feedback that determine how strong the weakest link in the theoretical chain is. The entire scientific enterprise is only as valid as the empirical ties between its theoretical concepts and their objective referents. The corrective feedback mechanism itself is preferably a multiple system operating at all conceptual levels: at simple ones that deal with theoretical details, at intermediate ones consisting of piecemeal efforts that aim to reach limited objectives, and at the highest ones where false predictions might potentially result in global catastrophes and human suffering.

It seems incredible that this kind of feedback mechanism should still be misunderstood and misrepresented so often in academic circles. Scholars frequently seem more interested in the superficial brilliance of their abstractions, conceptual sophistication, a global applicability of their theoretical speculations, and the persuasiveness and social impact of their rhetoric than in finding reliable and verifiably representative descriptions of the objective phenomena under investigation. An absence of a "dialogue with reality" cannot but facilitate their transformation from scientists into oracles. Also, many seem to wait and to hope for the heroic moment of insight when a falling apple and the process of logical analysis will lead them to an immortal discovery of some fundamental, revolutionary, and universal law of nature. They forget that even Newton relied on a wealth of observational data, incidently but systematically and accurately compiled, the kind of data that is very scarce in the social sciences. And, one might add, even Newton's laws were subsequently shown—on the basis of further empirical findings—to be only close approximations for the special, limited case of low velocities.

Such a trap of wishful thinking does not seem to go unnoticed by the writers at *Business Week*, where they state with apparent optimism: "Some economists are already looking for a modern Keynes whose sudden insight will generate a theory to explain what is happening today, but the majority think that understanding will come piece by piece, as they accumulate experience with the new problems that face them."[10]

The consequences of our actions, in the final analysis, affect the teacher, our skills, and our knowledge, and not least our students. Ultimately, they are the monitors of our intellectual honesty. Universal laws are independent of human desires and represent an uninvited and often exasperating, but uncompromising and incorruptible judge of how well advised our actions have been. Such undertakings as "the ingenious use of reconstructed statistics," on the other hand, are usually not very conducive to learning scientific objectivity and restraint. In the academic world of obedient and emotionally infused abstractions, a comfortable world in many ways shielded from objective feedback, the acquisition of dispassionate scientific objectivity and meticulous intellectual honesty is not, and never will be, an easy process. Daniel Bell mused pensively about "young intellectuals . . . who take their own sensibility and experiences, rather than reason or tradition, as the touchstone of truth" and concluded: "In the end, however, they lack the technical knowledge, or even the willingness to acquire it, that could test their abstractions against a social reality."[11]

Handicapping tendencies of this kind can make the centrality of methodology important. I feel that most of us agree on that. Where I seem to go further is my conviction that the entire focus of the social sciences, at least at the present time, should be not on what is possible but on what is not possible. I believe that teaching methodology by examining what it can do for us is not enough. We must also teach its limitations and its unwarranted temptations. We must somehow teach our students, and ourselves, to be less credulous, less naive, less easily "influenced by the ideas and tempers of the times," and to be content with what Popper referred to as "piecemeal engineering." To accomplish this task, we may have to spend more time on the philosophy of science and on examining relevant epistemological issues, particularly those that relate to the idea of free men living in a pluralistic and democratic society.

It was S. E. Glenn who pointed out that "obviously a prevalence of reasoning in terms of the logic of the verb 'to do' ties in with nominalism, while a prevalence of reasoning in terms of the logic of the verb 'to be' ties in with universalism."[12] It seems easy to demonstrate that the first epistemological approach, relying on the authority of observable facts and empirically verifiable propositions, is intrinsically associated with scientific and democratic strategies and that the second, relying on the authority and interpretative genius of a philosopher-king, has magical and authoritarian overtones. It should then be rather evident why I suggest that the social sciences should operate within "the logic of the verb 'to do' " rather than "the logic of the verb 'to be' " (but not, for that matter, within the logic of the verb "to control") and that their primary objective should be "to describe."

NOTES

1. Karl R. Popper, "Prediction and Prophecy in the Social Sciences," in *Conjectures and Refutations: The Growth of Scientific Knowledge* (New York: Basic Books, 1962), p. 336.

2. Popper, p. 340.

3. Popper, p. 342.

4. B. F. Skinner, *Science and Human Behavior* (New York: Free Press, 1965), p. 112.

5. "Theory Deserts the Forecasters," *Business Week*, June 29, 1974, p. 50.

6. Ibid.

7. Ibid, p. 51.

8. "A Loss of Faith in Pollsters," *Business Week*, June 1, 1974, p. 25.

9. Ibid.

10. "Theory Deserts the Forecasters," p. 50.

11. Daniel Bell, *The Reforming of General Education* (New York: Columbia University Press, 1966), pp. 307-308.

12. E. S. Glenn, "Semantic Difficulties in International Communication," in *The Use and Misuse of Language*, S. I. Hayakawa, ed. (Greenwich, Conn.: Fawcett Publications, 1962), p. 56.

A Proposal for
a New Division of the Curriculum

Gray Dorsey
Washington University

The university curriculum is generally considered to contain three broad areas of professional specialization—the humanities, the natural sciences, the social sciences—and general education. General education seeks to draw together from the areas of professional specialization the appropriate contribution of each to wisdom, which is understood as the requisite knowledge, perspective, and value commitments for a person to have a satisfactory life experience and to make a responsible contribution to the communities in which he participates.

This curriculum is not sufficient. It does not include the systematic study of facts, potentialities, and alternatives of immense significance and of great current concern. The feelings of helplessness and apprehension about these factors contribute substantially, I suggest, to the popular attitudes reported in the major papers: that general education is not worth pursuing; that science, understood as being limited to rational explanation, is either a pernicious obstacle to grasping truth or, on the other hand, a fully sufficient means of grasping truth; that the humanities are to be respected but ignored; and that the social sciences are topical, shallow, and inconsequential.

The facts I refer to are those of recent scientific discoveries. The potentialities are for technological and social changes. The alternatives, at least in part, offer choices between humane and inhumane practices, procedures, institutions, and conditions. These matters are dealt with in the university's present curriculum, but not systematically.

As Stephen Toulmin has recently pointed out, matters that in the present university curriculum are studied by scientists were, before 1840, dealt with by "mathematical, experimental, or natural philosophers, gentlemen naturalists, virtuosi, savants, and curious inquirers into pneumatic chemistry, optics, or vegetable staticks."[1] William Whewell's coining of the word "scientist," in his 1840 address before the British Association for the Advancement of Science, helped to create a profession that brought to the study of these matters unifying general principles and standards of excellence and responsibility. The analogous development in the present would bring into a single profession (subject to standards of excellence and responsibility) the areas of concern of all those who, under the guise of urban planners, scientologists, ecologists, consciousness-raisers, shamans, and public-interest lawyers, seek satisfying lives and decent communities amid a confusing welter of social and technological potentialities arising from recent scientific discoveries.

The need to deal in a more systematic way with technological potentialities, particularly those that may cause massive harm to the biosphere or infringe outrageously on the integrity of human personality, has already been felt and acted upon by persons in positions of political power. The most systematic and comprehensive result to date is the Report of the Panel on Technology Assessment of the National Academy of Sciences,[2] which was responding to an initiative by Representative Emilio Q. Daddario, chairman of the Subcommittee on Science, Research, and Development of the House Committee on Science and Astronautics. The Technology Assessment Act of 1972[3] provides for the establishment of an Office of Technology Assessment as an aid to Congress in the identification and consideration of existing and probable impacts of technology.

What qualifications should one have in order to identify and consider the impacts of technology? Does "consideration" involve judgments that some impacts are good and some bad? What training is pertinent to qualify one to be a technology assessor? Where is such training to be had? Are the standards of good and bad to be composed of the values that are the stuff of the humanities? How is the choice to be made of the appropriate value, or mix of values, to be used as a standard in a given instance? What mode of reasoning will assure explicit, open, repeatable, objective application of standards to technological impact?

These questions, and others equally pertinent, suggest that the Office of Technology Assessment will need to draw upon a profession that does not exist. This instance of felt need should not be permitted to define the curricular scope of the new profession. New technological potentialities arise from a change in the human condition. All potentialities arising from that change should be included in the subject matter of the new profession. The change in the human condition is the radical increase in human power over the environment.

Humankind has developed tremendous power over the geosphere. The gross nature of the earth's inert matter was not fixed for all time by the thousands of millions of years of geochemical and biochemical processes prior to the advent of human beings. The "natural" materials of the earth's crust are products of geogenesis, the process of change in the inert matter of the geosphere, or of biogenesis and geogenesis, in the case of plants and animals that once existed in the biosphere and then came into the geosphere by decomposition or fossilization. Most of the strategic materials of modern industrial production, however, are not "natural" materials; they have been produced by physical, chemical, and electrical processes and reactions initiated and directed by human beings. Iron and aluminum are products of human intervention that have long been essential to industrial production. Plastics, polymers, and the new metals of supersonic aircraft and rocket-powered spacecraft are more recent examples.

Humankind also has developed tremendous power over the biosphere. Nuclear and thermonuclear power devices with enough explosive power and radioactivity to wipe out human and many other forms of life are already in underground silos and in cruising submarines, awaiting only a set of signals to send them to their targets. The threat perceived by ecologists is that human beings will exhaust the life-support capacity of the earth—the capacity to make oxygen, to purify water, to grow food, and to supply energy. Humankind is on the threshold of controlling human life and behavior in various ways: cloning countless genetically exact copies of a human being; breeding human beings to genetic specifications; controlling human behavior through operant conditioning, or through changing the electrochemical brain system by drugs, electrode implants, or surgical procedures.

New potentialities for human control over the environment that are, in effect, new potentialities for human life, are discovered by the specialized forms of human thought called science. Actualizing a given potentiality requires development of material means—technology—but it also requires development of nonmaterial means—society. Human beings are the first form of life, out of hundreds of millions of life forms in the thousand-million-year history of the biosphere, to be given a measure of control over actualizing potentialities of life.

Many forms of life, prior to the human form, have utilized a form of society in actualizing life potentialities, but all of these forms of life relied upon morphological adaptation and specialization. The insects, a highly successful phylum, developed the capacity to gather food, fight off enemies, and reproduce in almost every environment on earth, in hot climates and cold, in tropical rain forests, on the most arid deserts, at the seashore, on mountain slopes. But no one insect can function successfully in all of these environments. Instead, the insects developed species structurally adapted to one or another of these environments. There is firm evidence of at least ten thousand species. Further, not every insect within a species can perform every function necessary to sustain life in the environment to which that species is adapted. Individual insects often are structurally specialized to a single function, such as gathering food, fighting, or reproducing. The functions to which sets of individual insects are specialized are auxiliary and complementary. When all sets of individuals perform their functions, insect society results.

Human society does not result from morphological adaptation and specialization. There are no human beings adapted to a specific food source or topography; none are specialized to tearing, striking, running, flying, or swimming. Human beings rely on society to actualize potentialities of life, but through the intervention of human intelligence, which is general, cumulative, and reflective, enabling human beings to take over from nature some direction of events and processes external to their own organisms. Human beings have learned about the various environments, how to make various responses and how to teach other human beings to make them, how to organize the direct cooperative actions, how to distribute auxiliary and complementary functions by assignment and assumption, and how to regulate and govern interrelationships between individuals. Above all, human beings have become conscious of themselves as thinking beings, with ends to which they are not automatically directed by nature, situated in a world in which they must seek ends through knowledge and intentionally directed social structures and actions.

It would be the task of the new area of professional specialization I am proposing to build up a body of systematic knowledge concerning life potentialities; to devise and demonstate the soundness of open, explicit, objective modes of reasoning to select standards and apply them to life potentialities of different types; to develop professional standards of excellence and responsibility; to develop procedures and institutions to assure that representative, or official, choices regarding life potentialities will be fair, informed, and impartial; and to develop materials and techniques of instruction concerning all these things. Perhaps "ethicist" is the appropriate word to designate the practitioner of this new profession. Although "ethicist" is not a new word, this usage would give it a new scope.

The proposed new division of the curriculum does not, in my opinion, presuppose censorship of scientific research. It does presuppose censorship of the technological and social *uses* of scientific discoveries. This is fraught with possibilities of abuse, but it is necessary. Suppose that one of the great multinational corporations proposed to produce by genetic engineering several thousand humanoids specialized to perform certain sets of functions and impervious to extreme cold, for use in mining operations in Siberia under a concession contract with the Soviet Union. Permanently subordinate, limited-function drones are found in insect societies. Indeed the staggering rates of reproduction of individuals and the profusion of species in evolutionary history indicate that every form of life, prior to human beings, actualized every life potentiality presented by its environment and its own stage of development. Surely, some potentialities must be rejected by human beings. When control over actualization of life potentialities passed from natural morphology to human thought and action were we given only the obligation to learn how, and not the obligation to decide whether? Slavery has now been abolished nearly everywhere on earth. Surely it would not be an improper restriction on scientific technology if the United States exercised its authority to prevent the corporation from creating humanlike creatures and holding them in permanent slavery because scientific knowledge could be utilized to regress human beings genetically into creatures having only the specific characteristics desired?

An important part of the subject matter of the new division would be the study of what structure of decision making is appropriate for each type of decision. Decisions of limitation, the paradigm of which is an action depriving another person of freedom or property, might best be made by a small professional group, a deliberative decision-making structure like the courts. Decisions of permission may require a different structure. In view of the immense and irreversible damage that some technologically feasible products could inflict on the biosphere —such as the catalytic reduction of the ozone shield in the lower stratosphere by the nitrogen oxides emitted by SSTs—it may become necessary, with respect to large areas of human activity, to reverse a long-standing principle of Anglo-American law permitting any act that cannot be proved specifically injurious to another in favor of a principle requiring prior proof of the safety of proposed products or actions. For the adoption of such a principle, the decision structure of a constitutional convention, or that used for constitutional amendments, might be appropriate. For other decisions, such as organization of the enterprises that would actualize the economic, humanitarian, or esthetic potentialities of a scientific discovery, the broad participation, ma-jority-vote decision structure of representative legislative institutions, or perhaps of popular referendum, might be the most appropriate. The important thing is that we build up the knowledge, standards, proce-dures, and institutions so that, consistently with democratic prefer-ences, we can make open, explicit, objective decisions about which life potentialities arising from scientific discoveries are opportunities for developing more satisfying lives and more decent communities and which ones are evils to be avoided.

NOTES

1. Stephen Toulmin, "The Alexandrian Trap," *Encounter*, XLII, No. 1 (Jan. 1974), p. 61.

2. See Part I of L. Tribe, *Channelling Technology Through Law* (Chicago: Bracton Press, 1973)

3. Public Law 92-484, 92nd Congress, 42 U.S.C.A. 1862.

On the Condition of Political Science

Joseph Dunner
Yeshiva University

Almost every issue to which Professor Glazer has alluded deserves serious discussion. Having taught political science in this country and abroad for close to forty years and having observed throughout those years the ups and downs not only in the study of politics but in sociology and economics as well, I am not surprised to hear Cassandra's warning of misfortune once again. It is to this aspect of Professor Glazer's position—the note of despair that he expresses—that I wish to address myself.

Is it really an indictment of the intrinsic value of the social sciences if the dean of Harvard College reports that the Harvard freshmen in the spring of 1973 considered the courses in the social sciences more time-wasting and duller than the courses in the natural sciences and the humanities? Or if an article in *Change* tells us that the survivors of a college class of 1961, seven years after their graduation, pronounce their grief about having missed various courses in the natural sciences and the humanities but did not list a single social-science course that they wish they had taken? Without wanting to appear boastful, I have not had diminished enrollments in any of the political-science classes I taught at Harvard, Grinnell, the University of Freiburg, and, for the last ten years, Yeshiva University. For I am quite sure that some of my colleagues throughout the country have had similar good experiences that contradict the data furnished by Professor Glazer. I venture the guess that these colleagues, like myself, are among those political scientists who have resisted the trend that some sociologists (not Max Weber, not Émile Durkheim, not my teachers and friends Karl Mannheim and Robert McIver, but some people of inferior vintage) have rather successfully imposed upon the whole discipline of political science. This is a trend known as behavioralism.

No social scientist, no political scientist, will object to refinements in the construction of questionnaires in voting and public-opinion studies. No genuine political scientist has ever displayed the sort of contempt for empirical research that our behavioralistic contemporaries have for political thought, for intuitive, traditional wisdom, for value judgments based on moral foundations. During the International Political Science meetings in Paris many years ago, I asked one of the founders of the behavioralistic school in the American political-science fraternity what he would say to his students if they asked him whether he, the allegedly value-free social scientist, had any way of discriminating between Hitlerism and Stalinism on the one hand and a free polity like that of the United States or Great Britain on the other hand. I received no answer.

This, I believe, is the reason for the malaise found in the social sciences and in political science in particular. In most of our universities political science is taught by computer technicians, who do not understand the fundamental difference between sociopolitical and physical phenomena, and by so-called behavioralists, who enjoy sizable foundation grants because of their promise to dissolve the uniqueness of historical events and the human personality into quantifiable units concocted by their own spleens and written up as the last words of wisdom in the *American Political Science Review* and similar periodicals. I can understand that the reaction of their students is to switch to those disciplines in which they get the real thing and not a frantic imitation. As a student, I would also have abandoned a political science that behavioralism had managed to turn into an artificially limited, utterly boring, and sterile storeroom of banalities.

I attribute much of the nihilistic rebellion of American students in the 1960s to the dull passivity and pseudoscientific neutralism of those political scientists who, imbued with the behavioralistic fad, had forgotten that the social scientist first of all has the duty to promote rationality rather than surrender to the irrational. This, of course, is a value judgment on my part, and I am quite aware of it, just as I am aware of the fact that differing values and beliefs affect different political perspectives. I see the task of the political scientist to be one of showing his students how political analysis is infused with the values of the analyst; how the masters of political science, those men whose names withstood the screening process of history, have examined past and present political structures and relations; how cautious one must be in the use of political terms having different meanings for different cultures and ideologies; and how truly exciting the unfolding of the political in man has been throughout the ages.

I am the last person who would denigrate the study of what we so arbitrarily call the humanities. The very fact that most political scientists in this country are unfamiliar with philosophy and master, at best, their mother tongue and its literature is one of the major reasons for the dullness of their teaching and their preoccupation with such trivia as "inputs," "outputs," "asymmetric relations," or that key to all value-free behavioralistic knowledge—the "authoritative allocation of values."

Unless our young people want to live in steady fear of the physical world about them, they must be urged to gain as much of a systematized knowledge of physics, chemistry, geology, and the other branches of natural science as they can get. But what could be more interesting to human beings than the inquiry into man's relationship with his fellowmen? What could be more challenging than the study of the ethics and values of societies and topics such as liberalism, conservatism, democracy, dictatorship, authority, freedom, change, and revolution?

I am convinced that those teachers of political science who, in the Aristotelian tradition, address themselves to the great issues of politics will not find their classrooms empty, provided of course, they have not taken the advice of the behavioralists and neglected their own studies of political thought. These political scientists will acquire students eager to study, eager to debate, eager to choose their personal models. Following Max Weber's wholesome advice, they will not try to relieve their students of the burden to make up their minds as to their own position in political life. In the end they might find themselves surrounded by young revolutionaries, but they will at least be revolutionaries who know why they prefer radical change and not the sort of pseudorevolutionaries we experienced a few years ago—the spoiled kids of well-to-do families who, out of sheer boredom, destroyed for the sake of destruction.

New Beginnings in General Education

Aldo S. Bernardo

Verrazzano College

The renewed interest in the role of general education at the college level for students of the 1970s, 1980s and 1990s is justifiable primarily as an antidote to the educational upheavals that occurred during the 1960s. The paradox of the 1960s, in the field of education, was that while the Mario Savios were complaining about and revolting against the shameful manner in which undergraduate education had been relegated to the role of handmaiden to graduate education, the non-student refugees from the Vietnam War were declaring the right of students to be educated under conditions of total anarchy. As cowardly faculties conceded that perhaps the students—and not they—constituted the nucleus of the university, total anarchy did win the day for the most part, thereby allowing the educational scale to hit bottom on the left side, just as it had hit bottom on the right side in the fascist countries before World War II.

What had really happened, of course, was that educators had discovered that the educational structures they had hastily built in the late 1940s and early 1950s following World War II had been resting on underpinnings of clay. The great general-education vogue of the period had never been thought through carefully. Breadth was confused with how many departments could split the pie rather than being conceived in terms of what it really meant within the context of the liberal arts. The potpourri that resulted on most campuses already contained the germ of the inevitable destruction of the entire structure. All that was needed were the hordes of either overspecialized PhDs or ersatz PhDs that were rushed through the mill, and the self-destruct mechanism was activated. What happened to American education in the 1960s was as inevitable as the atomic bomb.

The return to utopia is proving just as blind. The magic stone is still being sought through mysterious intertwinings and combinations of departmental offerings. Educators have become incapable of the overview because the dense foliage simply makes it impossible to emerge from the dark wood. The individual trees have become so monstrous that educators can no longer discern the forest. The confusion between administrative and academic structure is almost total. There is not a single department today that would dare admit that perhaps it has no significant role in the general education of a student, just as there was no such department in the 1950s. This is why any discussion of the subject is futile.

What is needed is a return to a kind of tabula rasa. Every undergraduate program should be rebuilt with the same spirit of inquiry that marks the work of the well-prepared and well-trained scholar. All such attempts should be beyond departmental interests. Indeed, the ideal environment would be a staff that would prefer to remain departmentless. What matters most is that a well-conceived general-education program should assure every able student of a perspective that is in time and beyond time. Such a perspective, almost from time immemorial, has been—to use an image borrowed from Petrarch—the view from atop the mount of time that allows one to see in one fell swoop how past, present, and future are linked together. Only in this manner can one truly begin sensing the meaning of the admonition of the Delphic oracle: Know thyself.

It is the heritage of the past that undergraduates must begin to grasp realistically. This heritage means just that and nothing more. The incredible hubris that characterizes so many universities is linked to a belief that somehow a campus must encompass the entire universe, and that the truly educated mind resembles the Widener Library at Harvard. The heritage that matters most in truly educating the student of tomorrow is the one that has provided him with his present identity. If he does not understand why he is a Western man, how could we ever expect him to understand what is meant by a non-Western man? If he is not made to see in some depth the signs and dimensions that marked the beginning of Western man, how could he see what Western man has become? If he then is not made to see and understand those qualities that have been assumed by those members of this heritage with whom he is in daily contact, how can we expect him to be civil, compassionate, broadminded and forbearing?

In providing this kind of program, most if not all members of a given faculty must be involved. Perhaps at first they will have to learn together with the students, but this should not prove too difficult if we restrict ourselves to a single course partaking minimally of the old Western Civilization or humanities sequences. What is desperately needed is a course that runs for four years and examines in some depth those great moments in the history of the modern disciplines that made them what they are today. This will not only make the chemist broadly aware of how chemistry evolved, but it will give him some insight into and respect for the nature of political science, sociology, literature, philosophy, and so forth. To know something about one of the liberal arts is almost insignificant if one does not also understand what the liberal arts are and how they interrelate.

At Verrazzano College we are trying to accomplish this by designing a total curriculum that starts by allowing all students to concentrate in one of the traditional disciplines without dividing the disciplines into departments. We then carefully structure their remaining time by requiring all students to pursue four years of a course entitled "The Western Heritage," four years of another course known as "The Mediterranean Heritage" (which involves the study of the language and development of a Mediterranean people and one year of study in that country), and one year of a third course entitled "The American Heritage," done in the senior year. By then requiring all students to structure their program so that ultimately they graduate as majors in the humanities, social sciences, or sciences, we assure them of a significant experience in both breadth and depth, which in turn should provide them with a desirable perspective for tomorrow's world.

Thoughts on a Social-Science Curriculum

Feliks Gross
City University of New York,
Brooklyn College

Our universities are not isolated cloisters, but are a part of the complex fabric of contemporary society. Their problems as well as philosophy have to be considered within this social context. For the relations between goals and the scope of higher learning in this country, the most technologically advanced on the globe, were greatly affected by the rapid change in its social structure. The process was far more complex however. The civil-rights movement, a major war, and ideological changes occurred at the same time. Then came the intellectual crisis, decadence and confusion, with fads, drugs, noisy music, violence, and political cultism.

Let us consider the social changes first before we move on to problems of educational philosophy, objectives, and curriculum.

A new class emerged after World War II, a class of college students, teachers, and graduates. Of course, there have been students and college professors for centuries. But they did not constitute a "class." When the modern beginnings of a community of researchers and scholars first appeared, sometime during the Renaissance in Florence and other cities, they were communities of a select few.

After World War II, the growth of college communities was rapid indeed. The crisis of the universities became intense precisely in the sixth decade of our century. In 1960, 380,000 faculty members of various ranks taught in American universities. In 1961, this number was still higher. In addition, 200,000 academicians—highly qualified university and college people—were employed in research. Since some may have taught and carried out research projects, we may safely assume that there were 500,000 members of teaching and research faculties. At the same time, student enrollment passed the four million figure, only to advance toward seven million by the end of the decade. Let us assume, however, the initial figures: an academic community of about five million people. This five-million figure almost equals the number of people active in agriculture at that time. Mechanization and "scientification" of agriculture effected a rapid decline of those actively employed in this important area, and in the sixth decade, employment in agriculture moved rapidly from 15 to 10 percent of the labor force.

This was also a time of declining employment of unskilled as well as certain skilled industrial and mine workers. For example, employment in coal mining declined in the United States to 156,000. We need only compare two sets of figures to get a striking image of change: 156,000 coal miners versus 500,000 college and research faculty—and five million people employed directly in agriculture vis-à-vis five million college and university participants (including students and faculty). One coal miner for three faculty members—indeed a striking change when compared with the first Industrial Revolution.[1]

Indeed, a new class made its entrance into history. This class does not have, as yet, a name in English, although the Russians and the Poles coined a term, "intelligentsia," which first appeared about 1850, when it was used by the literary and political essayist Bielinski. This class has arrived and is characterized by sentiments of common interest and identity. Few anticipated its advent: among Americans—perhaps forgotten today—was Lewis Corey; among Europeans, Henri De Man. A number of other commentators on modern times who looked at the changes with an unbiased mind, free from current fads, saw it coming. A new social stratification, quite different from that of the nineteenth century, developed, and it does not necessarily fit into Marx's prophecies. At the turn of the century Karl Kautsky, a prominent Marxist, was already puzzled by the growth of this new "middle class."

Our theoretical equipment and orientation has not been too helpful in perceiving this change. The standard sociological approach—our classroom frame of reference for the lower, middle, and upper classes—makes us see a climbing crowd, moving from the lower to the higher levels of the ladder in search of profit, status, and success. The Marxist approach perceives two basic classes—proletariat and capitalist. None of these approaches fits modern changes, which are primarily a consequence of occupational shifts. But the great change was anticipated clearly and even accurately by the United States Census Bureau and especially by the Labor Department, as well as by the corresponding branches of many state governments.

Thus, an influential and large class appeared; it had favorable employment and working conditions and stability, and a substantial section had tenure and a permanent, unshakable position.

II

The growth of this new social class coincided with two major historical events: the civil-rights movement and the Vietnam War. Both events were, of course, a legitimate challenge to an educated class, and it would have been bad indeed if this whole mass of teachers and students had remained passive. It is certainly to the credit of this class that it contributed so much to the trend toward racial democracy that began in the South. While the European student movements of the thirties (at least the student majorities) embraced narrow nationalism and even racism enthusiastically, the vast majority of American youth and faculty took a strong, humane position.

A historian may describe the impact of the war in a more accurate way, but it seems to me that there has not been a single war in American history that did not generate protests. This was certainly true of the Spanish-American War. The protest by itself was, of course, legitimate, and again it might be said, whatever views we hold, that a democracy without dissent does not reflect a vigorous political society. Dissent is a most natural, as well as obvious, fruit of freedom: it is its necessary consequence.

However, the picture begins to change. It is not the protest that is at issue here, only how it was expressed. A working democracy such as ours offers many means of nonviolent expression that are effective and visible. We witnessed violence and wanton destruction initiated by extremist groups, the destruction of libraries, fires, bombs, and campaigns of vilification on campuses throughout the country. Emotional and irrational appeals favored crowd and mob action. This activity was carried on by a minority, true, but they set the political style. Those tactical movements had a striking resemblance to techniques used by fascist movements between the two world wars. It was not the ideology of radical rhetoric, but the tactics, the *modus operandi*, that bore this similarity.

The confluence of these three processes—the revolutionary change in occupational structure and the emergence of a new and powerful educated class, the civil-rights movement and accompanying social unrest, and the Vietnam War—created a social and political situation in which small, tightly organized groups of a dedicated few could operate effectively, supplying initiative and leading and manipulating multitudes and opinions.

These groups sprang up on university and college campuses. New "microparties" appeared, which called themselves nonviolent although their members fully approved and applied violence as long as they had the stick. When others took it, it was called brutality.

The majority of the protesters were ethically motivated. Their actions were a consequence of a complex combination of moral and psychological factors and motives, but this is not the time to consider all of these in a detailed and adequate way. It is a topic, and an important one, that calls for still further study. What also appeared, however, was an unusual appetite for power. This hunger for power was, so it seems to me, limited to small "out-elite" groups, clustered in small vanguardist microparties. The slogans calling for "power for the people" appeared on the walls of the schools. The "people" were the new microparties of the few with their Jacobin "legitimacy" and their arrogance in claiming to be representative of a nation. These self-appointed parties claimed to represent the will of the people and therefore, without even asking "the people" for a vote (not unlike Castro), they (a handful of students) claimed the right to rule, order, and force action since they, and no one else, knew what was good for the people. The masses supposedly did not know what was good for them, of course, since they have a "false consciousness." The workers especially did not fit into the definitions of the classroom and failed to follow the behavior patterns assigned to them by these simplistic ideologies. Therefore they too had a "false consciousness." There was never in modern history a movement calling itself "revolutionary" that was more antilabor than these new microparties of the sixties. The new crop of "revolutionaries" came largely from comfortable and roomy suburban homes and well-to-do families. They often plotted their games in New York townhouses. They allied themselves with small but dynamic groups of racial minorities, youth that favored violence. Here the struggle against discrimination supplied a rationalization for the means employed.

Factories and city tenements were the political base of working-class movements; farms and villages, of the farmers' movement. Universities and colleges were the obvious base for the new power-seekers who came from the educated classes.

Of course, I do not think for a moment that power was their manifest and only goal, although they did not deny their demand for power. They had their ideology, they certainly believed. But, as frequently happens in political movements, motives were mixed.

These were the groups that made a bid for the control of the universities. Their goals were political. Colleges and universities, for them, were not centers of research and learning, but bases for political action.

But they also made demands that appealed to many: to end the war, for free access to colleges and universities, democratization of schools and admission of minorities that, at one time, had only a narrow and limited access to higher education. Those were demands that appealed to the grassroots and supplied the small, dynamic microparties with a social base they could use.

The attempts to capture universities were often successful. In such times of political and ideological crisis, during a highly unpopular war, the colleges were vulnerable. Three elements were essential: a weak and terrified college administration, an indifferent and confused faculty, and small, vigorous, organized "microparties," willing to act and determined about their goals. In many schools, all these elements were present.

In hindsight, there might have been some genius in the reluctant yielding to demands in order to avoid more violent clashes. One could have foreseen the familiar scenes: in my college, a group of five or six students easily disrupted a massive commemoration of an anniversary that was attended by representatives of many universities, and Cornell was conquered by a handful of "militants." But after all, in our own times, the Austrian government yielded to three gunmen. Weakness is a symptom of our times. Nevertheless, those groups imposed conditions on universities and also affected curricula. They occupied, without difficulty, presidents' offices, writing their slogans on the walls. Hardworking cleaners and painters, masons and electricians, who came to repair the damages, wondered about the tax money spent on education, and left impressed by the comfort of college lounges and swimming pools, compared with the crowded quarters of their cities.

III

The fourth important variable, next to the emergence of a new class, the antiwar and civil-rights movements, must be mentioned here since it had its impact on universities. It was what may be called the "great intellectual confusion," an intellectual crisis with the disturbing symptoms of decadence.

The relativization of values led to the loss of a sense of direction. General protest against the "oppressive society" and "repression" in one of the most, if not *the most*, liberal and free societies in human history, combined with the search for a new society, were associated with feelings of alienation and loneliness. A mass of youth, often monied but wearing dirty clothes and jeans, practiced a cult of drugs and marijuana. More often than not, they were unhappy youth, deserving sympathy and understanding. Still, new prophets appeared with such slogans as "pot is fun"; these might be poets, confused university instructors, or some popular or popularity-seeking anthropologists. Of course, in the past people drank whiskey and there were unhappy drug-users, but never had drug use risen to such proportions nor the demand for the use of drugs become a political program.

In the country of Roger Williams and Henry Thoreau, in the country that gave mankind institutions of toleration and religious, cultural, and political pluralism, new prophets on luxurious California campuses preached a faith of ideological intolerance for the sake, of course, of toleration and progress. As in the third and fourth centuries, new Oriental cults made their inroads. These philosophies appeared next to the political cults of Mao Tse-tung, whose picture appeared in bookstores on college streets, even in college offices, next to ones of Ho Chi Minh.

This political and cultural movement was accompanied by a new, loud deafening music that was often reduced to rhythm and wild yelling-singing, while thousands of young listeners were moving their hands, heads, and bodies as though they were in a dream or a trance, like Turkish dervishes. Violence and sex became, not a legitimate or a major theme, but an obsession. For some, artistic taste became either refined and bizarre or simply poor, even decadent. Posters representing photos of human excrement were sold on Broadway and in Greenwich Village as objects of art. *Playboy* was not only amusing for some, but it now also had the pretense of authority. And this cultural confusion moved through the universities and affected its programs and courses.

An excellent New York college, known for its scholastic achievements, advertised courses in astrology in a widely circulated daily, while a school famous for its contribution to the humanities and social sciences, with a faculty of world-renowned scholars, advertised courses (I suppose not seminars) in pornography. Of course, pornography was always a part of the life of the cities; it reflects human needs and as a phenomenon should not escape the attention of psychologists, anthropologists, or sociologists. Still, pornography humiliates the human beings involved and is akin to slavery. A special course in this field is only a symptom of the crisis. The crisis of the universities was the crisis of whole sections of the American intelligentsia.

IV

The philosophy behind the curriculum has to be considered within the context, on one hand, of the social, political, and cultural situation and, on the other hand, of the overall philosophy of the university. These times of crisis and change had a profound effect on colleges and universities. Some effects, to be sure, were positive: the opening up of the schools for racial, once underprivileged, minorities, the attempts to bring students into active participation in university decisions. But the colleges and universities frequently yielded to the pressures and demands of dynamic but often minor groups that claimed to represent the community. Colleges and universities, in so many cases, failed in assessing their own social function and role, in responding with their own clear and forward-looking philosophies and objectives. Survival was the goal, and in order to survive, the administration frequently yielded to strong political pressures. As a consequence of these times, curricula in some colleges are out of balance, to put it mildly, and in some cases a logical curriculum sequence has been destroyed. In one community college, a student could complete a substantial part of his term with (1) karate, (2) physical education, (3) some ethnic studies, and (4) some additional credit for "community work," whatever that means. We now get students in advanced undergraduate social-science courses with no background in history, mathematics, or geography.

In the ethnic studies of one minority group, a college may offer two or three pages in a list of courses, while the vital field of meteorology is represented by only two courses. Canada, our vast, interesting and closest neighbor, from which we can learn much, does not appear in most of the metropolitan college bulletins since there has been no pressure group to ask for it. In vain may we look for any extensive course offerings on the Arctic or Antarctica, regions not so very distant anymore and yet, in so many respects, enormously promising for study. They are two of the few remaining and challenging frontiers.

How do students react today? In my experience at least, many of them blame the schools, and rightly, for the deficiencies in their education. The present situation and prevailing philosophy was affected by the events and times, when many academic executives lost control of the steering wheel and yielded to pressures.

For many decades the strength of American education was in the colleges. On the whole, the European high school was better—or it might be proper to say, more scholarly, more academic—but the liberal-arts college not only compensated for the early years of schooling but also advanced a student in general education beyond the level of those with continental backgrounds. The American student had more independence and courage to think and write on his own, and his education was far more modern. These are, of course, my impressions. Therefore, with increased college enrollment, the strategic area of post-elementary education moves toward the college level.

The situation of colleges in the seventies has changed substantially. The American academic generation does not last more than two or three years, not the thirty years of classical times. After two, sometimes, three years, there is a new crop of students, who may be quite different from their predecessors. From my narrow, personal experience as a classroom teacher, I can say that the undergraduate student is weaker, less interested, not as willing to work and study, not as enthusiastic as those we knew ten years ago. Sometimes one yearns for the times of unrest and turbulence, which at least were symptoms of strong interest and searching. There are still substantial numbers of students who are as good as ever, and the graduate students generally are almost as good. On the other hand, students have appeared in city colleges, or at least at Brooklyn, who formerly could not have even dreamed of qualifying for college, and now they have a chance to attend college.

American youth have also changed in their attitudes. Today I see students of the sixties, many of whom have kept their progressive outlook but have revised their views on violence and the role of the universities. A European has a tendency to persist, to keep and "dogmatize" his political views, whether of the left or right. He is slow to change, only revising his views after many years. In the United States, due to the fact that a rigid and systematic political ideology of a single prophet is not easily accepted, at least by substantial sections of students, and that dogmatism, political or philosophical, is adverse to their entire mode of thinking, a revision of particular views (although not of basic values, principles, and institutions) is generally accepted. As a consequence, American students' flexibility is incomparably greater. In part at least, this contributes to the unusual political resilience of this nation.

V

With all of this in mind, we may consider the goals, functions, philosophy, and curriculum of the university. First of all, we must acknowledge what the college and university is not: it is not a base for political action; it is primarily a seat of learning. Simple as this statement is, it needs reaffirmation in view of current fads. Secondly, a university or college does not have one single goal and function but is multifunctional. Its multifunctional nature has to be acknowledged in considering a curriculum.

A complex society like ours has many specialized institutions, and they have their definite functions. There is no picnicking on the floor of museums and a boxing arena is not the reading room of a library. Political action is a necessary part of the democratic process. Desire for and action to win political power is a legitimate part of this process. The universities, however, are not a political arena but a place of learning. Cubanization of Latin American universities as well as of numerous German universities is a warning indeed. Yet, vigorous, even angry, debates and a careful study of political ideas, plans, and movements, as controversial as they may be different in their content, are a legitimate and necessary field of activity for the university.

There is, however, not one single objective, one single creed the university should serve, nor one single function it should have. Obvious as this may be, it must be restated in times when, on the order of Chairman Mao, "cultural revolutions" are initiated and manipulated, and a single primitive dogma, spelled out in a little red song-book, is imposed by means of force.

The universities cannot return to the pattern of restricted, elitist establishments for the selected few who are to lead the state and industry, in addition to training competent technicians and scholars. The broad base of university admissions secures for it a wide choice of talents, interests, and ideas; it opens opportunities to many who may, with difficulty, face formalized and petrified forms of examinations, but who may have scholarly curiosity, interest, and talent. Science and scholarship have very little to do with democracy. The former is a system of ideas subject to certain rules of validation. The validity of our findings has little to do with our norms of liberty. Nevertheless, access to studies may be democratic or elitist. Conditions for the discovery of truth call for freedom in the choice of subjects, hypotheses, and methods. The humanities call for freedom in the choice of ideas and interests. A broad base of admissions must be combined with the acceptance of basic principles, of the core values upon which the university is built, and of basic rules for the maintenance of freedom. Thus, the condition of citizenship in a university community is the acceptance of a minimum set of values—norms without which the university cannot exist.

We now have two premises: first, that the university is not a political arena nor an elitist school for the ruling classes. Secondly, its basic norm is freedom of inquiry, and this norm can be safeguarded only by the acceptance of some basic norms and rules as shared values and as conditions of participation. We have also noted that the university is multifunctional and pluralistic. One of its major functions is the transmission of knowledge and learning.

A few years ago, on an Indian reservation in New Mexico, I spoke to a Plains Indian, an intelligent and alert young man. On sheds nearby I saw a few deerskins stretched out on boards. I learned that hunting was still widely practiced and that no limits were set on the hunting season. In the Indian community's school—in the high-school curriculum—the emphasis was put on Indian dances and lore. I asked what kind of employment they expect for the younger generation. My friend showed me a new construction—a branch of some computer factory or lab—and suggested, not without pride, that this was the future for the young: electronics. However, training to become a medicine man is quite different from preparation for a physician or a physicist or a mathematician. Schools cannot escape the imperatives of competence. In a multifunctional university there is room for full freedom of choice, but competence requires systematic curricular orientation.

VI

The fact that the face, the "social base," the population of colleges has changed cannot be without effect on our curriculum.

The liberal-arts colleges of past decades, excellent though they were, had only an ancillary interest in the future employment of students and certainly did not concern themselves with the future earnings of graduates. These concerns were left to graduate or professional education. For decades, if not for centuries, the liberal-arts college was a school for the upper-middle class. State and city colleges were different, it is true; yet the national style was set in the private colleges. And, we may as well remember, many of our state universities are land-grant colleges; many of them grew from teachers' colleges and otherwise excellent agricultural colleges.

Open enrollment in New York City carries with it responsibility. Most of our students will have to earn their livings after their undergraduate work is completed. These are not colleges of the wealthy. Our curriculum cannot overlook these facts. Consequently, courses should emphasize solid, competent education. A worthless diploma is just that—worth nothing.

In consequence of the fact that the high school, at least in New York, has been considerably weakened in its scholarly quality and in view of the broadening of the educational base, the freshman and sophomore curriculum calls for considerable reconstruction. In addition, political pressures have considerably affected introductory levels of study. To remedy high-school deficiencies, the first two years of college should be organized around a strong core of required courses in the basic disciplines: history, mathematics, science, sociology, political science, English, and one foreign language. Geography integrated with astronomy, meteorology, and geology should be reintroduced as a required course. This basic core for all students should be very strong indeed.

Let me say a few words in defense of history, languages, and geography. Historicism is a basic element in our mode of thought. I am arguing here with James B. Conant, and perhaps with A. N. Whitehead, that historical thinking is essential in developing a scientific outlook. Being familiar with American and European teaching of history, let me say something about the excellence of American historians. The independence of their thinking and criticism, their diligence in ascertaining data and gathering accurate facts, their diversified methods and philosophy make history a superb discipline for educating the younger generation in critical and balanced judgment.

A new type of geography is essential in view of our new ecological problems.

Last, but not least, we must include a foreign language, preferably Spanish or French, since one or the other is spoken by our neighbors to the south and north and both are "link-languages," languages associated with great cultures. We must move slowly toward bilingualism in our modern world. Our methods of teaching languages are deficient. I once had a guide in Casablanca, a Berber, who was illiterate but spoke eleven languages. There is something wrong with our foreign-language instruction, if after years of study our students experience difficulties in reading a foreign text or simply in conversing. Intensive research in how a second language is acquired is badly needed.

Within such a curriculum the social sciences will only gain. This type of rigorous education will also favor and develop intellectual discipline and attention span and will pave the way for a vast choice of electives. In addition, art or music should be represented among courses required in the senior year and among electives during the junior year. A strong program of requirements will still leave enough time for electives.

The development of intellectual and personal self-discipline has been neglected. This would be taken care of by way of systematic and difficult subject matter. Education cannot always be pleasant, entertaining, and amusing. Nor is it true that there is no hierarchy of importance in subject matters. The college curriculum has to return to the concepts of intellectual competence and self-discipline. In a pluralistic approach, a student has to be exposed to various viewpoints, especially in such subjects as the social sciences and history. Still, plu-

271

ralism also calls for a sense of direction; the alternative is confusion. This sense of direction will be supplied by colloquia in ethics. By this, I do not mean the rigid imposition of norms, but rather individual attempts to discover values, goals, standards of conduct and life goals in a free exchange of views. This calls for change in the forms and techniques of education. The use of exams, term papers, and midterms should be abandoned in such seminars. In a new type of colloquia students and teachers could exchange views and ideas freely, free of the compulsions imposed by grades and finals. The great civilization of the Mediterranean is a civilization of conversation, of the table; let me call this culture "mensatic" from the Latin *mensa*. It is not an accident that Plato and Galileo wrote in dialogue form. In a dialogue, diverse, contradictory views can be expressed. Ethics lends itself to this form of dialogue, where diverse and opposing views can be expressed.

And now, let me narrow down in my lengthy presentation to the field of the social sciences. Various proposals have been made for introductory courses. Some have even suggested that statistics should become a basic, core offering.

We are in a time of confusion, and among many of our colleagues authoritarian rule and dictatorships are not necessarily unpopular, providing that these have been labeled "progressive democracy." People are within their full rights to profess any political religion they choose. But in political and social studies the distinction and classification of concepts is elementary. In introductory courses, the student should indeed learn the difference between democracy, dictatorship, tyranny, and despotism, concepts that today may be embodied in different forms but which have not lost their validity since the times of Aristotle and Montesquieu.

The classification of and clear distinction between concepts and institutions are contradictory to dogmatism and the a priori acceptance of definition. Those distinctions are based on empirical and historical data. Now we can move to the next area of consideration.

In sociology particularly, a student has to learn to gather empirical and secondary quantitative data, relate the data and facts, and draw conclusions. Our offerings have been increasingly narrowed down to textbook study. This calls for a proper balance, a combination of research skills and attitudes with theory. Research, even simple research, is also education in critical evaluation of data and independent judgment.

To make these offerings relevant for the student, even vital, one must relate to the research the important problems of our times. They should be brought to the attention of the student at the beginning, since those problems supply the challenge, create the interest in theory and method and in further study. Introductory courses in sociology should devote a part of the term to population and ecology problems, or at least to an introduction to demography. The misery and poverty and exploitation of the environment that accompany war and political domination—these are issues that bring students to study social sciences. We must begin our instruction here, where their motivation is initially strongest. From there we may move into the difficult areas of methods and theory and to higher levels of abstraction—understanding the nature and workings of a society.

At this point, we face new issues. Universities and colleges, dedicated to inductive and empirical orientation, look to the past and present rather than toward the future. The future suggests thoughtful planning, choice of alternatives, evaluation of risks, and allocations. Our curricula should, so it seems to me, be open to new attempts at charting new routes of human progress.

The major dilemma before us is to develop new approaches and methods that would permit us to submit these continually changing conditions to scholarly, even scientific, analysis. Usually we apply a nineteenth-century theoretical frame of reference to the entirely new, indeed revolutionary, and rapidly changing conditions of our time. "I am shooting at a moving target," commented one of my colleagues working in the field of international politics. In the social sciences, not only the static system but above all the moving, dynamic process calls for adequate and flexible theory. Here are areas, or at least some of the areas, for more advanced studies.

A university or a college cannot advance without a sense of responsibility and direction. "Direction" also implies a sense of values and some goals. The university is itself a community and ought to have enough strength to resist political pressure while paying utmost attention to the needs of the wider community and mankind.

At a time when the globe has been reduced to a crowded spaceship of quarrelsome and often fighting passengers, at a time when new, once unknown problems call for calm and competent answers, the responsibility of the university increases. It is not the cry for power and privilege, but the appeal to reason, knowledge, and responsibility that demands a renewal of the values that our academic institutions are built upon. Freedom of inquiry and broad access to education are among them.

NOTES

1. For statistical source materials and further data, see Feliks Gross, "Le Changement Structurel de la Societe aux États Unis," *Annales*, 21 Annee, No. 3 (May-June 1, 1966), pp. 488-517

The Specter at the Feast

Reuben Abel
New School for Social Research

A specter is haunting this discussion of the philosophy of the curriculum—the specter of nihilism. We humanists are forever embarrassed at the uncertainty of our conclusions, whereas the logicians and the mathematicians can define precisely the validity of their inferences. We can never, alas, determine absolutely the truth or falsity of any proposition about history, nor of any interpretation of literature, nor of any evaluation of art. Therefore (it is implied), anything goes! No indubitable judgments can be made in the humanities. Every man can be his own historian. Any one criticism of poetry is as valid as any other.

But this is a false model of our situation. We are not faced with the alternatives of *aut Caesar aut nullus*—either absolutism or nihilism. Relativism does not mean the absence of standards. Rather, we can see in this context the role of analysis, of methodology, and of training. The judgments that we make about history, or about literature, or about art—like judgments made about logic or about science or about anything whatever—must be justified by reasons, or they will not command the respect of rational men. No proposition in the humanities is ever a priori true or false. I have read, for example, that the Protestant Reformation was caused by Martin Luther's constipation, and indeed no one can disprove that claim. But it must be compared with alternative explanations; the evidence for it must be carefully criticized and

evaluated. That the assertion can be made does not qualify it as justified or as confirmed, by comparison with other historical hypotheses.

Let us exorcise that specter. Propositions in the humanities are as
reliable as we can make them.

Contributors

Reuben Abel   **New School for Social Research**

Professor Abel, chairman of the Humanities Division of the New School, is also adjunct professor of philosophy in the graduate faculty. He is the author of *The Pragmatic Humanism of F. C. S. Schiller* and *Man Is the Measure*, and he edited *Humanistic Pragmatism*.

M. H. Abrams   **Cornell University**

Class of 1916 professor of English at Cornell, Professor Abrams is the author of *The Milk of Paradise, A Glossary of Literary Terms, The Mirror and the Lamp: Romantic Theory and the Critical Tradition* and *Natural Supernaturalism: Tradition and Revolution in Romantic Literature,* and an editor of *The Norton Anthology of English Literature.* He was the recipient of the Phi Beta Kappa Christian Gauss Prize in 1954 and the James Russell Lowell Prize in 1972.

Robert L. Bartley   **The Wall Street Journal**

Starting as a staff reporter on the *Wall Street Journal* in 1962, Mr. Bartley subsequently covered politics, foreign policy, urban problems, and intellectual life, and eventually became editor of the editorial page of the *Journal* in 1972. *Time* magazine has suggested that he "may exert more influence on U.S. businessmen than any other journalist." He is a member of Sigma Delta Chi.

Ronald Berman   **National Endowment for the Humanities**

Dr. Berman is chairman of the Endowment. He is the author of *Henry King and the 17th Century, A Reader's Guide to Shakespeare's Plays,* and *America in the Sixties: An Intellectual History.* He received Phi Beta Kappa's Gold Medal for Distinguished Service in 1974.

Aldo S. Bernardo   Verrazzano College

President of Verrazzano College in Saratoga Springs, New York, Dr. Bernardo is on a leave of absence as codirector of the Center for Medieval and Early Renaissance Studies at the State University of New York, Binghamton, a center which he helped found. Holder of the Italian Order of Merit, he is the author of several works on Italian literature, including *Petrarch, Laura and the 'Triumphs.'*

Wm. Theodore deBary   Columbia University

Provost and vice-president in charge of academic affairs at Columbia, Professor deBary is the Horace Carpentier professor of Oriental studies. He is the coauthor of three distinguished works on the sources of Japanese, Indian, and Chinese tradition, translator of the Japanese *Five Women Who Loved Love,* and editor of *A Guide to Oriental Classics, Approaches to Asian Civilizations,* and *The Buddhist Tradition.* Dr. deBary has served as president of the Association for Asian Studies and is a member of the American Council of Learned Societies.

Gray Dorsey   Washington University

Dr. Dorsey is Nagel professor of jurisprudence and international law in the School of Law, Washington University, St. Louis. He is the author of *American Freedoms* and editor of *Constitutional Freedom and the Law* and *Validation of New Forms of Social Organization.*

Joseph Dunner   Yeshiva University

Professor Dunner is the David Petegorsky professor of political science and international relations at Yeshiva. A foreign correspondent for European newspapers during the early thirties and a press officer in Europe during and immediately after World War II, he is the author of *The Republic of Israel: Its History and Its Promise* and *Baruch Spinoza and Western Democracy,* and the editor and coauthor of *Major Aspects of International Politics* and *Dictionary of Political Science.*

Nathan Glazer   Harvard University

Dr. Glazer is professor of education and social structure at Harvard. He is the coauthor with Daniel P. Moynihan of *Beyond the Melting Pot,* and the author of *American Judaism, The Social Basis of American Communism,* and *Remembering the Answers: Essays on the American Student Revolt.* He is a coeditor of the magazine *The Public Interest.*

Feliks Gross   City University of New York

Professor of sociology at Brooklyn College and a member of the graduate faculty of City University, Dr. Gross is the author of *The Polish Worker, Violence in*

Politics, Il Paese: Values and Social Change in an Italian Village, and *The Revolutionary Party.* He was the senior Fulbright lecturer at the University of Rome in 1974.

Gertrude Himmelfarb   City University of New York

Dr. Himmelfarb is professor of history at City University. The author of *Lord Acton, Darwin and the Darwinian Revolution, Victorian Minds,* and *On Liberty and Liberalism,* she was a Phi Beta Kappa visiting scholar and is a fellow of the Royal Historical Society and the American Academy of Arts and Sciences.

Gerald Holton   Harvard University

Professor of physics at Harvard, Dr. Holton was a codirector of the Harvard Project Physics and a coauthor of the resulting *Project Physics Course* (1970). He has been a member of the Institute for Advanced Study at Princeton, a member of the National Academy of Sciences' committee for scholarly communications with the People's Republic of China, and an exchange professor at Leningrad University. He is the author of *Introduction to Concepts and Theories in Physical Science, The Twentieth Century Sciences: Studies in Intellectual Biography,* and *The Thematic Origins of Scientific Thought: Kepler to Einstein.*

Sidney Hook   New York University

Emeritus professor of philosophy at New York University, Dr. Hook is a fellow of the American Academy of Arts and Sciences and a senior research fellow at the Hoover Institution on War, Revolution and Peace, Stanford, California. He was formerly the chairman of the Washington Square College of Arts and Sciences. Professor Hook was an organizer of the Conference on Methods in Philosophy and Science, the Conference on Scientific Spirit and Democratic Faith, the American Committee for Cultural Freedom, and University Centers for Rational Alternatives. He is the author of *Political Power and Personal Freedom, Education for Modern Man, Academic Freedom and Academic Anarchy,* and *Education and the Taming of Power.*

Charles Issawi   Columbia University

Dr. Issawi is the Ragnar Nurkse professor of economics at Columbia and the author of *The Economic History of Iran; Oil, the Middle East and the World; Issawi's Laws of Social Motion;* and other economic studies of the Middle East and North Africa. For seven years he was a member of the Middle East unit of the economic department of the United Nations Secretariat.

Mortimer R. Kadish   Case Western Reserve University

Chairman of the department of philosophy at Case Western Reserve, Professor Kadish has been a Guggenheim fellow and a fellow of the American Council of

Learned Societies. He is the author of a novel, *Point of Honor,* of *Reason and Controversy in the Arts,* and, with S. H. Kadish, of *Discretion To Disobey.*

Paul Oskar Kristeller   Columbia University

Dr. Kristeller was the Frederick Woodbridge professor at Columbia until he became professor emeritus in 1973. He has been a member of the Institute for Advanced Study at Princeton, and he received the Serena Medal for Italian studies from the British Academy. Professor Kristeller has also been a Guggenheim fellow and is a fellow of the American Academy of Arts and Sciences, as well as of various French, Italian, and German academies. He is the author of *Eight Philosophers of the Italian Renaissance* and *Renaissance Concepts of Man and Other Essays.*

Paul Kurtz   State University of New York

Dr. Kurtz, professor of philosophy at the State University of New York at Buffalo and editor of *The Humanist* magazine, is the author of *The Fullness of Life* and *Decision and the Condition of Man.*

Herbert I. London   New York University

Professor of social studies and director of the University Without Walls program at New York University, an experimental program in individualized instruction, Professor London has served as an adviser to numerous urban educational projects and as a consultant to the Hudson Institute on drug programs, national conscription, and legalized gambling. He is an executive director of the Center for the Arts in Provincetown, Massachusetts, and is the author of *Fitting In: Crosswise at Generation Gap.*

Ernest Nagel   Columbia University

Formerly the John Dewey professor of philosophy and now University professor emeritus at Columbia, Dr. Nagel is the author of *Sovereign Reason, Logic Without Metaphysics, Gödel's Proof* (with J. R. Neuman), and *The Structure of Science.* He is a fellow of the American Academy of Arts and Sciences and a corresponding fellow of the British Academy.

Henry R. Novotny   California State College

Dr. Novotny is associate professor of psychology at California State at Bakersfield and a psychological consultant to the California Correctional Institution at Tehachapi. He also holds degrees in chemical engineering and physics.

Frederick A. Olafson   University of California

Dr. Olafson, chairman of the department of philosophy at the University of California, San Diego, is the author of *Principles and Persons: An Ethical Inter-*

pretation of Existentialism and *Ethics and Twentieth Century Thought*. He has been a Guggenheim fellow.

Michael Rabin   Hebrew University

Dr. Rabin is the rector of Hebrew University in Jerusalem, Israel.

Howard B. Radest   Ramapo College

Dr. Radest is the director of the School of American Studies and professor of philosophy at Ramapo College in New Jersey. Author of *On Life and Meaning* and *Toward Common Ground* and editor of *To Seek a Humane World*, Dr. Radest is a consultant to the New Jersey Public Broadcasting Authority.

Joseph J. Schwab   University of Chicago

Professor emeritus of education and William Rainey Harper professor of natural sciences at the University of Chicago, Dr. Schwab is a visiting fellow at the Center for the Study of Democratic Institutions, Santa Barbara, California. He is the author of *Teaching of Science as Enquiry; Teachers Handbook, Biological Sciences Curriculum Study;* and *College Curriculum and Student Protest.*

Robert F. Sexton   University of Kentucky

Dr. Sexton, executive director of the Office for Experiential Education at the University of Kentucky, is the past chairman of the board of directors of the National Center for Public Service Internship Programs. He is the author of *The Public Papers of Governor Louie B. Nunn* (in press), and has written papers on Kentucky history and experiential education.

Thomas Sowell   University of California

Professor of economics at the University of California at Los Angeles, Dr. Sowell is the author of *Black Education: Myths and Tragedies, Say's Law: An Historical Analysis, Classical Economics Reconsidered*, and *Race and Economics.*

John B. Stephenson   University of Kentucky

Dr. Stephenson is the dean of undergraduate studies at the University of Kentucky. He is the author of *Shiloh: A Mountain Community* and the coeditor of *Appalachia in the Sixties.*

Miro M. Todorovich   City University of New York

Dr. Todorovich, associate professor of physics at Bronx Community College, City University, is executive secretary of the University Centers for Rational Alternatives.